Dorothy la Désirée

Jurgen

A COMEDY OF JUSTICE

By

James Branch Cabell

With Illustrations and Decorations by
FRANK C. PAPÉ

DOVER PUBLICATIONS, INC.
NEW YORK

Published in Canada by General Publishing
Company, Ltd., 30 Lesmill Road, Don Mills,
Toronto, Ontario.
Published in the United Kingdom by Constable
and Company, Ltd., 10 Orange Street, London
WC2H 7EG.

This Dover edition, first published in 1977, is an
unabridged and unaltered republication of the
work as published by John Lane/The Bodley Head,
London, in 1921. The frontispiece was in color in
the John Lane edition but here appears in black
and white. An introduction by Hugh Walpole has
been omitted. The complete Foreword from the
nineteenth edition as published by Robert M.
McBride and Company, New York, in 1926, has
been added to make the Dover edition as complete
as possible.

International Standard Book Number: 0-486-23507-6
Library of Congress Catalog Card Number: 77-74612

Manufactured in the United States of America
Dover Publications, Inc.
180 Varick Street
New York, N. Y. 10014

TO

BURTON RASCOE

Before each tarradiddle,
Uncowed by sciolists,
Robuster persons twiddle
Tremendously big fists.

"Our gods are good," they tell us ;
"Nor will our gods defer
Remission of rude fellows'
Ability to err."

So this, your JURGEN, travels
Content to compromise
Ordainments none unravels
Explicitly . . . and sighs.

"Others, with better moderation, do either entertain the vulgar history of Jurgen as a fabulous addition unto the true and authentic story of St. Iurgenius of Poictesme, or else we conceive the literal acception to be a misconstruction of the symbolical expression : apprehending a veritable history, in an emblem or piece of Christian poesy. And this emblematical construction hath been received by men not forward to extenuate the acts of saints."

PHILIP BORSDALE.

"A forced construction is very idle. If readers of *The High History of Jurgen* do not meddle with the allegory, the allegory will not meddle with them. Without minding it at all, the whole is as plain as a pikestaff. It might as well be pretended that we cannot see Poussin's pictures without first being told the allegory, as that the allegory aids us in understanding *Jurgen*."

E. NOEL CODMAN.

"Too urbane to advocate delusion, too hale for the bitterness of irony, this fable of Jurgen is, as the world itself, a book wherein each man will find what his nature enables him to see ; which gives us back each his own image ; and which teaches us each the lesson that each of us desires to learn."

JOHN FREDERICK LEWISTAM.

CONTENTS

LIST OF PLATES

"*Of* JURGEN *eke they maken mencioun,*
That of an old wyf gat his youthe agoon,
And gat himselfe a shirte as bright as fyre
Wherein to jape, yet gat not his desire
In any countrie ne condicioun."

A FOREWORD

" Nescio quid certè est : et Hylax in limine latrat."

A FOREWORD
WHICH ASSERTS NOTHING

N Continental periodicals not more than a dozen articles in all would seem to have given accounts or partial translations of the Jurgen legends. No thorough investigation of this epos can be said to have appeared in print, anywhere, prior to the publication, in 1913, of the monumental *Synopses of Aryan Mythology* by Angelo de Ruiz. It is unnecessary to observe that in this exhaustive digest Professor de Ruiz has given (VII, p. 415 *et sequentia*) a summary of the greater part of these legends as contained in the collections of Verville and Bülg; and has discussed at length and with much learning the esoteric meaning of these folk-stories and their bearing upon questions to which the "solar theory" of myth explanation has given rise. To his volumes, and to the pages of Mr. Lewistam's *Key to the Popular Tales of Poictesme,* must be referred all those who may elect to think of Jurgen as the resplendent, journeying and procreative sun.

Equally in reading hereinafter will the judicious waive all allegorical interpretation, if merely because the suggestions hitherto advanced are inconveniently various. Thus Verville finds the Nessus shirt a symbol of retribution, where Bülg, with rather wide divergence, would have it represent the dangerous gift of genius. Then it may be remembered that Dr. Codman says, without any hesitancy, of Mother Sereda: "This Mother Middle is the world generally (an obvious anagram of *Erda es*), and this Sereda rules not merely the middle of the working-days but the midst of everything. She is the factor of *middleness,* of mediocrity, of an avoidance of extremes, of the eternal compromise begotten by use and wont. She is the Mrs. Grundy of the Léshy; she is Comstockery: and her shadow is common-sense." Yet Codman speaks with certainly no more authority than Prote, when the latter, in his *Origins of Fable,* declares this epos is "a parable of . . . man's vain journeying in search of that rationality and justice which his nature craves, and discovers nowhere in the universe: and the shirt is an emblem of this instinctive craving, as . . the shadow symbolizes conscience. Sereda typifies a surrender to life as it is, a giving up of man's rebellious self-centredness and selfishness: the anagram being *se dare."*

Thus do interpretations throng and clash, and neatly equal the commentators in number. Yet possibly each one of these unriddlings, with no doubt a host of others, is conceivable: so that wisdom will dwell upon none of them very seriously.

With the origin and the occult meaning of the folklore of Poictesme this book at least is in no wise concerned: its unambitious aim has been merely to familiarize English readers with the Jurgen epos for the tale's sake. And this tale of old years is one which, by rare fortune, can be given to English readers almost unabridged, in view of the singular delicacy and pure-mindedness of the Jurgen mythos: in all, not more than a half-dozen deletions have seemed expedient (and have been duly indicated) in order to remove such sparse and unimportant outcroppings

of mediæval frankness as might conceivably offend
the squeamish.

Since this volume is presented simply as a story to
be read for pastime, neither morality nor symbolism
is hereinafter educed, and no "parallels" and "authorities" are quoted. Even the gaps are left unabridged by guesswork: whereas the historic and
mythological problems perhaps involved are relinquished to those really thoroughgoing scholars whom
erudition qualifies to deal with such topics, and
tedium does not deter. . . .

In such terms, and thus far, ran the Foreword to
the first issues of this book, whose later fortunes have
made necessary the lengthening of the Foreword with
a postscript. The needed addition—this much at least
chiming with good luck—is brief. It is just that fragment which some scholars, since the first appearance
of this volume, have asserted—upon what perfect
frankness must describe as not indisputable grounds
—to be a portion of the thirty-second chapter of the
complete form of *La Haulte Histoire de Jurgen.*

And in reply to what these scholars assert, discretion says nothing. For this fragment was, of course,
unknown when the High History was first put into
English, and there in consequence appears, here, little
to be won either by endorsing or denying its claims
to authenticity. Rather, does discretion prompt the
appending, without any gloss or scholia, of this fragment, which deals with

The Judging of Jurgen.

Now a court was held by the Philistines to decide
whether or no King Jurgen should be relegated to
limbo. And when the judges were prepared for judging, there came into the court a great tumblebug,

rolling in front of him his loved and properly housed young ones. With the creature came pages, in black and white, bearing a sword, a staff and a lance.

This insect looked at Jurgen, and its pincers rose erect in horror. The bug cried to the three judges, "Now, by St. Anthony! this Jurgen must forthwith be relegated to limbo, for he is offensive and lewd and lascivious and indecent."

"And how can that be?" says Jurgen.

"You are offensive," the bug replied, "because this page has a sword which I choose to say is not a sword. You are lewd because that page has a lance which I prefer to think is not a lance. You are lascivious because yonder page has a staff which I elect to declare is not a staff. And finally, you are indecent for reasons of which a description would be objectionable to me, and which therefore I must decline to reveal to anybody."

"Well, that sounds logical," says Jurgen, "but still, at the same time, it would be no worse for an admixture of common-sense. For you gentlemen can see for yourselves, by considering these pages fairly and as a whole, that these pages bear a sword and a lance and a staff, and nothing else whatever; and you will deduce, I hope, that all the lewdness is in the insectival mind of him who itches to be calling these things by other names."

The judges said nothing as yet. But they that guarded Jurgen, and all the other Philistines, stood to this side and to that side with their eyes shut tight, and all these said: "We decline to look at the pages fairly and as a whole, because to look might seem to imply a doubt of what the tumblebug has decreed. Besides, as long as the tumblebug has reasons which he declines to reveal, his reasons stay unanswerable, and you are plainly a prurient rascal who are making trouble for yourself."

"To the contrary," says Jurgen, "I am a poet, and I make literature."

"But in Philistia to make literature and to make trouble for yourself are synonyms," the tumblebug explained. "I know, for already we of Philistia have been pestered by three of these makers of literature. Yes, there was Edgar, whom I starved and hunted until I was tired of it: then I chased him up a back alley one night, and knocked out those annoying brains of his. And there was Walt, whom I chivvied and battered from place to place, and made a paralytic of him: and him, too, I labelled offensive and lewd and lascivious and indecent. Then later there was Mark, whom I frightened into disguising himself in a clown's suit, so that nobody might suspect him to be a maker of literature: indeed, I frightened him so that he hid away the greater part of what he had made until after he was dead, and I could not get at him. That was a disgusting trick to play on me, I consider. Still, these are the only three detected makers of literature that have ever infested Philistia, thanks be to goodness and my vigilance, but for both of which we might have been no more free from makers of literature than are the other countries."

"Now, but these three," cried Jurgen, "are the glory of Philistia: and of all that Philistia has produced, it is these three alone, whom living ye made least of, that to-day are honored wherever art is honored, and where nobody bothers one way or the other about Philistia."

"What is art to me and my way of living?" replied the tumblebug, wearily. "I have no concern with art and letters and the other lewd idols of foreign nations. I have in charge the moral welfare of my young, whom I roll here before me, and trust with St. Anthony's aid to raise in time to be God-fearing tumblebugs like me, delighting in what is proper to their nature. For the rest, I have never minded dead men being well-spoken-of. No, no, my lad: once whatever I may do means nothing to you, and once you are really rotten, you will find the tumblebug friendly enough. Meanwhile I am paid to protest that living persons are offensive and lewd and lascivious and indecent, and one must live."

Then the Philistines who stood to this side and to that side said in indignant unison: "And we, the reputable citizenry of Philistia, are not at all in sympathy with those who would take any protest against the tumblebug as a justification of what they are pleased to call art. The harm done by the tumblebug seems to us very slight, whereas the harm done by the self-styled artist may be very great."

Jurgen now looked more attentively at this queer creature: and he saw that the tumblebug was malodorous, certainly, but at bottom honest and well-meaning; and this seemed to Jurgen the saddest thing he had found among the Philistines. For the tumblebug was sincere in his insane doings, and all Philistia honored him sincerely, so that there was nowhere any hope for this people.

Therefore King Jurgen addressed himself, as his need was, to submit to the strange customs of the Philistines. "Now do you judge me fairly," cried Jurgen to his judges, "if there be any justice in this mad country. And if there be none, do you relegate me to limbo or to any other place, so long as in that place this tumblebug is not omnipotent and sincere and insane."

And Jurgen waited. . . .

DUMBARTON GRANGE,
April, 1926

CHAPTER I

WHY JURGEN DID THE MANLY THING

is a tale which they narrate in Poictesme, saying: In the old days lived a pawn-broker named Jurgen; but what his wife called him was very often much worse than that. She was a high-spirited woman, with no especial gift for silence. Her name, they say, was Adelais, but people by ordinary called her Dame Lisa.

They tell, also, that in the old days, after putting up the shop-windows for the night, Jurgen was passing the Cistercian Abbey, on his way home: and one of the monks had tripped over a stone in the road-way. He was cursing the devil who had placed it there.

"Fie, brother!" says Jurgen, "and have not the devils enough to bear as it is?"

"I never held with Origen," replied the monk; "and besides, it hurt my great-toe confoundedly."

"None the less," observes Jurgen, "it does not behove God-fearing persons to speak with disrespect of the divinely ap-pointed Prince of Darkness. To your further confusion, consider this monarch's industry! Day and night you may detect him toiling at the task Heaven set him.

3

That is a thing can be said of few communicants and of no monks. Think, too, of his fine artistry, as evidenced in all the perilous and lovely snares of this world, which it is your business to combat, and mine to lend money upon. Why, but for him we would both be vocationless! Then, too, consider his philanthropy, and deliberate how insufferable would be our case if you and I, and all our fellow parishioners, were to-day hobnobbing with other beasts in the Garden which we pretend to desiderate on Sundays! To arise with swine and lie down with the hyena?—Oh, intolerable!"

Thus he ran on, devising reasons for not thinking too harshly of the Devil. Most of it was an abridgment of some verses Jurgen had composed, in the shop when business was slack.

" I consider that to be stuff and nonsense," was the monk's glose.

" No doubt your notion is sensible," observed the pawnbroker : " but mine is the prettier."

Then Jurgen passed the Cistercian Abbey, and was approaching Bellegarde, when he met a black gentleman, who saluted him and said :

" Thanks, Jurgen, for your good word."

" Who are you, and why do you thank me ? " asks Jurgen.

" My name is no great matter. But you have a kind heart, Jurgen. May your life be free from care! "

" Save us from hurt and harm, friend, but I am already married."

" Eh, sirs, and a fine clever poet like you ! "

" Yet it is a long while now since I was a practising poet."

" Why, to be sure ! You have the artistic temperament, which is not exactly suited to the restrictions of domestic life. Then I suppose your wife has her own personal opinion about poetry, Jurgen."

" Indeed, sir, her opinion would not bear repetition, for I am sure you are unaccustomed to such language."

" This is very sad. I am afraid your wife does not quite understand you, Jurgen."

" Sir," says Jurgen, astounded, " do you read people's inmost thoughts ? "

The black gentleman seemed much dejected. He pursed his lips, and fell to counting upon his fingers : as they moved his sharp nails glittered like flame-points.

" Now but this is a very deplorable thing," says the black gentleman, " to have befallen the first person I have found ready to speak a kind word for evil. And in all these centuries, too ! Dear me, this is a most regrettable instance of mismanagement ! No matter, Jurgen, the morning is brighter than the evening. How I will reward you, to be sure ! "

So Jurgen thanked the simple old creature politely. And when Jurgen reached home his wife was nowhere to be seen. He looked on all sides and questioned everyone, but to no avail. Dame Lisa had vanished in the midst of getting supper ready—suddenly, completely and inexplicably, just as (in Jurgen's figure) a windstorm passes and leaves behind it a tranquillity which seems, by contrast, uncanny. Nothing could explain the mystery, short of magic : and Jurgen on a sudden recollected the black gentleman's queer promise. Jurgen crossed himself.

" How unjustly now," says Jurgen, " do some people get an ill name for gratitude ! And now do I perceive how wise I am, always to speak pleasantly of everybody, in this world of tale-bearers."

Then Jurgen prepared his own supper, went to bed, and slept soundly.

" I have implicit confidence," says he, " in Lisa. I have particular confidence in her ability to take care of herself in any surroundings."

That was all very well : but time passed, and presently it began to be rumoured that Dame Lisa walked on

Morven. Her brother, who was a grocer and a member of the town-council, went thither to see about this report. And sure enough, there was Jurgen's wife walking in the twilight and muttering incessantly.

" Fie, sister ! " says the town-councillor, " this is very unseemly conduct for a married woman, and a thing likely to be talked about."

" Follow me ! " replied Dame Lisa. And the town-councillor followed her a little way in the dusk, but when she came to Amneran Heath and still went onward, he knew better than to follow.

Next evening the elder sister of Dame Lisa went to Morven. This sister had married a notary, and was a shrewd woman. In consequence, she took with her this evening a long wand of peeled willow-wood. And there was Jurgen's wife walking in the twilight and muttering incessantly.

" Fie, sister ! " says the notary's wife, who was a shrewd woman, " and do you not know that all this while Jurgen does his own sewing, and is once more making eyes at Countess Dorothy ? "

Dame Lisa shuddered ; but she only said, " Follow me ! "

And the notary's wife followed her to Amneran Heath, and across the heath, to where a cave was. This was a place of abominable repute. A lean hound came to meet them there in the twilight, lolling his tongue : but the notary's wife struck thrice with her wand, and the silent beast left them. And Dame Lisa passed silently into the cave, and her sister turned and went home to her children, weeping.

So the next evening Jurgen himself came to Morven, because all his wife's family assured him this was the manly thing to do. Jurgen left the shop in charge of Urien Villemarche, who was a highly efficient clerk. Jurgen followed his wife across Amneran Heath until they reached the cave. Jurgen would willingly have been elsewhere.

For the hound squatted upon his haunches, and seemed to grin at Jurgen ; and there were other creatures abroad, that flew low in the twilight, keeping close to the ground like owls ; but they were larger than owls and were more discomforting. And, moreover, all this was just after sunset upon Walburga's Eve, when almost anything is rather more than likely to happen.

So Jurgen said, a little peevishly : " Lisa, my dear, if you go into the cave I will have to follow you, because it is the manly thing to do. And you know how easily I take cold."

The voice of Dame Lisa, now, was thin and wailing, a curiously changed voice. " There is a cross about your neck. You must throw that away."

Jurgen was wearing such a cross, through motives of sentiment, because it had once belonged to his dead mother. But now, to pleasure his wife, he removed the trinket, and hung it on a barberry bush ; and with the reflection that this was likely to prove a deplorable business, he followed Dame Lisa into the cave.

CHAPTER II

HE tale tells that all was dark there, and Jurgen could see no one. But the cave stretched straight forward and downward, and at the far end was a glow of light. Jurgen went on and on, and so came presently to a centaur : and this surprised him not a little, because Jurgen knew that centaurs were imaginary creatures.

Certainly they were curious to look at, for here was the body of a fine bay horse, and rising from its shoulders, the sun-burnt body of a young fellow who regarded Jurgen with grave and not unfriendly eyes. The Centaur was lying beside a fire of cedar and juniper wood : near him was a platter containing a liquid with which he was anointing his hoofs. This stuff, as the Centaur rubbed it in with his fingers, turned the appearance of his hoofs to gold.

"Hail, friend," says Jurgen, "if you be the work of God."

"Your protasis is not good Greek," observed the Centaur, "because in Hellas we did not make such reservations. Besides, it is not so much my origin as my destination which concerns you."

"Well, friend, and whither are you going?"

"To the garden between dawn and sunrise, Jurgen."

"Surely, now, but that is a fine name for a garden! and it is a place I would take joy to be seeing."

"Up upon my back, Jurgen, and I will take you

thither," says the Centaur, and heaved to his feet.
Then said the Centaur, when the pawnbroker hesitated :
" Because, as you must understand, there is no other
way. For this garden does not exist, and never did
exist, in what men humorously called real life ; so that
of course only imaginary creatures such as I can
enter it."

" That sounds very reasonable," Jurgen estimated :
" but as it happens, I am looking for my wife, whom I
suspect to have been carried off by a devil, poor fellow ! "

And Jurgen began to explain to the Centaur what had
befallen.

The Centaur laughed. " It may be for that reason I
am here. There is, in any event, only one remedy in
this matter. Above all devils and above all gods—they
tell me, but certainly above all centaurs—is the power of
Koshchei the Deathless, who made things as they are."

" It is not always wholesome," Jurgen submitted, " to
speak of Koshchei. It seems especially undesirable in a
dark place like this."

" None the less, I suspect it is to him you must go for
justice."

" I would prefer not doing that," said Jurgen, with
unaffected candour.

" You have my sympathy : but there is no question
of preference where Koshchei is concerned. Do you
think, for example, that I am frowzing in this underground place by my own choice ? and knew your name
by accident ? "

Jurgen was frightened, a little. " Well, well ! but it
is usually the deuce and all, this doing of the manly
thing. How, then, can I come to Koshchei ? "

" Roundabout," says the Centaur. " There is never
any other way."

" And is the road to this garden roundabout ? "

" Oh, very much so, inasmuch as it circumvents both
destiny and common sense."

" Needs must, then," says Jurgen : " at all events, I am willing to taste any drink once."

" You will be chilled, though, travelling as you are. For you and I are going a queer way, in search of justice, over the grave of a dream and through the malice of time. So you had best put on this shirt above your other clothing."

" Indeed it is a fine snug shining garment, with curious figures on it. I accept such raiment gladly. And whom shall I be thanking for his kindness, now ? "

" My name," said the Centaur, " is Nessus."

" Well, then, friend Nessus, I am at your service."

And in a trice Jurgen was on the Centaur's back, and the two of them had somehow come out of the cave, and were crossing Amneran Heath. So they passed into a wooded place, where the light of sunset yet lingered, rather unaccountably. Now the Centaur went westward. And now about the pawnbroker's shoulders and upon his breast and over his lean arms glittered like a rainbow the many-coloured shirt of Nessus.

For a while they went through the woods, which were composed of big trees standing a goodish distance from one another, with the Centaur's gilded hoofs rustling and sinking in a thick carpet of dead leaves, all grey and brown, in level stretches that were unbroken by any undergrowth. And then they came to a white roadway that extended due west, and so were done with the woods. Now happened an incredible thing in which Jurgen would never have believed had he not seen it with his own eyes : for now the Centaur went so fast that he gained a little by a little upon the sun, thus causing it to rise in the west a little by a little ; and these two sped westward in the glory of a departed sunset. The sun fell full in Jurgen's face as he rode straight toward the west, so that he blinked and closed his eyes, and looked first toward this side, then the other. Thus it was that the country about him, and the persons

And these two sped westward in the glory of a departed sunset

they were passing, were seen by him in quick bright flashes, like pictures suddenly transmuted into other pictures; and all his memories of this shining highway were, in consequence, always confused and incoherent.

He wondered that there seemed to be so many young women along the road to the garden. Here was a slim girl in white, teasing a great brown and yellow dog that leaped about her clumsily; here a girl sat in the branches of a twisted and gnarled tree, and back of her was a broad muddied river, copper-coloured in the sun; and here shone the fair head of a tall girl on horseback, who seemed to wait for someone: in fine, the girls along the way were numberless, and Jurgen thought he recollected one or two of them.

But the Centaur went so swiftly that Jurgen could not be sure.

CHAPTER III

THE GARDEN BETWEEN DAWN AND SUNRISE

THUS it was that Jurgen and the Centaur came to the garden between dawn and sunrise, entering this place in a fashion which it is not convenient to record. But as they passed over the bridge three fled before them, screaming. And when the life had been trampled out of the small furry bodies which these three had misused, there was none to oppose the Centaur's entry into the garden between dawn and sunrise.

This was a wonderful garden: yet nothing therein was strange. Instead, it seemed that everything hereabouts was heart-breakingly familiar and very dear to Jurgen. For he had come to a broad lawn which slanted northward to a well-remembered brook: and multitudinous maples and locust-trees stood here and there, irregularly, and were being played with very lazily by an irresolute west wind, so that foliage seemed to toss and ripple everywhere like green spray: but autumn was at hand, for the locust-trees were dropping a Danaë's shower of small round yellow leaves. Around the garden was an unforgotten circle of blue hills. And this was a place of lucent twilight, unlit by either sun or stars, and with no shadows anywhere in the diffused faint radiancy that revealed this garden, which is not visible to any man except in the brief interval between dawn and sunrise.

"Why, but it is Count Emmerick's garden at

Storisende," says Jurgen, " where I used to be having such fine times when I was a lad."

" I will wager," said Nessus, " that you did not use to walk alone in this garden."

" Well, no; there was a girl."

" Just so," assented Nessus. " It is a local by-law: and here are those who comply with it."

For now had come toward them, walking together in the dawn, a handsome boy and girl. And the girl was incredibly beautiful, because everybody in the garden saw her with the vision of the boy who was with her.

" I am Rudolph," said this boy, " and she is Anne."

" And are you happy here ? " asked Jurgen.

" Oh yes, sir, we are tolerably happy: but Anne's father is very rich, and my mother is poor, so that we cannot be quite happy until I have gone into foreign lands and come back with a great many lakhs of rupees and pieces of eight."

" And what will you do with all this money, Rudolph ? "

" My duty, sir, as I see it. But I inherit defective eyesight."

" God speed to you, Rudolph ! " said Jurgen, " for many others are in your plight."

Then came to Jurgen and the Centaur another boy with the small blue-eyed person in whom he took delight. And this fat and indolent-looking boy informed them that he and the girl who was with him were walking in the glaze of the red mustard jar, which Jurgen thought was gibberish : and the fat boy said that he and the girl had decided never to grow any older, which Jurgen said was excellent good sense if only they could manage it.

" Oh, I can manage that," said this fat boy, reflectively, " if only I do not find the managing of it uncomfortable."

Jurgen for a moment regarded him, and then gravely shook hands.

" I feel for you," said Jurgen, " for I perceive that you,

too, are a monstrous clever fellow: so life will get the best of you."

"But is not cleverness the main thing, sir?"

"Time will show you, my lad," says Jurgen, a little sorrowfully. "And God speed to you, for many others are in your plight."

And a host of boys and girls did Jurgen see in the garden. And all the faces that Jurgen saw were young and glad and very lovely and quite heart-breakingly confident, as young persons beyond numbering came toward Jurgen and passed him there, in the first glow of dawn: so they all went exulting in the glory of their youth, and foreknowing life to be a puny antagonist from whom one might take very easily anything which one desired. And all passed in couples—"as though they came from the Ark," said Jurgen. But the Centaur said they followed a precedent which was far older than the Ark.

"For in this garden," said the Centaur, "each man that ever lived has sojourned for a little while, with no company save his illusions. I must tell you again that in this garden are encountered none but imaginary creatures. And stalwart persons take their hour of recreation here, and go hence unaccompanied, to become aldermen and respected merchants and bishops, and to be admired as captains upon prancing horses, or even as kings upon tall thrones; each in his station thinking not at all of the garden ever any more. But now and then come timid persons, Jurgen, who fear to leave this garden without an escort: so these must need go hence with one or another imaginary creature, to guide them about alleys and by-paths, because imaginary creatures find little nourishment in the public highways, and shun them. Thus must these timid persons skulk about obscurely with their diffident and skittish guides, and they do not ever venture willingly into the thronged places where men get horses and build thrones."

"And what becomes of these timid persons, Centaur?"

"Why, sometimes they spoil paper, Jurgen, and sometimes they spoil human lives."

"Then are these accursed persons," Jurgen considered.

"You should know best," replied the Centaur.

"Oh, very probably," said Jurgen. "Meanwhile here is one who walks alone in this garden, and I wonder to see the local by-laws thus violated."

Now Nessus looked at Jurgen for a while without speaking; and in the eyes of the Centaur was so much of comprehension and compassion that it troubled Jurgen. For somehow it made Jurgen fidget and consider this an unpleasantly personal way of looking at anybody.

"Yes, certainly," said the Centaur, "this woman walks alone. But there is no help for her loneliness, since the lad who loved this woman is dead."

"Nessus, I am willing to be reasonably sorry about it. Still, is there any need of pulling quite such a portentously long face? After all, a great many other persons have died, off and on: and for anything I can say to the contrary, this particular young fellow may have been no especial loss to anybody."

Again the Centaur said, "You should know best."

CHAPTER IV

THE DOROTHY WHO DID NOT UNDERSTAND

OR now had come to Jurgen and the Centaur a gold-haired woman, clothed all in white, and walking alone. She was tall, and lovely and tender to regard : and hers was not the red and white comeliness of many ladies that were famed for beauty, but rather it had the even glow of ivory. Her nose was large and high in the bridge, her flexible mouth was not of the smallest : and yet whatever other persons might have said, to Jurgen this woman's countenance was in all things perfect. Perhaps this was because he never saw her as she was. For certainly the colour of her eyes stayed a matter never revealed to him : grey, blue or green, there was no saying : they varied as does the sea ; but always these eyes were lovely and friendly and perturbing.

Jurgen remembered that : for Jurgen saw this was Count Emmerick's second sister, Dorothy la Désirée, whom Jurgen very long ago (a many years before he met Dame Lisa and set up in business as a pawn-broker) had hymned in innumerable verses as Heart's Desire.

"And this is the only woman whom I ever loved," Jurgen remembered, upon a sudden. For people cannot always be thinking of these matters.

So he saluted her, with such deference as is due to a countess from a tradesman, and yet with unforgotten tremors waking in his staid body. But the strangest was yet to be seen, for he noted now that this was not a handsome woman in middle life but a young girl.

" I do not understand," he said, aloud : " for you are Dorothy. And yet it seems to me that you are not the Countess Dorothy who is Heitman Michael's wife."

And the girl tossed her fair head, with that careless lovely gesture which the Countess had forgotten. " Heitman Michael is well enough, for a nobleman, and my brother is at me day and night to marry the man : and certainly Heitman Michael's wife will go in satin and diamonds at half the courts of Christendom, with many lackeys to attend her. But I am not to be thus purchased."

" So you told a boy that I remember, very long ago. Yet you married Heitman Michael, for all that, and in the teeth of a number of other fine declarations."

" Oh no, not I," said this Dorothy, wondering. " I never married anybody. And Heitman Michael has never married anybody, either, old as he is. For he is twenty-eight, and looks every day of it ! But who are you, friend, that have such curious notions about me ? "

" That question I will answer, just as though it were put reasonably. For surely you perceive I am Jurgen."

" I never knew but one Jurgen. And he is a young man, barely come of age——" Then as she paused in speech, whatever was the matter upon which this girl now meditated, her cheeks were tenderly coloured by the thought of it, and in her knowledge of this thing her eyes took infinite joy.

And Jurgen understood. He had come back somehow to the Dorothy whom he had loved, but departed, and past overtaking by the fleet hoofs of centaurs, was the boy who had once loved this Dorothy, and who had rhymed of her as his Heart's Desire : and in the garden there was of this boy no trace. Instead, the girl was talking to a staid and paunchy pawnbroker, of forty-and-something.

So Jurgen shrugged, and looked toward the Centaur : but Nessus had discreetly wandered away from them, in search of four-leafed clovers. Now the east had grown brighter, and its crimson began to be coloured with gold.

" Yes, I have heard of this other Jurgen," says the pawnbroker. " Oh, Madame Dorothy, but it was he that loved you ! "

" No more than I loved him. Through a whole summer have I loved Jurgen."

And the knowledge that this girl spoke a wondrous truth was now to Jurgen a joy that was keen as pain. And he stood motionless for a while, scowling and biting his lips.

" I wonder how long the poor devil loved you ! He also loved for a whole summer, it may be. And yet again, it may be that he loved you all his life. For twenty years and for more than twenty years I have debated the matter : and I am as well informed as when I started."

" But, friend, you talk in riddles."

" Is not that customary when age talks with youth ? For I am an old fellow, in my forties : and you, as I know now, are near eighteen,—or rather, four months short of being eighteen, for it is August. Nay, more, it is the August of a year I had not looked ever to see again ; and again Dom Manuel reigns over us, that man of iron whom I saw die so horribly. All this seems very improbable."

Then Jurgen meditated for a while. He shrugged.

" Well, and what could anybody expect me to do about it ? Somehow it has befallen that I, who am but the shadow of what I was, now walk among shadows, and we converse with the thin intonations of dead persons. For, Madame Dorothy, you who are not yet eighteen, in this same garden there was once a boy who loved a girl, with such love as it puzzles me to think of now. I believe that she loved him. Yes, certainly it is a cordial to the tired and battered heart which nowadays pumps blood for me, to think that for a little while, for a whole summer, these two were as brave and comely and clean a pair of sweethearts as the world has known."

Thus Jurgen spoke. But his thought was that this was a girl whose equal for loveliness and delight was not to be found between two oceans. Long and long ago that doubtfulness of himself which was closer to him than his skin had fretted Jurgen into believing the Dorothy he had loved was but a piece of his imaginings. But certainly this girl was real. And sweet she was, and innocent she was, and light of heart and feet, beyond the reach of any man's inventiveness. No! Jurgen had not invented her; and it strangely contented him to know as much.

"Tell me your story, sir," says she, "for I love all romances."

" Ah, my dear child, but I cannot tell you very well of just what happened. As I look back, there is a blinding glory of green woods and lawns and moonlit nights and dance music and unreasonable laughter. I remember her hair and eyes, and the curving and the feel of her red mouth, and once when I was bolder than ordinary—— But that is hardly worth raking up at this late day. Well, I see these things in memory as plainly as I now seem to see your face : but I can recollect hardly anything she said. Perhaps, now I think of it, she was not very intelligent, and said nothing worth remembering. But the boy loved her, and was happy, because her lips and heart were his, and he, as the saying is, had plucked a diamond from the world's ring. True, she was a count's daughter and the sister of a count : but in those days the boy quite firmly intended to become a duke or an emperor or something of that sort, so the transient discrepancy did not worry them."

" I know. Why, Jurgen is going to be a duke, too," says she, very proudly, " though he did think, a great while ago, before he knew me, of being a cardinal, on

account of the robes. But cardinals are not allowed to
marry, you see—— And I am forgetting your story,
too! What happened then?"

"They parted in September—with what vows it
hardly matters now—and the boy went into Gâtinais, to
win his spurs under the old Vidame de Soyecourt. And
presently—oh, a good while before Christmas!—came
the news that Dorothy la Désirée had married rich
Heitman Michael."

"But that is what I am called! And, as you know,
there is a Heitman Michael who is always plaguing me.
Is that not strange? for you tell me all this happened a
great while ago."

"Indeed, the story is very old, and old it was when
Methuselah was teething. There is no older and more
common story anywhere. As the sequel, it would be
heroic to tell you this boy's life was ruined. But I do
not think it was. Instead, he had learned all of a sudden
that which at twenty-one is heady knowledge. That
was the hour which taught him sorrow and rage, and
sneering, too, for a redemption. Oh, it was armour
that hour brought him, and a humour to use it, because
no woman now could hurt him very seriously. No, never
any more!"

"Ah, the poor boy!" she said, divinely tender, and
smiling as a goddess smiles, not quite in mirth.

"Well, women, as he knew by experience now, were
the pleasantest of playfellows. So he began to play.
Rampaging through the world he went in the pride of
his youth and in the armour of his hurt. And songs he
made for the pleasure of kings, and sword-play he made
for the pleasure of men, and a whispering he made for
the pleasure of women, in places where renown was, and
where he trod boldly, giving pleasure to everybody, in
those fine days. But the whispering, and all that followed
the whispering, was his best game, and the game he
played for the longest while, with many brightly coloured

playmates who took the game more seriously than he did.   And their faith in the game's importance, and in him and his high-sounding nonsense, he very often found amusing : and in their other chattels too he took his natural pleasure.   Then, when he had played sufficiently, he held a consultation with divers waning appetites ; and he married the handsome daughter of an estimable pawnbroker in a fair line of business.   And he lived with his wife very much as two people customarily live together.   So, all in all, I would not say his life was ruined."

"Why, then, it was," said Dorothy.   She stirred uneasily, with an impatient sigh ; and you saw that she was vaguely puzzled.   "Oh, but somehow I think you are a very horrible old man : and you seem doubly horrible in that glittering queer garment you are wearing."

"No woman ever praised a woman's handiwork, and each of you is particularly severe upon her own.   But you are interrupting the saga."

"I do not see "—and those large bright eyes, of which the colour was so indeterminable and so dear to Jurgen, seemed even larger now—" but I do not see how there could well be any more."

"Still, human hearts survive the benediction of the priest, as you may perceive any day.   This man, at least, inherited his father-in-law's business, and found it, quite as he had anticipated, the fittest of vocations for a cashiered poet.   And so, I suppose, he was content.   Ah, yes ; but after a while Heitman Michael returned from foreign parts, along with his lackeys, and plate, and chest upon chest of merchandise, and his fine horses, and his wife.   And he who had been her lover could see her now, after so many years, whenever he liked.   She was a handsome stranger.   That was all.   She was rather stupid.   She was nothing remarkable, one way or another. This respectable pawnbroker saw that quite plainly : day by day he writhed under the knowledge.   Because, as I must tell you, he could not retain composure in her presence, even now. No, he was never able to do that."

The girl somewhat condensed her brows over this information. " You mean that he still loved her. Why, but of course ! "

" My child," says Jurgen, now with a reproving forefinger, " you are an incurable romanticist. The man disliked her and despised her. At any event, he assured himself that he did. Well, even so, this handsome stupid stranger held his eyes, and muddled his thoughts, and put errors into his accounts : and when he touched her hand he did not sleep that night as he was used to sleep. Thus he saw her, day after day. And they whispered that this handsome and stupid stranger had a liking for young men who aided her artfully to deceive her husband : but she never showed any such favour to the respectable pawnbroker. For youth had gone out of him, and it seemed that nothing in particular happened. Well, that was his saga. About her I do not know. And I shall never know ! But certainly she got the name of deceiving Heitman Michael with two young men, or with five young men it might be, but never with a respectable pawnbroker."

" I think that is an exceedingly cynical and stupid story," observed the girl. " And so I shall be off to look for Jurgen. For he makes love very amusingly," says Dorothy, with the sweetest, loveliest meditative smile that ever was lost to heaven.

And a madness came upon Jurgen, there in the garden between dawn and sunrise, and a disbelief in such injustice as now seemed incredible.

" No, Heart's Desire," he cried, " I will not let you go. For you are dear and pure and faithful, and all my evil dream, wherein you were a wanton and befooled me, was not true. Surely, mine was a dream that can never be true so long as there is any justice upon earth. Why, there is no imaginable God who would permit a boy to be robbed of that which in my evil dream was taken from me ! "

" And still I cannot understand your talking, about this dream of yours—— ! "

" Why, it seemed to me I had lost the most of myself; and there was left only a brain which played with ideas, and a body that went delicately down pleasant ways. And I could not believe as my fellows believed, nor could I love them, nor could I detect anything in aught they said or did save their exceeding folly : for I had lost their cordial common faith in the importance of what use they made of half-hours and months and years ; and because a jill-flirt had opened my eyes so that they saw too much, I had lost faith in the importance of my own actions, too. There was a little time of which the passing might be made endurable ; beyond gaped unpredictable darkness : and that was all there was of certainty anywhere. Now tell me, Heart's Desire, but was not that a foolish dream ? For these things never happened. Why, it would not be fair if these things ever happened ! "

And the girl's eyes were wide and puzzled and a little frightened. " I do not understand what you are saying : and there is that about you which troubles me unspeakably. For you call me by the name which none but Jurgen used, and it seems to me that you are Jurgen ; and yet you are not Jurgen."

" But I am truly Jurgen. And look you, I have done what never any man has done before ! For I have won back to that first love whom every man must lose, no matter whom he marries. I have come back again, passing very swiftly over the grave of a dream and through the malice of time, to my Heart's Desire ! And how strange it seems that I did not know this thing was inevitable ! "

" Still, friend, I do not understand you."

" Why, but I yawned and fretted in preparation for some great and beautiful adventure which was to befall me by and by, and dazedly I toiled forward. Whereas behind me all the while was the garden between dawn and sunrise, and therein you awaited me ! Now assuredly, the life of every man is a quaintly builded tale, in which the right and proper ending comes first. Thereafter time runs forward, not as schoolmen fable in a straight line, but in a vast closed curve, returning to the place of its starting. And it is by a dim foreknowledge of this, by some faint prescience of justice and reparation being given them by and by, that men have heart to live. For I know now that I have always known this thing. What else was living good for unless it brought me back to you ? "

But the girl shook her small glittering head, very sadly. " I do not understand you, and I fear you. For you talk foolishness and in your face I see the face of Jurgen as one might see the face of a dead man drowned in muddy water."

" Yet I am truly Jurgen, and, as it seems to me, for the first time since we were parted. For I am strong and admirable—even I, who sneered and played so long, because I thought myself a thing of no worth at all. That which has been since you and I were young together is as a mist that passes : and I am strong and admirable, and all my being is one vast hunger for you, my dearest, and I will not let you go, for you, and you alone, are my Heart's Desire."

Now the girl was looking at him very steadily, with a small puzzled frown, and with her vivid young soft lips a little parted. And all her tender loveliness was glorified by the light of a sky that had turned to dusty palpitating gold.

" Ah, but you say that you are strong and admirable : and I can only marvel at such talking. For I see that which all men see."

And then Dorothy showed him the little mirror which was attached to the long chain of turquoise matrix about her neck : and Jurgen studied the frightened foolish aged face that he found in the mirror.

Thus drearily did sanity return to Jurgen : and his flare of passion died, and the fever and storm and the impetuous whirl of things was ended, and the man was very weary. And in the silence he heard the piping cry of a bird that seemed to seek for what it could not find.

" Well, I am answered," said the pawnbroker : " and yet I know that this is not the final answer. Dearer than any hope of heaven was that moment when awed surmises first awoke as to the new strange loveliness which I had seen in the face of Dorothy. It was then I noted the new faint flush suffusing her face from chin to brow so often as my eyes encountered and found new lights in the shining eyes which were no longer entirely frank in meeting mine. Well, let that be, for I do not love Heitman Michael's wife.

" It is a grief to remember how we followed love, and found his service lovely. It is bitter to recall the sweetness of those vows which proclaimed her mine eternally, —vows that were broken in their making by prolonged and unforgotten kisses. We used to laugh at Heitman Michael then ; we used to laugh at everything. Thus for a while, for a whole summer, we were as brave and comely and clean a pair of sweethearts as the world has known. But let that be, for I do not love Heitman Michael's wife.

" Our love was fair but short-lived. There is none that may revive him since the small feet of Dorothy trod out this small love's life. Yet when this life of ours too is over—this parsimonious life which can allow us no more love for anybody—must we not win back, somehow, to that faith we vowed against eternity, and be content again, in some fair-coloured realm ? Assuredly I think this thing will happen. Well, but let that be, for I do not love Heitman Michael's wife."

" Why, this is excellent hearing," observed Dorothy,

" because I see that you are converting your sorrow into the raw stuff of verses. So I shall be off to look for Jurgen, since he makes love quite otherwise and far more amusingly."

And again, whatever was the matter upon which this girl now meditated, her cheeks were tenderly coloured by the thought of it, and in her knowledge of this thing her eyes took infinite joy.

Thus it was for a moment only: for she left Jurgen now, with the friendliest light waving of her hand; and so passed from him, not thinking of this old fellow any longer, as he could see, even in the instant she turned from him. And she went toward the dawn, in search of that young Jurgen whom she, who was perfect in all things, had loved, though only for a little while, not undeservedly.

CHAPTER V

REQUIREMENTS OF BREAD AND BUTTER

"ESSUS," says Jurgen, "and am I so changed? For that Dorothy whom I loved in youth did not know me."

"Good and evil keep very exact accounts," replied the Centaur, "and the face of every man is their ledger. Meanwhile the sun rises, it is already another workday: and when the shadows of those two who come to take possession fall full upon the garden, I warn you, there will be astounding changes brought about by the requirements of bread and butter. You have not time to revive old memories by chatting with the others to whom you babbled aforetime in this garden."

"Ah, Centaur, in the garden between dawn and sunrise there was never any other save Dorothy la Désirée."

The Centaur shrugged. "It may be you forget; it is certain that you underestimate the local population. Some of the transient visitors you have seen, and in addition hereabouts dwell the year round all manner of imaginary creatures. The fairies live just southward, and the gnomes too. To your right is the realm of the Valkyries: the Amazons and the Cynocephali are their allies: all three of these nations are continually at loggerheads with their neighbours, the Baba-Yagas, whom Morfei cooks for, and whose monarch is Oh, a person very dangerous to name. Northward dwell the Lepracauns and the Men of Hunger, whose king is Clobhair. My people, who are ruled by Chiron, live even further to the north. The Sphinx pastures on yonder mountain; and now the Chimæra is old and generally derided, they say that Cerberus visits the Sphinx at twilight, although I was never the person to disseminate scandal——"

"Centaur," said Jurgen, "and what is Dorothy doing here?"

"Why, all the women that any man has ever loved live here," replied the Centaur, "for very obvious reasons."

"That is a hard saying, friend."

Nessus tapped with his forefinger upon the back of Jurgen's hand. "Worm's-meat! this is the destined food, do what you will, of small white worms. This by and by will be a struggling pale corruption, like seething milk. That too is a hard saying, Jurgen. But it is a true saying."

"And was that Dorothy whom I loved in youth an imaginary creature?"

"My poor Jurgen, you who were once a poet! She was your masterpiece. For there was only a shallow, stupid and airy, high-nosed and light-haired miss, with no remarkable good looks,—and consider what your ingenuity made from such poor material! You should be proud of yourself."

"No, Centaur, I cannot very well be proud of my folly: yet I do not regret it. I have been befooled by a bright shadow of my own raising, you tell me, and I concede it to be probable. No less, I served a lovely shadow; and my heart will keep the memory of that loveliness until life ends, in a world where other men follow pantingly after shadows which are not even pretty."

"There is something in that, Jurgen: there is also something in an old tale we used to tell in Thessaly, about a fox and certain grapes."

"Well, but look you, Nessus, there is an emperor that reigns now in Constantinople and occasionally does business with me.   Yes, and I could tell you tales of by what shifts he came to the throne——"

"Men's hands are by ordinary soiled in climbing," quoth the Centaur.

"And 'Jurgen,' this emperor says to me, not many months ago, as he sat in his palace, crowned and dreary and trying to cheat me out of my fair profit on some emeralds,—'Jurgen, I cannot sleep of nights, because of that fool Alexius, who comes into my room with staring eyes and the bowstring still about his neck.   And my Varangians must be in league with that silly ghost, because I constantly order them to keep Alexius out of my bedchamber, and they do not obey me, Jurgen.   To be King of the East is not to the purpose, Jurgen, when one must submit to such vexations.'   Yes, it was Cæsar Pharamond himself said this to me : and I deduce the shadow of a crown has led him into an ugly pickle, for all that he is the mightiest monarch in the world.   And I would not change with Cæsar Pharamond, not I who am a respectable pawnbroker, with my home in fee and my bit of tilled land.   Well, this is a queer world, to be sure : and this garden is visited by no stranger things than pop into a man's mind sometimes, without his knowing how."

"Ah, but you must understand that the garden is speedily to be remodelled.   Yonder you may observe the two whose requirements are to rid the place of all fantastic unremunerative notions ; and who will develop the natural resources of this garden according to generally approved methods."

And from afar Jurgen could see two figures coming out of the east, so tall that their heads rose above the encircling hills and glistened in the rays of a sun which was not yet visible.   One was a white pasty-looking giant, with a crusty expression : he walked with the aid of a cane. The other was of a pale yellow colour : his face was oily, and he rode on a vast cow that was called Ædhumla.

"Make way there, brother, with your staff of life," says the yellow giant, "for there is much to do hereabouts."

"Ay, brother, this place must be altered a deal before it meets with our requirements," the other grumbled. "May I be toasted if I know where to begin!"

Then as the giants turned dull and harsh faces toward the garden, the sun came above the circle of blue hills, so that the mingled shadows of these two giants fell across the garden. For an instant Jurgen saw the place oppressed by that attenuated mile-long shadow, as in heraldry you may see a black bar painted sheer across some brightly emblazoned shield. Then the radiancy of everything twitched and vanished, as a bubble bursts.

And Jurgen was standing in the midst of a field, very neatly ploughed, but with nothing as yet growing in it. And the Centaur was with him still, it seemed, for there were the creature's hoofs, but all the gold had been washed or rubbed away from them in travelling with Jurgen.

"See, Nessus!" Jurgen cried, "the garden is made desolate. Oh, Nessus, was it fair that so much loveliness should be thus wasted?"

"Nay," said the Centaur, "nay!" Long and wailingly he whinnied, "Nay!"

And when Jurgen raised his eyes he saw that his companion was not a centaur, but only a strayed riding-horse.

"Were you the animal, then," says Jurgen, "and was it a quite ordinary animal, that conveyed me to the garden between dawn and sunrise?" And Jurgen laughed disconsolately. "At all events, you have clothed me in a curious fine shirt. And, now I look, your bridle is marked with a coronet. So I will return you to the castle at Bellegarde, and it may be that Heitman Michael will reward me."

Then Jurgen mounted this horse and rode away from the ploughed field wherein nothing grew as yet. As they left the furrows they came to a signboard with writing on it, in a peculiar red and yellow lettering.

Jurgen paused to decipher this.

" Read me ! " was written on the signboard : " read me, and judge if you understand ! So you stopped in your journey because I called, scenting something unusual, something droll. Thus, although I am nothing, and even less, there is no one that sees me but lingers here. Stranger, I am a law of the universe. Stranger, render the law what is due the law ! "

Jurgen felt cheated. " A very foolish signboard, indeed ! for how can it be ' a law of the universe,' when there is no meaning to it ? " says Jurgen. " Why, for any law to be meaningless would not be fair."

CHAPTER VI

SHOWING THAT SEREDA IS FEMININE

HEN, having snapped his fingers at that foolish signboard, Jurgen would have turned easterly, toward Bellegarde : but his horse resisted. The pawnbroker decided to accept this as an omen.

"Forward, then!" he said, "in the name of Koshchei." And thereafter Jurgen permitted the horse to choose its own way.

Thus Jurgen came through a forest, wherein he saw many things not salutary to notice, to a great stone house like a prison, and he sought shelter there. But he could find nobody about the place, until he came to a large hall, newly swept. This was a depressing apartment, in its chill neat emptiness, for it was unfurnished save for a bare deal table, upon which lay a yardstick and a pair of scales. Above this table hung a wicker cage containing a blue bird, and another wicker cage containing three white pigeons. And in this hall a woman, no longer young, dressed all in blue, and wearing a white towel by way of head-dress was assorting curiously coloured cloths.

She had very bright eyes, with wrinkled lids ; and now as she looked up at Jurgen her shrunk jaws quivered.

"Ah," says she, "I have a visitor. Good day to you, in your glittering shirt. It is a garment I seem to recognise."

"Good day, grandmother! I am looking for my wife, whom I suspect to have been carried off by a devil, poor

Then JURGEN knew with whom he talked

fellow ! Now, having lost my way, I have come to pass the night under your roof."

" Very good : but few come seeking Mother Sereda of their own accord."

Then Jurgen knew with whom he talked : and inwardly he was perturbed, for all the Léshy are unreliable in their dealings.

So when he spoke it was very civilly. " And what do you do here, grandmother ? "

" I bleach. In time I shall bleach that garment you are wearing. For I take the colour out of all things. Thus you see these stuffs here, as they are now. Clotho spun the glowing threads, and Lachesis wove them, as you observe, in curious patterns, very marvellous to see : but when I am done with these stuffs there will be no more colour or beauty or strangeness anywhere apparent than in so many dish-clouts."

" Now I perceive," says Jurgen, " that your power and dominion is more great than any other power which is in the world."

He made a song of this, in praise of the Léshy and their Days, but more especially in praise of the might of Mother Sereda and of the ruins that have fallen on Wednesday. To Chetverg and Utornik and Subbota he gave their due. Pyatinka and Nedelka also did Jurgen commend for such demolishments as have enregistered their names in the calendar of saints, no less. Ah, but there was none like Mother Sereda : hers was the centre of that power which is the Léshy's. The others did but nibble at temporal things, like furtive mice : she devastated, like a sandstorm, so that there were many dust-heaps where Mother Sereda had passed, but nothing else.

And so on, and so on. The song was no masterpiece, and would not be bettered by repetition. But it was all untrammelled eulogy, and the old woman beat time to it with her lean hands : and her shrunk jaws quivered, and she nodded her white-wrapped head this way and

that way, with a rolling motion, and on her thin lips was
a very proud and foolish smile.

"That is a good song," says she; "oh, yes, an excellent
song! But you report nothing of my sister Pandelis who
controls the day of the Moon."

"Monday!" says Jurgen: "yes, I neglected Monday,
perhaps because she is the oldest of you, but in part
because of the exigencies of my rhyme scheme. We must
let Pandelis go unhymned. How can I remember everything when I consider the might of Sereda?"

"Why, but," says Mother Sereda, "Pandelis may not
like it, and she may take holiday from her washing some
day to have a word with you. However, I repeat, that is
an excellent song. And in return for your praise of me,
I will tell you that, if your wife has been carried off by
a devil, your affair is one which Koshchei alone can
remedy. Assuredly, I think it is to him you must go for
justice."

"But how may I come to him, grandmother?"

"Oh, as to that, it does not matter at all which road
you follow. All highways, as the saying is, lead roundabout to Koshchei. The one thing needful is not to
stand still. This much I will tell you also for your song's
sake, because that was an excellent song, and nobody ever
made a song in praise of me before to-day."

Now Jurgen wondered to see what a simple old
creature was this Mother Sereda, who sat before him
shaking and grinning and frail as a dead leaf, with her
head wrapped in a common kitchen-towel, and whose
power was so enormous.

"To think of it," Jurgen reflected, "that the world I
inhabit is ordered by beings who are not one-tenth so
clever as I am! I have often suspected as much, and it
is decidedly unfair. Now let me see if I cannot make
something out of being such a monstrous clever fellow."

Jurgen said aloud: "I do not wonder that no practising
poet ever presumed to make a song of you. You are too

majestical. You frighten these rhymesters, who feel themselves to be unworthy of so great a theme. So it remained for you to be appreciated by a pawnbroker, since it is we who handle and observe the treasures of this world after you have handled them."

" Do you think so ? " says she, more pleased than ever. " Now, may be that was the way of it. But I wonder that you who are so fine a poet should ever have become a pawnbroker."

" Well, and indeed, Mother Sereda, your wonder seems to me another wonder : for I can think of no profession better suited to a retired poet. Why, there is the variety of company ! for high and low and even the genteel are pressed sometimes for money : then the ploughman slouches into my shop, and the duke sends for me privately. So the people I know, and the bits of their lives I pop into, give me a deal to romance about."

" Ah, yes, indeed," says Mother Sereda, wisely, " that well may be the case. But I do not hold with romance, myself."

" Moreover, sitting in my shop, I wait there quiet-like while tribute comes to me from the ends of earth. Every-thing which men and women have valued anywhere comes sooner or later to me : and jewels and fine knickknacks that were the pride of queens they bring me, and wedding rings, and the baby's cradle with his little tooth marks on the rim of it, and silver coffin-handles, or it may be an old frying-pan, they bring me, but all comes to Jurgen. So that just to sit there in my dark shop quiet-like, and wonder about the history of my belongings and how they were made mine, is poetry, and is the deep and high and ancient thinking of a god who is dozing among what time has left of a dead world, if you understand me, Mother Sereda."

" I understand : oho, I understand that which pertains to gods, for a sufficient reason."

" And then another thing, you do not need any turn

for business : people are glad to get whatever you choose
to offer, for they would not come otherwise. So you get
the shining and rough-edged coins that you can feel the
proud king's head on, with his laurel-wreath like millet
seed under your fingers ; and you get the flat and greenish
coins that are smeared with the titles and the chins and
hooked noses of emperors whom nobody remembers or
cares about any longer : all just by waiting there quiet-
like, and making a favour of it to let customers give you
their belongings for a third of what they are worth.
And that is easy labour, even for a poet."

"I understand : I understand all labour."

"And people treat you a deal more civilly than any real
need is, because they are ashamed of trafficking with you
at all. I dispute if a poet could get such civility shown him
in any other profession. And finally, there is the long
idleness between business interviews, with nothing to do
save sit there quiet-like and think about the queerness of
things in general : and that is always rare employment for
a poet, even without the tatters of so many lives and
homes heaped up about him like spillikins. So that I
would say in all, Mother Sereda, there is certainly no
profession better suited to an old poet than the profession
of pawnbroking."

"Certainly, there may be something in what you tell
me," observes Mother Sereda. "I know what the Little
Gods are, and I know what work is, but I do not think
about these other matters, nor about anything else. I
bleach."

"Ah, and a great deal more I could be saying, too,
godmother, but for the fear of wearying you. Nor would
I have run on at all about my private affairs were it not
that we two are so close related. And kith makes kind,
as people say."

"But how can you and I be kin ? "

"Why, heyday, and was I not born upon a Wednesday ?
That makes you my godmother, does it not ? "

" I do not know, dearie, I am sure. Nobody ever cared to claim kin with Mother Sereda before this," says she, pathetically.

" There can be no doubt, though, on the point, no possible doubt. Sabellius states it plainly. Artemidorus Minor, I grant you, holds the question debatable, but his reasons for doing so are tolerably notorious. Besides, what does all his flimsy sophistry avail against Nicanor's fine chapter on this very subject? Crushing, I consider it. His logic is final and irrefutable. What can anyone say against Sævius Nicanor?—ah, what indeed? " demanded Jurgen.

And he wondered if there might not have been perchance some such persons somewhere, after all. Their names, in any event, sounded very plausible to Jurgen.

" Ah, dearie, I was never one for learning. It may be as you say."

" You say ' it may be,' godmother. That embarrasses me, rather, because I was about to ask for my christening gift, which in the press of other matters you overlooked some forty years back. You will readily conceive that your negligence, however unintentional, might possibly give rise to unkindly criticism : and so I felt I ought to mention it, in common fairness to you."

" As for that, dearie, ask what you will within the limits of my power. For mine are all the sapphires and turquoises and whatever else in this dusty world is blue ; and mine likewise are all the Wednesdays that have ever been or ever will be : and any one of these will I freely give you in return for your fine speeches and your tender heart."

" Ah, but, godmother, would it be quite just for you to accord me so much more than is granted to other persons ? "

" Why, no : but what have I to do with justice ? I bleach. Come now, then, do you make a choice ! for I can assure you that my sapphires are of the first water, and that many of my oncoming Wednesdays will be well worth seeing."

"No, godmother, I never greatly cared for jewelry: and the future is but dressing and undressing, and shaving, and eating, and computing percentage, and so on; the future does not interest me now. So I shall modestly content myself with a second-hand Wednesday, with one that you have used and have no further need of: and it will be a Wednesday in the August of such and such a year."

Mother Sereda agreed to this. "But there are certain rules to be observed," says she, "for one must have system."

As she spoke, she undid the towel about her head, and she took a blue comb from her white hair: and she showed Jurgen what was engraved on the comb. It frightened Jurgen, a little: but he nodded assent.

"First, though," says Mother Sereda, "here is the blue bird. Would you not rather have that, dearie, than your Wednesday? Most people would."

"Ah, but, godmother," he replied, "I am Jurgen. No, it is not the blue bird I desire."

So Mother Sereda took from the wall the wicker cage containing the three white pigeons: and going before him, with small hunched shoulders, and shuffling her feet along the flagstones, she led the way into a courtyard, where, sure enough, they found a tethered he-goat. Of a dark blue colour this beast was, and his eyes were wiser than the eyes of a beast.

Then Jurgen set about that which Mother Sereda said was necessary.

CHAPTER VII

OF COMPROMISES ON A WEDNESDAY

O it was that, riding upon a horse whose bridle was marked with a coronet, the pawnbroker returned to a place, and to a moment, which he remembered. It was rather queer to be a fine young fellow again, and to foresee all that was to happen for the next twenty years.

As it chanced, the first person he encountered was his mother Azra, whom Coth had loved very greatly but not long. And Jurgen talked with Azra of what clothes he would be likely to need in Gâtinais, and of how often he would write to her. She disparaged the new shirt he was wearing, as was to be expected, since Azra had always preferred to select her son's clothing rather than trust to Jurgen's taste. His new horse she admitted to be a handsome animal; and only hoped he had not stolen it from anybody who would get him into trouble. For Azra, it must be recorded, had never any confidence in her son; and was the only woman, Jurgen felt, who really understood him.

And now as his beautiful young mother impartially petted and snapped at him, poor Jurgen thought of that very real dissension and severance which in the oncoming years was to arise between them; and of how she would die without his knowing of her death for two whole months; and of how his life thereafter would be changed, somehow, and the world would become an unstable place in which you could no longer put cordial faith. And he

39

foreknew all the remorse he was to shrug away, after the
squandering of so much pride and love.   But these things
were not yet : and besides, these things were inevitable.

"And yet that these things should be inevitable is
decidedly not fair," said Jurgen.

So it was with all the persons he encountered.   The
people whom he loved when at his best as a fine young
fellow were so very soon, and through petty causes, to
become nothing to him, and he himself was to be con-
verted into a commonplace tradesman.   And living
seemed to Jurgen a wasteful and inequitable process.

Then Jurgen left the home of his youth, and rode
toward Bellegarde, and tethered his horse upon the heath,
and went into the castle.   Thus Jurgen came to Dorothy.
She was lovely and dear, and yet, by some odd turn, not
quite so lovely and dear as the Dorothy he had seen in
the garden between dawn and sunrise.   And Dorothy, like
everybody else, praised Jurgen's wonderful new shirt.

"It is designed for such festivals," said Jurgen,
modestly—"a little notion of my own.   A bit extreme,
some persons might consider it, but there is no pleasing
everybody.   And I like a trifle of colour."

For there was a masque that night at the castle of
Bellegarde : and wildly droll and sad it was to Jurgen to
remember what was to befall so many of the participants.

Jurgen had not forgotten this Wednesday, this ancient
Wednesday upon which Messire de Montors had brought
the Confraternity of St. Médard from Brunbelois, to
enact a masque of The Birth of Hercules, as the vaga-
bonds were now doing, to hilarious applause.   Jurgen
remembered it was the day before Bellegarde discovered
that Count Emmerick's guest, the Vicomte de Puysange,
was in reality the notorious outlaw, Perion de la Forêt.
Well, yonder the yet undetected impostor was talking
very earnestly with Dame Melicent : and Jurgen knew
all that was in store for this pair of lovers.

Meanwhile, as Jurgen reflected, the real Vicomte de

Puysange was at this moment lying in a delirium, yonder at Benoit's : to-morrow the true Vicomte would be recognised, and within the year the Vicomte would have married Félise de Soyecourt, and later Jurgen would meet her, in the orchard ; and Jurgen knew what was to happen then also.

And Messire de Montors was watching Dame Melicent, sidewise, while he joked with little Ettarre, who was this night permitted to stay up later than usual, in honour of the masque : and Jurgen knew that this young bishop was to become Pope of Rome, no less ; and that the child he joked with was to become the woman for possession of whom Guiron des Rocques and the surly-looking small boy yonder, Maugis d'Aigremont, would contend with each other until the country hereabouts had been devastated, and the castle wherein Jurgen now was had been besieged, and this part of it burned. And wildly droll and sad it was to Jurgen thus to remember all that was going to happen to these persons, and to all the other persons who were frolicking in the shadow of their doom and laughing at this trivial masque.

For here—with so much of ruin and failure impending, and with sorrow prepared so soon to smite a many of these revellers in ways foreknown to Jurgen ; and with death resistlessly approaching so soon to make an end of almost all this company in some unlovely fashion that Jurgen foreknew exactly,—here laughter seemed unreasonable and ghastly. Why, but Reinault yonder, who laughed so loud, with his cropped head flung back : would Reinault be laughing in quite this manner if he knew the round strong throat he thus exposed was going to be cut like the throat of a calf, while three Burgundians held him ? Jurgen knew this thing was to befall Reinault Vinsauf before October was out. So he looked at Reinault's throat, and shudderingly drew in his breath between set teeth.

" And he is worth a score of me, this boy ! " thought

Jurgen : " and it is I who am going to live to be an old fellow, with my bit of land in fee, years after dirt clogs those bright generous eyes, and years after this fine big-hearted boy is wasted ! And I shall forget all about him, too. Marion l'Edol, that very pretty girl behind him, is to become a blotched and toothless haunter of alleys, a leering plucker at men's sleeves ! And blue-eyed Colin here, with his baby mouth, is to be hanged for that matter of coin-clipping—let me recall, now,—yes, within six years of to-night ! Well, but in a way, these people are blessed in lacking foresight. For they laugh, and I cannot laugh, and to me their laughter is more terrible than weeping. Yes, they may be very wise in not glooming over what is inevitable ; and certainly I cannot go so far as to say they are wrong : but still, at the same time—— ! And assuredly, living seems to me in everything a wasteful and inequitable process."

Thus Jurgen, while the others passed a very pleasant evening.

And presently, when the masque was over, Dorothy and Jurgen went out upon the terrace, to the east of Bellegarde, and so came to an unforgotten world of moonlight. They sat upon a bench of carved stone near the balustrade which overlooked the highway : and the boy and the girl gazed wistfully beyond the highway, over luminous valleys and tree-tops. Just so they had sat there, as Jurgen perfectly remembered, when Mother Sereda first used this Wednesday.

" My Heart's Desire," says Jurgen, " I am sad to-night. For I am thinking of what life will do to us, and what offal the years will make of you and me."

" My own sweetheart," says she, " and do we not know very well what is to happen ? " And Dorothy began to talk of all the splendid things that Jurgen was to do, and of the happy life which was to be theirs together.

" It is horrible," he said : " for we are more fine than we will ever be hereafter. We have a splendour for which the world has no employment. It will be wasted. And such wastage is not fair."

"But presently you will be so and so," says she: and fondly predicts all manner of noble exploits which, as Jurgen remembered, had once seemed very plausible to him also. Now he had clearer knowledge as to the capacities of the boy of whom he had thought so well.

"No, Heart's Desire: no, I shall be quite otherwise."

"—and to think how proud I shall be of you! 'But then I always knew it,' I shall tell everybody, very condescendingly——"

"No, Heart's Desire: for you will not think of me at all."

"Ah, sweetheart! and can you really believe that I shall ever care a snap of my fingers for anybody but you?"

Then Jurgen laughed a little; for Heitman Michael came now across the lonely terrace, in search of Madame Dorothy: and Jurgen foreknew this was the man to whom within two months of this evening Dorothy was to give her love and all the beauty that was hers, and with whom she was to share the ruinous years which lay ahead.

But the girl did not know this, and Dorothy gave a little shrugging gesture. "I have promised to dance with him, and so I must. But the old fellow is a great plague."

For Heitman Michael was nearing thirty, and this to Dorothy and Jurgen was an age that bordered upon senility.

"Now, by heaven," said Jurgen, "wherever Heitman Michael does his next dancing it will not be hereabouts."

Jurgen had decided what he must do.

And then Heitman Michael saluted them civilly. "But I fear I must rob you of this fair lady, Master Jurgen," says he.

Jurgen remembered that the man had said precisely this a score of years ago; and that Jurgen had mumbled polite regrets, and had stood aside while Heitman Michael bore off Dorothy to dance with him. And this dance

had been the beginning of intimacy between Heitman
Michael and Dorothy.

"Heitman," says Jurgen, "the bereavement which you
threaten is very happily spared me, since, as it happens,
the next dance is to be mine."

"We can but leave it to the lady," says Heitman
Michael, laughing.

"Not I," says Jurgen. "For I know too well what
would come of that. I intend to leave my destiny to no
one."

"Your conduct, Master Jurgen, is somewhat strange,"
observed Heitman Michael.

"Ah, but I will show you a thing yet stranger. For,
look you, there seem to be three of us here on this terrace.
Yet I can assure you there are four."

"Read me the riddle, my boy, and have done."

"The fourth of us, Heitman, is a goddess that wears
a speckled garment and has black wings. She can boast
of no temples, and no priests cry to her anywhere, because
she is the only deity whom no prayers can move or any
sacrifices placate. I allude, sir, to the eldest daughter
of Nox and Erebus."

"You speak of death, I take it."

"Your apprehension, Heitman, is nimble. Even so, it
is not quick enough, I fear, to forerun the whims of god-
desses. Indeed, what person could have foreseen that
this implacable lady would have taken such a strong fancy
for your company?"

"Ah, my young bantam," replies Heitman Michael,
"it is quite true that she and I are acquainted. I may
even boast of having despatched one or two stout warriors
to serve her underground. Now, as I divine your meaning, you plan that I should decrease her obligation by
sending her a whippersnapper."

"My notion, Heitman, is that since this dark goddess
is about to leave us, she should not, in common gallantry,
be permitted to go hence unaccompanied. I propose,

therefore, that we forthwith decide who is to be her escort."

Now Heitman Michael had drawn his sword. " You are insane. But you extend an invitation which I have never yet refused."

" Heitman," cries Jurgen, in honest gratitude and admiration, " I bear you no ill-will. But it is highly necessary you die to-night, in order that my soul may not perish too many years before my body."

With that he too whipped out his sword.

So they fought. Now Jurgen was a very acceptable swordsman, but from the start he found in Heitman Michael his master. Jurgen had never reckoned upon that, and he considered it annoying. If Heitman Michael perforated Jurgen the future would be altered, certainly, but not quite as Jurgen had decided it ought to be remodelled. So this unlooked-for complication seemed preposterous, and Jurgen began to be irritated by the suspicion that he was getting himself killed for nothing at all.

Meanwhile his unruffled tall antagonist seemed but to play with Jurgen, so that Jurgen was steadily forced back toward the balustrade. And presently Jurgen's sword was twisted from his hand, and sent flashing over the balustrade, into the public highway.

" So now, Master Jurgen," says Heitman Michael, " that is the end of your nonsense. Why, no, there is not any occasion to posture like a statue. I do not intend to kill you. Why the devil's name, should I ? To do so would only get me an ill name with your parents : and besides, it is infinitely more pleasant to dance with this lady, just as I first intended." And he turned gaily toward Madame Dorothy.

But Jurgen found this outcome of affairs insufferable. This man was stronger than he, this man was of the sort that takes and uses gallantly all the world's prizes which mere poets can but respectfully admire. All was to do again : Heitman Michael, in his own hateful phrase, would act just as he had first intended, and Jurgen would be brushed aside by the man's brute strength. This man would take away Dorothy, and leave the life of Jurgen to become a business which Jurgen remembered with distaste. It was unfair.

So Jurgen snatched out his dagger, and drove it deep into the undefended back of Heitman Michael. Three times young Jurgen stabbed and hacked the burly soldier, just underneath the left ribs. Even in his fury Jurgen remembered to strike on the left side.

It was all very quickly done. Heitman Michael's arms jerked upward, and in the moonlight his fingers spread and clutched. He made curious gurgling noises. Then the strength went from his knees, so that he toppled backward. His head fell upon Jurgen's shoulder, resting there for an instant fraternally ; and as Jurgen shuddered away from the abhorred contact, the body of Heitman Michael collapsed. Now he lay staring upward, dead at the feet of his murderer. He was horrible looking, but he was quite dead.

" What will become of you ? " Dorothy whispered, after a while. " Oh, Jurgen, it was foully done ; that which you did was infamous ! What will become of you, my dear ? "

" I will take my doom," says Jurgen, " and without whimpering, so that I get justice. But I shall certainly insist upon justice." Then Jurgen raised his face to the bright heavens. " The man was stronger than I and wanted what I wanted. So I have compromised with necessity, in the only way I could make sure of getting that which was requisite to me. I cry for justice to the power that gave him strength and gave me weakness, and gave to each of us his desires. That which I have done, I have done. Now judge ! "

Then Jurgen tugged and shoved the heavy body of Heitman Michael, until it lay well out of sight, under the bench upon which Jurgen and Dorothy had been

JURGEN's sword was twisted from his hand,
and sent flashing over the ballustrade ...

FRANK C. PAPÉ

sitting. " Rest there, brave sir, until they find you. Come to me now, my Heart's Desire. Good! That is excellent. Here I sit with my true love, upon the body of my enemy. Justice is satisfied, and all is quite as it should be. For you must understand that I have fallen heir to a fine steed, whose bridle is marked with a coronet, —prophetically, I take it,—and upon this steed you will ride pillion with me to Lisuarte. There we will find a priest to marry us. We will go together into Gâtinais. Meanwhile, there is a bit of neglected business to be attended to." And he drew the girl close to him.

For Jurgen was afraid of nothing now. And Jurgen thought :

" Oh, that I could detain the moment ! that I could make some fitting verses to preserve this moment in my own memory ! Could I but get into words the odour and the thick softness of this girl's hair as my hands, that are a-quiver in every nerve of them, caress her hair ; and get into enduring words the glitter and the cloudy shadowings of her hair in this be-drenching moonlight ! For I shall forget all this beauty, or at best I shall remember this moment very dimly."

" You have done very wrong——" says Dorothy.

Says Jurgen, to himself : " Already the moment passes, this miserably happy moment wherein once more life shudders and stands heart-stricken at the height of bliss ! it passes, and I know even as I lift this girl's soft face to mine, and mark what faith and submissiveness and expectancy is in her face, that whatever the future holds for us, and whatever of happiness we two may know hereafter, we shall find no instant happier than this, which passes from us irretrievably while I am thinking about it, poor fool, in place of rising to the issue."

" —And heaven only knows what will become of you, Jurgen."

Says Jurgen, still to himself : " Yes, something must remain to me of all this rapture, though it be only guilt

and sorrow : something I mean to wrest from this high
moment which was once wasted fruitlessly. Now I am
wiser : for I know there is not any memory with less
satisfaction in it than the memory of some temptation
we resisted. So I will not waste the one real passion I
have known, nor leave unfed the one desire which ever
caused me for a heart-beat to forget to think about Jurgen's welfare. And thus, whatever happens, I shall
not always regret that I did not avail myself of this girl's
love before it was taken from me."

So Jurgen made such advances as seemed good to him.
And he noted, with amusing memories of how much
afraid he had once been of shocking his Dorothy's notions
of decorum, that she did not repulse him very vigorously.

"Here, over a dead body ! Oh, Jurgen, this is horrible !
Now, Jurgen, remember that somebody may come any
minute ! And I thought I could trust you ! Ah, and is
this all the respect you have for me ? " This much she
said in duty. Meanwhile the eyes of Dorothy were
dilated and very tender.

" Faith, I take no chances, this second time. And so
whatever happens, I shall not always regret that which I
left undone."

Now upon his lips was laughter, and his arms were
about the submissive girl. And in his heart was an un-
namable depression and a loneliness, because it seemed to
him that this was not the Dorothy whom he had seen in
the garden between dawn and sunrise. For in my arms
now there is just a very pretty girl who is not over-care-
ful in her dealings with young men, thought Jurgen, as
their lips met. Well, all life is a compromise ; and a
pretty girl is something tangible, at any rate. So he
laughed, triumphantly, and prepared for the sequel.

But as Jurgen laughed triumphantly, with his arm
beneath the head of Dorothy, and with the tender face of
Dorothy passive beneath his lips, and with unreasonable
wistfulness in his heart, the castle bell tolled midnight.

What followed was curious: for as Wednesday passed, the face of Dorothy altered, her flesh roughened under his touch, and her cheeks fell away, and fine lines came about her eyes, and she became the Countess Dorothy whom Jurgen remembered as Heitman Michael's wife. There was no doubt about it, in that be-drenching moonlight: and she was leering at him, and he was touching her everywhere, this horrible lascivious woman, who was certainly quite old enough to know better than to permit such liberties. And her breath was sour and nauseous. Jurgen drew away from her, with a shiver of loathing, and he closed his eyes, to shut away that sensual face.

"No," he said; "it would not be fair to what we owe to others. In fact, it would be a very heinous sin. We should weigh such considerations occasionally, madame."

Then Jurgen left his temptress, with simple dignity. "I go to search for my dear wife, madame, in a frame of mind which I would strongly advise you to adopt toward your husband."

And he went straightway down the terraces of Bellegarde, and turned southward to where his horse was tethered upon Amneran Heath: and Jurgen was feeling very virtuous.

CHAPTER VIII

OLD TOYS AND A NEW SHADOW

JURGEN had behaved with conspicuous nobility. Jurgen reflected: but he had committed himself. "I go in search of my dear wife," he had stated, in the exaltation of virtuous sentiments. And now Jurgen found himself alone in a world of moonlight just where he had last seen his wife.

"Well, well," he said, "now that my Wednesday is done with, and I am again a reputable pawnbroker, let us remember the advisability of sometimes doing the manly thing! It was into this cave that Lisa went. So into this cave go I, for the second time, rather than home to my unsympathetic relatives-in-law. Or at least, I think I am going——"

"Ay," said a squeaking voice, "this is the time. A ab hur hus!"

"High time!"

"Oh, more than time!"

"Look, the man in the oak!"

"Oho, the fire-drake!"

Thus many voices screeched and wailed confusedly. But Jurgen, staring about him, could see nobody: and all the tiny voices seemed to come from far overhead, where nothing was visible save the clouds, which of a sudden were gathering; for a wind was rising, and already the moon was overcast. Now for a while that noise high in the air became like a wrangling of sparrows, wherein no words were distinguishable.

Then said a small shrill voice distinctly : " Note now, sweethearts, how high we pass over the wind-vexed heath, where the gallows' burden creaks and groans, swaying to and fro in the night ! Now the rain breaks loose as a hawk from the fowler, and grave Queen Holda draws her tresses over the moon's bright shield. Now the bed is made, and the water drawn, and we the bride's maids seek for the lass who will be bride to Sclaug."

Said another : " Oh, search for a maid with golden hair, who is perfect, tender and pure, and fit for a king who is old as love, with no trace of love in him. Even now our grinning dusty master wakes from sleep, and his yellow fingers shake to think of her flower-soft lips who comes to-night to his lank embrace and warms the ribs that our eyes have seen. Who will be bride to Sclaug ? "

And a third said : " The wedding-gown we have brought with us, we that a-questing ride : and a maid will go hence on Phorgemon in Cleopatra's shroud. Hah, Will o' the Wisp will marry the couple——"

" No, no ! let Brachyotus ! "

" No, be it Kitt with the candlestick ! "

" Eman hetan, a fight, a fight ! "

" Oho, Tom Tumbler, 'ware of Stadlin ! "

" Hast thou the marmaritin, Tib ? "

" A ab hur hus ! "

" Come, Bembo, come away ! "

So they all fell to screeching and whistling and wrangling high over Jurgen's head, and Jurgen was not pleased with his surroundings.

" For these are the witches of Amneran about some deviltry or another in which I prefer to take no part. I now regret that I flung away a cross in this neighbourhood so very recently, and trust the action was understood. If my wife had not made a point of it, and had not positively insisted upon it, I would never have thought of doing such a thing. I intended no reflection upon anybody.

Even so, I consider this heath to be unwholesome. And upon the whole, I prefer to seek whatever I may encounter in this cave."

So in went Jurgen, for the second time.

And the tale tells that all was dark there, and Jurgen could see no one. But the cave stretched straight forward and downward, and at the far end was a glow of light. Jurgen went on and on, and so came to the place where he had found the Centaur. This part of the cave was now vacant. But behind where Nessus had lain in wait for Jurgen was an opening in the cave's wall, and through this opening streamed the light. Jurgen stooped and crawled through the orifice.

He stood erect. He caught his breath sharply. Here at his feet was, of all things, a tomb carved with the recumbent effigy of a woman. Now this part of the cave was lighted by lamps upon tall iron stands, so that everything was clearly visible, even to Jurgen, whose eyesight had of late years failed him. This was certainly a low, flat tombstone such as Jurgen had seen in many churches : but the tinted effigy thereupon was curious, somehow. Jurgen looked more closely. He touched the thing.

Then he recoiled, because there is no mistaking the feel of dead flesh. The effigy was not coloured stone : it was the body of a dead woman. More unaccountable still, it was the body of Félise de Puysange, whom Jurgen had loved very long ago in Gâtinais, a great many years before he set up in business as a pawnbroker.

Very strange it was to Jurgen again to see her face. He had often wondered what had become of this large brown woman ; had wondered if he were really the first man for whom she had put a deceit upon her husband ; and had wondered what sort of person Madame Félise de Puysange had been in reality.

"Two months it was that we played at intimacy, was it not, Félise ? You comprehend, my dear, I really remember very little about you. But I recall quite clearly the door left just a-jar, and how as I opened it gently I would see first of all the lamp upon your dressing-table, turned down almost to extinction, and the glowing dust upon its glass shade.   Is it not strange that our exceeding wickedness should have resulted in nothing save the memory of dust upon a lamp chimney ?   Yet you were very handsome, Félise.   I dare say I would have liked you if I had ever known you.   But when you told me of the child you had lost, and showed me his baby picture, I took a dislike to you.   It seemed to me you were betraying that child by dealing over-generously with me : and always between us afterwards was his little ghost. Yet I did not at all mind the deceits you put upon your husband.   It is true I knew your husband rather intimately——.   Well, and they tell me the good Vicomte was vastly pleased by the son you bore him some months after you and I had parted.   So there was no great harm done, after all——"

Then Jurgen saw there was another woman's body lying like an effigy upon another low flat tomb, and beyond that another, and then still others.   And Jurgen whistled.

"What, all of them !" he said.   "Am I to be confronted with every pound of tender flesh I have embraced ? Yes, here is Graine, and Rosamond, and Marcouève, and Elinor.   This girl, though, I do not remember at all. And this one is, I think, the little Jewess I purchased from Hassan Bey in Sidon, but how can one be sure ?   Still, this is certainly Judith, and this is Myrina.   I have half a mind to look again for that mole, but I suppose it would be indecorous.   Lord, how one's women do add up !   There must be several scores of them in all.   It is the sort of spectacle that turns a man to serious thinking. Well, but it is a great comfort to reflect that I dealt fairly with every one of them.   Several of them treated me most unjustly, too.   But that is past and done with : and I bear no malice toward such fickle and short-sighted creatures as could not be contented with one lover, and he the Jurgen that was ! "

Thereafter, Jurgen, standing among his dead, spread out his arms in an embracing gesture.

" Hail to you, ladies, and farewell ! for you and I have done with love. Well, love is very pleasant to observe as he advances, overthrowing all ancient memories with laughter. And yet for each gay lover who concedes the lordship of love, and wears intrepidly love's liveries, the end of all is death. Love's sowing is more agreeable than love's harvest : or, let us put it, he allures us into byways leading nowhither, among blossoms which fall before the first rough wind : so at the last, with much excitement and breath and valuable time quite wasted, we find that the end of all is death. Then would it have been more shrewd, dear ladies, to have avoided love ? To the contrary, we were unspeakably wise to indulge the high-hearted insanity that love induced ; since love alone can lend young people rapture, however transiently, in a world wherein the result of every human endeavour is transient, and the end of all is death."

Then Jurgen courteously bowed to his dead loves, and left them, and went forward as the cave stretched.

But now the light was behind him, so that Jurgen's shadow, as he came to a sharp turn in the cave, loomed suddenly upon the cave wall, confronting him. This shadow was clear-cut and unarguable.

Jurgen regarded it intently. He turned this way, then the other ; he looked behind him, raised one hand, shook his head tentatively ; then he twisted his head sideways with his chin well lifted, and squinted so as to get a profile view of this shadow. Whatever Jurgen did the shadow repeated, which was natural enough. The odd part was that it in nothing resembled the shadow which ought to attend any man, and this was an uncomfortable discovery to make in loneliness deep underground.

" I do not exactly like this," said Jurgen. " Upon my

word, I do not like this at all. It does not seem fair. It is perfectly preposterous. Well "—and here he shrugged —" well, and what could anybody expect me to do about it? Ah, what indeed! So I shall treat the incident with dignified contempt, and continue my exploration of this cave."

CHAPTER IX

THE ORTHODOX RESCUE OF GUENEVERE

OW the tale tells how the cave narrowed and again turned sharply, so that Jurgen came as through a corridor into quite another sort of underground chamber. Yet this also was a discomfortable place.

Here, suspended from the roof of the vault, was a kettle of quivering red flames. These lighted a very old and villainous-looking man in full armour, girded with a sword, and crowned royally : he sat erect upon a throne, motionless, with staring eyes that saw nothing. Back of him Jurgen noted many warriors seated in rows, and all staring at Jurgen with wide-open eyes that saw nothing. The red flaming of the kettle was reflected in all these eyes, and to observe this was not pleasant.

Jurgen waited non-committally. Nothing happened. Then Jurgen saw that at this unengaging monarch's feet were three chests. The lids had been ripped from two of them, and these were filled with silver coins. Upon the middle chest, immediately before the king, sat a woman, with her face resting against the knees of the glaring, withered, motionless old rascal.

"And this is a young woman. Obviously ! Observe the glint of that thick coil of hair ! the rich curve of the neck ! Oh, clearly, a tidbit fit to fight for, against any moderate odds ! "

So ran the thoughts of Jurgen. Bold as a dragon now, he stepped forward and lifted the girl's head.

Upon the middle chest sat a woman.

Her eyes were closed. She was, even so, the most beautiful creature Jurgen had ever imagined.

" She does not breathe. And yet, unless memory fails me, this is certainly a living woman in my arms. Evidently this is a sleep induced by necromancy. Well, it is not for nothing I have read so many fairy tales. There are orthodoxies to be observed in the awakening of every enchanted princess. And Lisa, wherever she may be, poor dear ! is nowhere in this neighbourhood, because I hear nobody talking. So I may consider myself at liberty to do the traditional thing by this princess. Indeed, it is the only fair thing for me to do, and justice demands it."

In consequence, Jurgen kissed the girl. Her lips parted and softened, and they assumed a not unpleasant sort of submissive ardour. Her eyes, enormous when seen thus closely, had languorously opened, had viewed him without wonder, and then the lids had fallen, about half-way, just as, Jurgen remembered, the eyelids of a woman ought to do when she is being kissed properly. She clung a little, and now she shivered a little, but not with cold : Jurgen perfectly remembered that ecstatic shudder convulsing a woman's body : everything, in fine, was quite as it should be. So Jurgen put an end to the kiss, which, as you may surmise, was a tolerably lengthy affair.

His heart was pounding as though determined to burst from his body, and he could feel the blood tingling at his finger-tips. He wondered what in the world had come over him, who was too old for such emotions.

Yet, truly, this was the loveliest girl that Jurgen had ever imagined. Fair was she to look on, with her shining grey eyes and small smiling lips, a fairer person might no man boast of having seen. And she regarded Jurgen graciously, with her cheeks flushed by that red flickering overhead, and she was very lovely to observe. She was clothed in a robe of flame-coloured silk, and about her neck was a collar of red gold. When she spoke her voice was music.

"I knew that you would come," the girl said, happily.

"I am very glad that I came," observed Jurgen.

"But time presses."

"Time sets an admirable example, my dear Princess——"

"Oh, messire, but do you not perceive that you have brought life into this horrible place? You have given of this life to me, in the most direct and speedy fashion. But life is very contagious. Already it is spreading by infection."

And Jurgen regarded the old king, as the girl indicated. The withered ruffian stayed motionless: but from his nostrils came slow augmenting jets of vapour, as though he were beginning to breathe in a chill place. This was odd, because the cave was not cold.

"And all the others too are snorting smoke," says Jurgen. "Upon my word I think this is a delightful place to be leaving."

First, though, he unfastened the king's sword-belt, and girded himself therewith, sword, dagger and all. "Now I have arms befitting my fine shirt," says Jurgen.

Then the girl showed him a sort of passage way, by which they ascended forty-nine steps roughly hewn in stone, and so came to daylight. At the top of the stairway was an iron trapdoor, and this door at the girl's instruction Jurgen lowered. There was no way of fastening the door from without.

"But Thragnar is not to be stopped by bolts or padlocks," the girl said. "Instead, we must straightway mark this door with a cross, since that is a symbol which Thragnar cannot pass."

Jurgen's hand had gone instinctively to his throat. Now he shrugged. "My dear young lady, I no longer carry the cross. I must fight Thragnar with other weapons."

" Two sticks will serve, laid crosswise——"

Jurgen submitted that nothing would be easier than to lift the trapdoor, and thus dislodge the sticks. " They will tumble apart without anyone having to touch them, and then what becomes of your crucifix ? "

" Why, how quickly you think of everything ! " she said, admiringly. " Here is a strip from my sleeve, then. We will tie the twigs together."

Jurgen did this, and laid upon the trapdoor a recognisable crucifix. " Still, when anyone raises the trapdoor whatever lies upon it will fall off. Without disparaging the potency of your charm, I cannot but observe that in this case it is peculiarly difficult to handle. Magician or no, I would put heartier faith in a stout padlock."

So the girl tore another strip, from the hem of her gown, and then another from her right sleeve, and with these they fastened their cross to the surface of the trapdoor, in such a fashion that the twigs could not be dislodged from beneath. They mounted the fine steed whose bridle was marked with a coronet, the girl riding pillion, and they turned westward, since the girl said this was best.

For, as she now told Jurgen, she was Guenevere, the daughter of Gogyrvan, King of Glathion and the Red Islands. So Jurgen told her he was the Duke of Logreus, because he felt it was not appropriate for a pawnbroker to be rescuing princesses : and he swore, too, that he would restore her safely to her father, whatever Thragnar might attempt. And all the story of her nefarious capture and imprisonment by King Thragnar did Dame Guenevere relate to Jurgen, as they rode together through the pleasant May morning.

She considered the Troll King could not well molest them. " For now you have his charmed sword, Caliburn, the only weapon with which Thragnar can be slain. Besides, the sign of the cross he cannot pass. He beholds and trembles."

"My dear Princess, he has but to push up the trapdoor from beneath, and the cross, being tied to the trapdoor, is promptly moved out of his way. Failing this expedient, he can always come out of the cave by the other opening, through which I entered. If this Thragnar has any intelligence at all and a reasonable amount of tenacity, he will presently be at hand."

"Even so, he can do no harm unless we accept a present from him. The difficulty is that he will come in disguise."

"Why, then, we will accept gifts from nobody."

"There is, moreover, a sign by which you may distinguish Thragnar. For if you deny what he says, he will promptly concede you are in the right. This was the curse put upon him by Miramon Lluagor, for a detection and a hindrance."

"By that unhuman trait," says Jurgen, "Thragnar ought to be very easy to distinguish."

CHAPTER X

PITIFUL DISGUISES OF THRAGNAR

EXT, the tale tells that as Jurgen and the Princess were nearing Gihon, a man came riding toward them, full armed in black, and having a red serpent with an apple in its mouth painted upon his shield.

"Sir knight," says he, speaking hollowly from the closed helmet, "you must yield to me that lady."

"I think," says Jurgen, civilly, "that you are mistaken."

So they fought, and presently, since Caliburn was a resistless weapon, and he who wore the scabbard of Caliburn could not be wounded, Jurgen prevailed; and gave the strange knight so heavy a buffet that the knight fell senseless.

"Do you think," says Jurgen, about to unlace his antagonist's helmet, "that this is Thragnar?"

"There is no possible way of telling," replied Dame Guenevere: "if it is the Troll King he should have offered you gifts, and when you contradicted him he should have admitted you were right. Instead, he proffered nothing, and to contradiction he answered nothing, so that proves nothing."

"But silence is a proverbial form of assent. At all events, we will have a look at him."

"But that too will prove nothing, since Thragnar goes about his mischiefs so disguised by enchantments as invariably to resemble somebody else, and not himself at all."

" Such dishonest habits introduce an element of uncertainty, I grant you," says Jurgen. " Still, one can rarely err by keeping on the safe side. This person is, in any event, a very ill-bred fellow, with probably immoral intentions. Yes, caution is the main thing, and in justice to ourselves we will keep on the safe side."

So without unloosing the helmet, he struck off the strange knight's head, and left him thus. The Princess was now mounted on the horse of their deceased assailant.

" Assuredly," says Jurgen then, " a magic sword is a fine thing, and a very necessary equipment, too, for a knight errant of my age."

" But you talk as though you were an old man, Messire de Logreus ! "

" Come now," thinks Jurgen, " this is a princess of rare discrimination. What, after all, is forty-and-something when one is well-preserved ? This uncommonly intelligent girl reminds me a little of Marcouève, whom I loved in Artein : besides, she does not look at me as women look at an elderly man. I like this princess, in fact, I adore this princess. I wonder now what would she say if I told her as much ? "

But Jurgen did not tempt chance that time, for just then they encountered a boy who had frizzed hair and painted cheeks. He walked mincingly, in a curious garb of black bespangled with gold lozenges, and he carried a gilded dung fork.

*　*　*

Then Jurgen and the Princess came to a black and silver pavilion standing by the roadside. At the door of the pavilion was an apple-tree in blossom : from a branch of this tree was suspended a black hunting-horn, silver-mounted. A woman waited there alone. Before her was a chess-board, with the ebony and silver pieces set ready for a game, and upon the table to her left hand glittered flagons and goblets of silver. Eagerly this woman rose and came toward the travellers.

"Oh, my dear Jurgen," says she, "but how fine you look in that new shirt you are wearing! But there was never a man had better taste in dress, as I have always said : and it is long I have waited for you in this pavilion, which belongs to a black gentleman who seems to be a great friend of yours. And he went into Crim Tartary this morning, with some missionaries, by the worst piece of luck, for I know how sorry he will be to miss you, dear. Now, but I am forgetting that you must be very tired and thirsty, my darling, after your travels. So do you and the young lady have a sip of this, and then we will be telling one another of our adventures."

For this woman had the appearance of Jurgen's wife, Dame Lisa, and of none other.

Jurgen regarded her with two minds. "You certainly seem to be Lisa. But it is a long while since I saw Lisa in such an amiable mood."

"You must know," says she, still smiling, "that I have learned to appreciate you since we were separated."

"The fiend who stole you from me may possibly have brought about that wonder. None the less, you have met me riding at adventure with a young woman. And you have assaulted neither of us, you have not even raised your voice. No! quite decidedly, here is a miracle beyond the power of any fiend."

"Ah, but I have been doing a great deal of thinking, Jurgen dear, as to our difficulties in the past. And it seems to me that you were almost always in the right."

Guenevere nudged Jurgen. "Did you note that? This is certainly Thragnar in disguise."

"I am beginning to think that at all events it is not Lisa." Then Jurgen magisterially cleared his throat. "Lisa, if you indeed be Lisa, you must understand I am through with you. The plain truth is that you tire me. You talk and talk : no woman breathing equals you at

mere volume and continuity of speech : but you say
nothing that I have not heard seven hundred and eighty
times, if not oftener."

"You are perfectly right, my dear," says Dame Lisa,
piteously. "But then I never pretended to be as clever
as you."

"Spare me your beguilements, if you please. And
besides, I am in love with this princess. Now spare me
your recriminations, also, for you have no real right to
complain. If you had stayed the person whom I promised the priest to love, I would have continued to think
the world of you. But you did nothing of the sort.
From a cuddlesome and merry girl, who thought whatever
I did was done to perfection, you elected to develop into
an uncommonly plain and short-tempered old woman."
And Jurgen paused. "Eh ? " said he, "and did you not
do this ? "

Dame Lisa answered sadly : "My dear, you are perfectly right, from your way of thinking. However, I
could not very well help getting older."

"But, oh, dear me ! " says Jurgen, "this is astonish-
ingly inadequate impersonation, as any married man would
see at once. Well, I made no contract to love any such
plain and short-tempered person. I repudiate the claims
of any such person, as manifestly unfair. And I pledge
undying affection to this high and noble Princess
Guenevere, who is the fairest lady that I have ever seen."

"You are right," wailed Dame Lisa, "and I was
entirely to blame. It was because I loved you, and
wanted you to get on in the world and be a credit to my
father's line of business, that I nagged you so. But you
will never understand the feelings of a wife, nor will you
understand that even now I desire your happiness above
all else. Here is our wedding-ring, then, Jurgen. I
give you back your freedom. And I pray that this
princess may make you very happy, my dear. For surely
you deserve a princess if ever any man did."

Jurgen shook his head. " It is astounding that a demon so much talked about should be so poor an impersonator. It raises the staggering supposition that the majority of married women must go to Heaven. As for your ring, I am not accepting gifts this morning, from anyone. But you understand, I trust, that I am hopelessly enamoured of the Princess on account of her beauty."

" Oh, and I cannot blame you, my dear. She is the loveliest person I have ever seen."

" Hah, Thragnar ! " says Jurgen, " I have you now. A woman might, just possibly, have granted her own homeliness : but no woman that ever breathed would have conceded the Princess had a ray of good looks."

So with Caliburn he smote, and struck off the head of this thing which foolishly pretended to be Dame Lisa.

" Well done ! oh, bravely done ! " cried Guenevere. " Now the enchantment is dissolved, and Thragnar is slain by my clever champion."

" I could wish there were some surer sign of that," said Jurgen. " I would have preferred that the pavilion and the decapitated Troll King had vanished with a peal of thunder and an earthquake and such other phenomena as are customary. Instead, nothing is changed except that the woman who was talking to me a moment since now lies at my feet in a very untidy condition. You conceive, madame, I used to tease her about that twisted little-finger, in the days before we began to squabble : and it annoys me that Thragnar should not have omitted even Lisa's crooked little-finger on her left hand. Yes, such painstaking carefulness worries me. For you conceive also, madame, it would be more or less awkward if I had made an error, and if the appearance were in reality what it seemed to be, because I was pretty trying sometimes. At all events, I have done that which seemed equitable, and I have found no comfort in the doing of it, and I do not like this place."

CHAPTER XI

APPEARANCE OF THE DUKE OF LOGREUS

SO Jurgen brushed from the table the chessmen that were set there in readiness for a game, and he emptied the silver flagons upon the ground. His reasons for not meddling with the horn he explained to the Princess : she shivered, and said that, such being the case, he was certainly very sensible. Then they mounted, and departed from the black and silver pavilion. They came thus without further adventure to Gogyrvan Gawr's city of Cameliard.

Now there was shouting and the bells all rang when the people knew their Princess was returned to them : the houses were hung with painted cloths and banners, and trumpets sounded, as Guenevere and Jurgen came to the King in his Hall of Judgment. And this Gogyrvan, that was King of Glathion and Lord of Enisgarth and Camwy and Sargyll, came down from his wide throne, and he embraced first Guenevere, then Jurgen.

" And demand of me what you will, Duke of Logreus," said Gogyrvan, when he had heard the champion's name, " and it is yours for the asking. For you have restored to me the best loved daughter that ever was the pride of a high king."

" Sir," replied Jurgen, reasonably, " a service rendered so gladly should be its own reward. So I am asking that you do in turn restore to me the Princess Guenevere, in honourable marriage, do you understand ? because I am a poor lorn widower, I am tolerably certain ; but I am quite certain I love your daughter with my whole heart."

Thus Jurgen, whose periods were confused by emotion.

"I do not see what the condition of your heart has to do with any such unreasonable request. And you have no good sense to be asking this thing of me when here are the servants of Arthur, that is now King of the Britons, come to ask for my daughter as his wife. That you are Duke of Logreus you tell me, and I concede a duke is all very well : but I expect you in return to concede a king takes precedence, with any man whose daughter is marriageable. But to-morrow, or the next day it may be, you and I will talk over your reward more privately. Meanwhile it is very queer and very frightened you are looking, to be the champion who conquered Thragnar."

For Jurgen was staring at the great mirror behind the King's throne. In this mirror Jurgen saw the back of Gogyrvan's crowned head, and beyond this, Jurgen saw a queer and frightened-looking young fellow, with sleek black hair, and an impudent nose, and wide-open bright brown eyes which were staring hard at Jurgen : and the lad's very red and very heavy lips were parted, so that you saw what fine strong teeth he had : and he wore a glittering shirt with curious figures on it.

"I was thinking," says Jurgen, and he saw the lad in the mirror was speaking too, "I was thinking that is a remarkable mirror you have there."

"It is like any other mirror," replies the King, "in that it shows things as they are. But if you fancy it as your reward, why, take it and welcome."

"And are you still talking of rewards !" cries Jurgen. "Why, if that mirror shows things as they are, I have come out of my borrowed Wednesday still twenty-one. Oh, but it was the clever fellow I was, to flatter Mother Sereda so cunningly, and to fool her into such generosity ! And I wonder that you who are only a king, with bleared

eyes under your crown, and with a drooping belly under
all your royal robes, should be talking of rewarding a fine
young fellow of twenty-one, for there is nothing you
have which I need be wanting now."

"Then you will not be plaguing me any more with
your nonsense about my daughter : and that is excellent
news."

"But I have no requirement to be asking your good
graces now," said Jurgen, " nor the good-will of any man
alive that has a handsome daughter or a handsome wife.
For now I have the aid of a lad that was very recently
made Duke of Logreus : and with his countenance I can
look out for myself, and I can get justice done me everywhere, in all the bedchambers of the world."

And Jurgen snapped his fingers, and was about to turn
away from the King. There was much sunlight in the
hall, so that Jurgen in this half-turn confronted his
shadow as it lay plain upon the flagstones. And Jurgen
looked at it very intently.

"Of course," said Jurgen presently, " I only meant in a
manner of speaking, sir : and was paraphrasing the splendid if hackneyed passage from Sornatius, with which you
are doubtless familiar, in which he goes on to say, so
much more beautifully than I could possibly express
without quoting him word for word, that all this was
spoken jestingly, and without the least intention of
offending anybody, oh, anybody whatever, I can assure
you, sir."

"Very well," said Gogyrvan Gawr : and he smiled, for
no reason that was apparent to Jurgen, who was still
watching his shadow sidewise. "To-morrow, I repeat, I
must talk with you more privately. To-day I am giving
a banquet such as was never known in these parts, because my daughter is restored to me, and because my
daughter is going to be queen over all the Britons."

So said Gogyrvan, that was King of Glathion and Lord
of Enisgarth and Camwy and Sargyll : and this was done.

And everywhere at the banquet Jurgen heard talk of this King Arthur who was to marry Dame Guenevere, and of the prophecy which Merlin Ambrosius had made as to the young monarch. For Merlin had predicted:

"He shall afford succour, and shall tread upon the necks of his enemies: the isles of the ocean shall be subdued by him, and he shall possess the forests of Gaul: the house of Romulus shall fear his rage, and his acts shall be food for the narrators."

"Why, then," says Jurgen, to himself, "this monarch reminds me in all things of David of Israel, who was so splendid and famous, and so greedy, in the ancient ages. For to these forests and islands and necks and other possessions, this Arthur Pendragon must be adding my one ewe lamb; and I lack a Nathan to convert him to repentance. Now, but this, to be sure, is a very unfair thing."

Then Jurgen looked again into a mirror: and presently the eyes of the lad he found therein began to twinkle.

"Have at you, David!" said Jurgen, valorously; "since, after all, I see no reason to despair."

CHAPTER XII

EXCURSUS OF YOLANDE'S UNDOING

NOW Jurgen, self-appointed Duke of Logreus, abode at the court of King Gogyrvan. The month of May passed quickly and pleasantly: but the monstrous shadow which followed Jurgen did not pass. Still, no one noticed it: that was the main thing. For himself, he was not afraid of shadows, and the queerness of this one was not enough to distract his thoughts from Guenevere, nor from his love-making with Guenevere.

For these were quiet times in Glathion, now that the war with Rience of Northgalis was satisfactorily ended: and love-making was now everywhere in vogue. By way of diversion, gentlemen hunted and fished and rode a-hawking and amicably slashed and battered one another in tournaments: but their really serious pursuit was love-making, after the manner of chivalrous persons, who knew that the King's trumpets would presently be summoning them into less softly furnished fields of action, from one or another of which they would return feet foremost on a bier. So Jurgen sighed and warbled and made eyes with many excellent fighting-men: and the Princess listened with many other ladies whose hearts were not of flint. And Gogyrvan meditated.

Now it was the kingly custom of Gogyrvan when his dinner was spread at noontide, not to go to meat until all such as demanded justice from him had been furnished with a champion to redress the wrong. One day as the gaunt old King sat thus in his main hall, upon a seat of green rushes covered with yellow satin, and with a cushion of yellow satin under his elbow, and with his barons ranged about him according to their degrees, a damsel came with a very heart-rending tale of the oppression that was on her.

Gogyrvan blinked at her, and nodded. "You are the handsomest woman I have seen in a long while," says he, irrelevantly. "You are a woman I have waited for. Duke Jurgen of Logreus will undertake this adventure."

There being no help for it, Jurgen rode off with this Dame Yolande, not very well pleased : but as they rode he jested with her. And so, with much laughter by the way, Yolande conducted him to the Green Castle, of which she had been dispossessed by Graemagog, a most formidable giant.

"Now prepare to meet your death, sir knight!" cried Graemagog, laughing horribly, and brandishing his club ; "for all knights who come hither I have sworn to slay."

"Well, if truth-telling were a sin you would be a very virtuous giant," says Jurgen, and he flourished Thragnar's sword, resistless Caliburn.

Then they fought, and Jurgen killed Graemagog. Thus was the Green Castle restored to Dame Yolande, and the maidens who attended her aforetime were duly released from the cellarage. They were now maidens by courtesy only, but so tender is the heart of women that they all wept over Graemagog.

Yolande was very grateful, and proffered every manner of reward.

"But, no, I will take none of these fine jewels, nor money, nor lands either," says Jurgen. "For Logreus, I must tell you, is a fairly well-to-do duchy, and the killing of giants is by way of being my favourite pastime. He is well paid that is well satisfied. Yet if you must reward me for such a little service, do you swear to do what you can to get me the love of my lady, and that will suffice."

Yolande, without any particular enthusiasm, consented to attempt this : and indeed Yolande, at Jurgen's request, made oath upon the Four Evangelists that she would do everything within her power to aid him.

" Very well," said Jurgen, " you have sworn, and it is you whom I love."

Surprise now made her lovely. Yolande was frankly delighted at the thought of marrying the young Duke of Logreus, and offered to send for a priest at once.

" My dear," says Jurgen, " there is no need to bother a priest about our private affairs."

She took his meaning, and sighed. " Now I regret," said she, " that I made so solemn an oath. Your trick was unfair."

" Oh, not at all," said Jurgen : " and presently you will not regret it. For indeed the game is well worth the candle."

" How is that shown, Messire de Logreus ? "

" Why, by candle-light," says Jurgen,—" naturally."

" In that event, we will talk no further of it until this evening."

So that evening Yolande sent for him. She was, as Gogyrvan had said, a remarkably handsome woman, sleek and sumptuous and crowned with a wealth of copper-coloured hair. To-night she was at her best in a tunic of shimmering blue, with a surcote of gold embroidery, and with gold embroidered pendent sleeves that touched the floor. Thus she was when Jurgen came to her.

" Now," says Yolande, frowning, " you may as well come out straightforwardly with what you were hinting at this morning."

But first Jurgen looked about the apartment, and it was lighted by a tall gilt stand whereon burned candles.

He counted these, and he whistled. " Seven candles ! upon my word, sweetheart, you do me great honour, for this is a veritable illumination. To think of it, now, that you should honour me, as people do saints, with seven candles ! Well, I am only mortal, but none the less I am Jurgen, and I shall endeavour to repay this sevenfold courtesy without discount."

" Oh, Messire de Logreus," cried Dame Yolande, " but what incomprehensible nonsense you talk ! You misinterpret matters, for I can assure you I had nothing of that sort in mind. Besides, I do not know what you are talking about."

" Indeed, I must warn you that my actions often speak more unmistakably than my words. It is what learned persons term an idiosyncrasy."

"—And I certainly do not see how any of the saints can be concerned in this. If you had said the Four Evangelists now——! For we were talking of the Four Evangelists, you remember, this morning—— Oh, but how stupid it is of you, Messire de Logreus, to stand there grinning and looking at me in a way that makes me blush ! "

" Well, that is easily remedied," said Jurgen, as he blew out the candles, " since women do not blush in the dark."

" What do you plan, Messire de Logreus ? "

" Ah, do not be alarmed ! " said Jurgen. " I shall deal fairly with you."

And in fact Yolande confessed afterward that, considering everything, Messire de Logreus was very generous. Jurgen confessed nothing : and as the room was profoundly dark nobody else can speak with authority as to what happened there. It suffices that the Duke of Logreus and the Lady of the Green Castle parted later on the most friendly terms.

" You have undone me, with your games and your candles and your scrupulous returning of courtesies," said Yolande, and yawned, for she was sleepy ; " but I fear that I do not hate you as much as I ought to."

" No woman ever does," says Jurgen, " at this hour." He called for breakfast, then kissed Yolande—for this, as Jurgen had said, was their hour of parting,—and he rode away from the Green Castle in high spirits.

"Why, what a thing it is again to be a fine young fellow!" said Jurgen. "Well, even though her big brown eyes protrude too much—something like a lobster's—she is a splendid woman, that Dame Yolande: and it is a comfort to reflect I have seen justice was done her."

Then he rode back to Cameliard, singing with delight in the thought that he was riding toward the Princess Guenevere, whom he loved with his whole heart.

CHAPTER XIII

PHILOSOPHY OF GOGYRVAN GAWR

AT Cameliard the young Duke of Logreus spent most of his time in the company of Guenevere, whose father made no objection overtly. Gogyrvan had his promised talk with Jurgen.

"I lament that Dame Yolande dealt over-thriftily with you," the King said, first of all: "for I estimated you two would be as spark and tinder, kindling between you an amorous conflagration to burn up all this nonsense about my daughter."

"Thrift, sir," said Jurgen, discreetly, "is a proverbial virtue, and fires may not consume true love."

"That is the truth," Gogyrvan admitted, "whoever says it." And he sighed.

Then for a while he sat in nodding meditation. To-night the old King wore a disreputably rusty gown of black stuff, with fur about the neck and sleeves of it, and his scant white hair was covered by a very shabby black cap. So he huddled over a small fire in a large stone fireplace carved with shields; beside him was white wine and red, which stayed untasted while Gogyrvan meditated upon things that fretted him.

"Now, then!" says Gogyrvan Gawr: "this marriage with the high King of the Britons must go forward, of course. That was settled last year, when Arthur and his devil-mongers, the Lady of the Lake and Merlin Ambrosius, were at some pains to rescue me at Carohaise. I estimate that Arthur's ambassadors, probably the devil-mongers themselves, will come for my daughter before June is out. Meanwhile, you two have youth and love for playthings, and it is spring."

" What is the season of the year to me," groaned Jurgen, " when I reflect that within a week or so the lady of my heart will be borne away from me for ever ? How can I be happy, when all the while I know the long years of misery and vain regret are near at hand ? "

" You are saying that," observed the King, " in part because you drank too much last night, and in part because you think it is expected of you. For in point of fact, you are as happy as anyone is permitted to be in this world, through the simple reason that you are young. Misery, as you employ the word, I consider to be a poetical trope : but I can assure you that the moment you are no longer young the years of vain regret will begin, either way."

" That is true," said Jurgen, heartily.

" How do you know ? Now then, put it I were insane enough to marry my daughter to a mere duke, you would grow damnably tired of her : I can assure you of that also, for in disposition Guenevere is her sainted mother all over again. She is nice looking, of course, because in that she takes after my side of the family : but, between ourselves, she is not particularly intelligent, and she will always be making eyes at some man or another. To-day it appears to be your turn to serve as her target, in a fine glittering shirt of which the like was never seen in Glathion. I deplore, but even so I cannot deny, your rights as the champion who rescued her : and I must bid you make the most of that turn."

" Meanwhile, it occurs to me, sir, that it is unusual to betroth your daughter to one man, and permit her to go freely with another."

" If you insist upon it," said Gogyrvan Gawr, " I can of course lock up the pair of you, in separate dungeons, until the wedding day. Meanwhile, it occurs to me you should be the last commentator to grumble."

" Why, I tell you plainly, sir, that critical persons would say you are taking very small care of your daughter's honour."

" To that there are several answers," replied the King. " One is that I remember my late wife as tenderly as possible, and I reflect I have only her word for it as to Guenevere's being my daughter. Another is that, though my daughter is a quiet and well-conducted young woman, I never heard King Thragnar was anything of this sort."

" Oh, sir," said Jurgen, horrified, " whatever are you hinting ? "

" All sorts of things, however, happen in caves, things which it is wiser to ignore in sunlight. So I ignore : I ask no questions : my business is to marry my daughter acceptably, and that only. Such discoveries as may be made by her husband afterward are his affair, not mine. This much I might tell you, Messire de Logreus, by way of answer. But the real answer is to bid you consider this : that a woman's honour is concerned with one thing only, and it is a thing with which the honour of a man is not concerned at all."

" But now you talk in riddles, King, and I wonder what it is you would have me do."

Gogyrvan grinned. " Obviously, I advise you to give thanks you were born a man, because that sturdier sex has so much less need to bother over breakage."

" What sort of breakage, sir ? " says Jurgen.

Gogyrvan told him.

Duke Jurgen for the second time looked properly horrified. " Your aphorisms, King, are abominable, and of a sort unlikely to quiet my misery. However, we were speaking of your daughter, and it is she who must be considered rather than I."

" Now I perceive that you take my meaning perfectly.

Yes, in all matters which concern my daughter I would
have you lie like a gentleman."

"Well, I am afraid, sir," said Jurgen, after a pause,
"that you are a person of somewhat degraded ideals."

"Ah, but you are young. Youth can afford ideals,
being vigorous enough to stand the hard knocks they earn
their possessor. But I am an old fellow cursed with a
tender heart and tolerably keen eyes. That combination,
Messire de Logreus, is one which very often forces me to
jeer out of season, simply because I know myself to be
upon the verge of far more untimely tears."

Thus Gogyrvan replied. He was silent for a while,
and he contemplated the fire. Then he waved a shrivelled
hand toward the window, and Gogyrvan began to speak,
meditatively :

"Messire de Logreus, it is night in my city of Cameliard. And somewhere one of those roofs harbours a girl
whom we will call Lynette. She has a lover—we will say
he is called Sagramor. The names do not matter. To-
night, as I speak with you, Lynette lies motionless in the
carved wide bed that formerly was her mother's. She is
thinking of Sagramor. The room is dark save where
moonlight silvers the diamond-shaped panes of ancient
windows. In every corner of the room mysterious
quivering suggestions lurk."

"Ah, sire," says Jurgen, "you also are a poet ! "

"Do not interrupt me, then ! Lynette, I repeat, is
thinking of Sagramor. Again they sit near the lake,
under an apple-tree older than Rome. The knotted
branches of the tree are upraised as in benediction : and
petals—petals, fluttering, drifting, turning,—interminable
white petals fall silently in the stillness. Neither speaks :
for there is no need. Silently he brushes a petal from the
blackness of her hair, and silently he kisses her. The
lake is dusky and hard-seeming as jade. Two lonely stars
hang low in the green sky. It is droll that the chest of
a man is hairy, oh, very droll ! And a bird is singing,

a silvery needle of sound moves fitfully in the stillness. Surely high Heaven is thus quietly coloured and thus strangely lovely. So at least thinks little Lynette, lying motionless like a little mouse, in the carved wide bed wherein Lynette was born."

" A very moving touch, that," Jurgen interpolated.

" Now, there is another sort of singing : for now the pot-house closes, big shutters bang, feet shuffle, a drunken man hiccoughs in his singing. It is a love-song he is murdering. He sheds inexplicable tears as he lurches nearer and nearer to Lynette's window, and his heart is all magnanimity, for Sagramor is celebrating his latest conquest. Do you not think that this or something very like this is happening to-night in my city of Cameliard, Messire de Logreus ? "

" It happens momently," said Jurgen, " everywhere. For thus is every woman for a little while, and thus is every man for all time."

" That being a dreadful truth," continued Gogyrvan, " you may take it as one of the many reasons why I jeer out of season in order to stave off far more untimely tears. For this thing happens : in my city it happens, and in my castle it happens. King or no, I am powerless to prevent its happening. So I can but shrug and hearten my old blood with a fresh bottle. No less, I regard the young woman, who is quite possibly my daughter, with considerable affection : and it would be salutary for you to remember that circumstance, Messire de Logreus, if ever you are tempted to be candid."

Jurgen was horrified. " But with the Princess, sir, it is unthinkable that I should not deal fairly."

King Gogyrvan continued to look at Jurgen. Gogyrvan Gawr said nothing, and not a muscle of him moved.

" Although of course," said Jurgen, " I would, in simple justice to her, not ever consider volunteering any information likely to cause pain."

" Again I perceive," said Gogyrvan, " that you understand me. Yet I did not speak of my daughter only, but of everybody."

"How then, sir, would you have me deal with everybody?"

"Why, I can but repeat my words," says Gogyrvan, very patiently: "I would have you lie like a gentleman. And now be off with you, for I am going to sleep. I shall not be wide awake again until my daughter is safely married. And that is absolutely all I can do for you."

"Do you think this is reputable conduct, King?"

"Oh, no!" says Gogyrvan, surprised. "It is what we call PHILANTHRO

CHAPTER XIV

PRELIMINARY TACTICS OF DUKE JURGEN

O Jurgen abode at court, and was tolerably content for a little while. He loved a princess, the fairest and most perfect of mortal women; and loved her (a circumstance to which he frequently recurred) as never any other man had loved in the world's history: and very shortly he was to stand by and see her married to another. Here was a situation to delight the chivalrous court of Glathion, for every requirement of romance was exactly fulfilled.

Now the appearance of Guenevere, whom Jurgen loved with an entire heart, was this:—She was of middling height, with a figure not yet wholly the figure of a woman. She had fine and very thick hair, and the colour of it was the yellow of corn floss. When Guenevere undid her hair it was a marvel to Jurgen to note how snugly this hair descended about the small head and slender throat, and then broadened boldly and clothed her with a loose soft foam of pallid gold. For Jurgen delighted in her hair; and with increasing intimacy, loved to draw great strands of it back of his head, crossing them there, and pressing soft handfuls of her perfumed hair against his cheeks as he kissed the Princess.

The head of Guenevere, be it repeated, was small: you wondered at the proud free tossing movements of that little head which had to sustain the weight of so much hair. The face of Guenevere was coloured tenderly and softly: it made the faces of other women seem the work of a sign-painter, just splotched in anyhow. Grey eyes had Guenevere, veiled by incredibly long black lashes that curved incredibly. Her brows arched rather high above her eyes : that was almost a fault. Her nose was delicate and saucy : her chin was impudence made flesh : and her mouth was a tiny and irresistible temptation.

"And so on, and so on ! But indeed there is no sense at all in describing this lovely girl as though I were taking an inventory of my shop-window," said Jurgen. "Analogues are all very well, and they have the unanswerable sanction of custom : none the less, when I proclaim that my adored mistress's hair reminds me of gold I am quite consciously lying. It looks like yellow hair, and nothing else : nor would I willingly venture within ten feet of any woman whose head sprouted with wires, of whatever metal. And to protest that her eyes are as grey and fathomless as the sea is very well also, and the sort of thing which seems expected of me : but imagine how horrific would be puddles of water slopping about in a lady's eye-sockets ! If we poets could actually behold the monsters we rhyme of, we would scream and run. Still, I rather like this sirvente."

For he was making a sirvente in praise of Guenevere. It was the pleasant custom of Gogyrvan's court that every gentleman must compose verses in honour of the lady of whom he was hopelessly enamoured; as well as that in these verses he should address the lady (as one whose name was too sacred to mention) otherwise than did her sponsors. So Duke Jurgen of Logreus duly rhapsodised of his Phyllida.

"I borrow for my dear love the appellation of that noted but by much inferior lady who was beloved by Ariphus of Belsize," he explained. "You will remember Poliger suspects she was a princess of the house of Scleroveus : and you of course recall Pisander's masterly summing-up of the probabilities, in his *Heraclea*."

" Oh, yes," they said.   And the courtiers of Gogyrvan
Gawr, like Mother Sereda, were greatly impressed by
young Duke Jurgen's erudition.

For Jurgen was Duke of Logreus nowadays, with his
glittering shirt and the coronet upon his bridle to show
for it.   Awkwardly this proved to be an earl's coronet,
but incongruities are not always inexplicable.

" It was Earl Giarmuid's horse.   You have doubtless
heard of Giarmuid : but to ask that is insulting."

" Oh, not at all.   It is humour.   We perfectly understand your humour, Duke Jurgen."

" And a very pretty fighter I found this famous Giarmuid as I travelled westward.   And since he killed my
steed in the heat of our conversation, I was compelled to
take over his horse, after I had given this poor Giarmuid proper interment.   Oh, yes, a very pretty fighter,
and I had heard much talk of him in Logreus.   He was
Lord of Orc and Persaunt, you remember, though of
course the estate came by his mother's side."

" Oh, yes," they said.   " You must not think that we
of Glathion are quite shut out from the great world.   We
have heard of all these affairs.   And we have also heard
fine things of your duchy of Logreus, messire."

" Doubtless," said Jurgen ; and turned again to his
singing.

" Lo, for I pray to thee, resistless Love," he descanted,
" that thou to-day make cry unto my love, to Phyllida
whom I, poor Logreus, love so tenderly, not to deny me
love !   Asked why, say thou my drink and food is love,
in days wherein I think and brood on love, and truly find
naught good in aught save love, since Phyllida hath taught
me how to love."

Here Jurgen groaned with nicely modulated ardour ;
and he continued : " If she avow such constant hate of
love as would ignore my great and constant love, plead
thou no more !   With listless lore of love woo Death
resistlessly, resistless Love, in place of her that saith such

scorn of love as lends to Death the lure and grace I love."

Thus Jurgen sang melodiously of his Phyllida, and meant thereby (as everybody knew) the Princess Guenevere. Since custom compelled him to deal in analogues, he dealt wholesale. Gems and metals, the blossoms of the field and garden, fires and wounds, and sunrises and perfumes, an armoury of lethal weapons, ice and a concourse of mythological deities were his starting-point. Then the seas and heavens were dredged of phenomena to be mentioned with disparagement, in comparison with one or another feature of Duke Jurgen's Phyllida. Zoology and history, and generally the remembered contents of his pawnshop, were overhauled and made to furnish targets for depreciation : whereas in dealing with the famous ladies loved by earlier poets, Duke Jurgen was positively insulting, allowing hardly a rag of merit. Still, he was careful to be just : and he allowed that these poor creatures might figure advantageously enough in eyes which had never beheld his Phyllida. And to all this information the lady whom he hymned attended willingly.

" She is a princess," reflected Jurgen. " She is quite beautiful. She is young, and whatever her father's opinion, she is reasonably intelligent, as women go. Nobody could ask more. Why, then, am I not out of my head about her ? Already she permits a kiss or two when nobody is around, and presently she will permit more. And she thinks I am quite the cleverest person living. Come, Jurgen, man ! is there no heart in this spry young body you have regained ? Come, let us have a little honest rapture and excitement over this promising situation ! "

But somehow Jurgen could not manage it. He was interested in what, he knew, was going to happen. Yes, undoubtedly he looked forward to more intimate converse with this beautiful young princess, but it was rather as one anticipates partaking of a favourite dessert. Jurgen felt that a liaison arranged for in this spirit was neither one thing nor the other.

"If only I could feel like a cold-blooded villain, now, I would at worst be classifiable. But I intend the girl no harm, I am honestly fond of her. I shall talk my best, broaden her ideas, and give her, I flatter myself, considerable pleasure : vulgar prejudices apart, I shall leave her no whit the worse. Why, the dear little thing, not for the ransom of seven emperors would I do her any hurt ! And in these matters discretion is everything, simply everything. No, quite decidedly, I am not a cold-blooded villain ; and I shall deal fairly with the Princess."

Thus Jurgen was disappointed by his own emotions, as he turned them from side to side, and prodded them, and shifted to a fresh viewpoint, only to find it no more favourable than the one relinquished : but he veiled the inadequacy of his emotions with very moving fervours. The tale does not record his conversations with Guenevere : for Jurgen now discoursed plain idiocy, as one purveys sweetmeats to a child in fond astonishment at the pet's appetite. And leisurely Jurgen advanced : there was no hurry, with weeks wherein to accomplish everything : meanwhile this routine work had a familiar pleasantness.

For the amateur co-ordinates matters, knowing that one thing axiomatically leads to another. There is no harm at all in respectful allusions to a love that comprehends its hopelessness : it was merely a fact which Jurgen mentioned, and was about to pass on; only Guenevere, in modesty, was forced to disparage her own attractions, as an inadequate cause for so much misery. Common courtesy demanded that Jurgen enter upon a rebuttal. To emphasise one point in this, the orator was forced to take the hand of his audience : but strangers did that every day, with nobody objecting; moreover, the hand was here, not so much seized as displayed by its detainer, as evidence of what he contended. How else was he to prove the Princess of Glathion had the loveliest hand in the world? It was not a matter he could request Guenevere to accept on hearsay: and Jurgen wanted to deal fairly with her.

Well, but before relinquishing the loveliest hand in the world a connoisseur will naturally kiss each fingertip: this is merely a tribute to perfection, and has no personal application. Besides, a kiss, wherever deposited, as Jurgen pointed out, is, when you think of it, but a ceremonial, of no intrinsic wrongfulness. The girl demurring against this apothegm—as custom again exacted,—was, still in common fairness, convinced of her error. So now, says Jurgen presently, you see for yourself. Is anything changed between us? Do we not sit here, just as we were before? Why, to be sure! a kiss is now attestedly a quite innocuous performance, with nothing very fearful about it one way or the other. It even has its pleasant side. Thus there is no need to make a pother over kisses or over an arm about you, when it is more comfortable sitting so: how can one reasonably deny to a sincere friend what is accorded to a cousin or an old cloak? It would be nonsense, as Jurgen demonstrated with a very apt citation from Napsacus.

Then, sitting so, in the heat of conversation a speaker naturally gesticulates: and a deal of his eloquence is dependent upon his hands. When anyone is talking it is discourteous to interrupt, whereas to lay hold of a gentleman's hand outright, as Jurgen parenthesised, is a little forward. No, he really did not think it would be quite proper for Guenevere to hold his hand. Let us preserve decorum, even in trifles.

"Ah, but you know that you are doing wrong!"

"I doing wrong! I, who am simply sitting here and talking my poor best in an effort to entertain you! Come now, Princess, but tell me what you mean!"

"You should know very well what I mean."

"But I protest to you I have not the least notion.

How can I possibly know what you mean when you
refuse to tell me what you mean ? ”

And since the Princess declined to put into words just
what she meant, things stayed as they were, for the
while.

Thus did Jurgen co-ordinate matters, knowing that one
thing axiomatically leads to another. And in short,
affairs sped very much as Jurgen had anticipated.

Now, by ordinary, Jurgen talked with Guenevere in
dimly lighted places. He preferred this, because then
he was not bothered by that unaccountable shadow whose
presence in sunlight put him out. Nobody ever seemed
to notice this preposterous shadow ; it was patent, indeed,
that nobody could see it save Jurgen : none the less, the
thing worried him. So even from the first he remembered Guenevere as a soft voice and a delectable perfume
in twilight, as a beauty not clearly visioned.

And Gogyrvan’s people worried him. The hook-nosed
tall old King had been by Jurgen dismissed from thought,
as an enigma not important enough to be worth the
trouble of solving. Gogyrvan at once seemed to be
schooling himself to patience under some private annoyance and to be revolving in his mind some private jest ;
he was queer, and probably abominable : but to grant the
old rascal his due, he was not meddlesome.

The people about Gogyrvan, though, were perplexing.
These men who considered that all you possessed was
loaned you to devote to the service of your God, your
King and every woman who crossed your path, could
hardly be behaving rationally. To talk of serving God
sounded as sonorously and as inspiritingly as a drum :
yes, and a drum had nothing but air in it. The priests
said so-and-so : but did anybody believe the gallant
Bishop of Merion, for example, was always to be depended
upon ?

“ I would like the opinion of Prince Evrawc’s wife as
to that,” said Jurgen, with a grin. For it was well known

that all affairs between this Dame Alundyne and the
Bishop were so discreetly managed as to afford no reason
for any scandal whatever.

As for serving the King, there in plain view was
Gogyrvan Gawr, for anyone who so elected, to regard
and grow enthusiastic over : Gogyrvan might be shrewd
enough, but to Jurgen he suggested very little of the
Lord's anointed. To the contrary, he reminded you of
Jurgen's brother-in-law, the grocer, without being graced
by the tradesman's friendly interest in customers.
Gogyrvan Gawr was a person whom Jurgen simply could
not imagine any intelligent Deity selecting as steward.
And finally, when it came to serving women, what sort
of service did women most cordially appreciate ? Jurgen
had his answer pat enough, but it was an answer not
suitable for utterance in a mixed company.

" No one of my honest opinions, in fact, is adapted to
further my popularity in Glathion, because I am a monstrous clever fellow who does justice to things as they
are. Therefore I must remember always, in justice to
myself, that I very probably hold traffic with madmen.
Yet Rome was a fine town, and it was geese who saved it.
These people may be right ; and certainly I cannot go
so far as to say they are wrong : but still, at the same
time—— Yes, that is how I feel about it."

Thus did Jurgen abide at the chivalrous court of
Glathion, and conform to all its customs. In the matter
of love-songs nobody protested more movingly that the
lady whom he loved (quite hopelessly, of course), em-
bodied all divine perfections : and when it came to
knightly service, the possession of Caliburn made the
despatching of thieves and giants and dragons seem
hardly sportsmanlike. Still, Jurgen fought a little, now
and then, in order to conform to the customs of Glathion :
and the Duke of Logreus was widely praised as a very
promising young knight.

And all the while he fretted because he could just

dimly perceive that ideal which was served in Glathion, and the beauty of this ideal, but could not possibly believe in it.   Here was, again, a loveliness perceived in twilight, a beauty not clearly visioned.

" Yet am not I a monstrous clever fellow," he would console himself, " to take them all in so completely ?   It is a joke to which, I think, I do full justice."

So Jurgen abode among these persons to whom life was a high-hearted journeying homeward.   God the Father awaited you there, ready to punish at need, but eager to forgive, after the manner of all fathers : that one became a little soiled in travelling, and sometimes blundered into the wrong lane, was a matter which fathers understood : meanwhile here was an ever-present reminder of His perfection incarnated in woman, the finest and the noblest of His creations.   Thus was every woman a symbol to be honoured magnanimously and reverently.   So said they all.

"Why, but to be sure ! " assented Jurgen.   And in support of his position, he very edifyingly quoted Ophelion, and Fabianus Papirius, and Sextius Niger to boot.

CHAPTER XV

OF COMPROMISES IN GLATHION

HE tale records that it was not a great while before, in simple justice to Guenevere, Duke Jurgen had afforded her the advantage of frank conversation in actual privacy. For conventions have to be regarded, of course. Thus the time of a princess is not her own, and at any hour of day all sorts of people are apt to request an audience just when some most improving conversation is progressing famously : but the Hall of Judgment stood vacant and unguarded at night.

"But I would never consider doing such a thing," said Guenevere : "and whatever must you think of me, to make such a proposal ! "

"That too, my dearest, is a matter which I can only explain in private."

"And if I were to report your insolence to my father——? "

"You would annoy him exceedingly : and from such griefs it is our duty to shield the aged."

"And besides, I am afraid."

"Oh, my dearest," says Jurgen, and his voice quavered, because his love and his sorrow seemed very great to him : "but, oh, my dearest, can it be that you have not faith in me ! For with all my body and soul I love you, as I have loved you ever since I first raised your face between my hands, and understood that I had never before known beauty. Indeed, I love you as, I think, no

man has ever loved any woman that lived in the long
time that is gone, for my love is worship, and no less.
The touch of your hand sets me to trembling, dear; and
the look of your grey eyes makes me forget there is anything of pain or grief or evil anywhere: for you are the
loveliest thing God ever made, with joy in the new skill
that had come to His fingers.   And you have not faith
in me! "

Then the Princess gave a little sobbing laugh of content and repentance, and she clasped the hand of her
grief-stricken lover.   " Forgive me, Jurgen, for I cannot
bear to see you so unhappy! "

" Ah, and what is my grief to you? " he asks of her,
bitterly.

" Much, oh, very much, my dear! " she whispered.

So in the upshot Jurgen was never to forget that
moment wherein he waited behind the door, and through
the crack between the half-open door and the door-frame
saw Guenevere approach irresolutely, a wavering white
blur in the dark corridor.   She came to talk with him
where they would not be bothered with interruptions:
but she came delightfully perfumed, in her night-shift,
and in nothing else.   Jurgen wondered at the way of
these women even as his arms went about her in the
gloom.   He remembered always the feel of that warm and
slender and yielding body, naked under the thin fabric
of the shift, as his arms first went about her: of all
their moments together that last breathless minute
before either of them had spoken stayed in his memory
as the most perfect.

And yet what followed was pleasant enough, for now it
was to the wide and softly cushioned throne of a king,
no less, that Guenevere and Jurgen resorted, so as to
talk where they would not be bothered with interruptions.   The throne of Gogyrvan was perfectly dark, under
its canopy, in the unlighted hall, and in the dark nobody
can see what happens.

Thereafter these two contrived to talk together nightly upon the throne of Glathion : but what remained in Jurgen's memory was that last moment behind the door, and the six tall windows upon the east side of the hall, those windows which were of commingled blue and silver, but were all an opulent glitter, throughout that time in the night when the moon was clear of the tree-tops and had not yet risen high enough to be shut off by the eaves. For that was all which Jurgen really saw in the Hall of Judgment. There would be a brief period wherein upon the floor beneath each window would show a narrow quadrangle of moonlight : but the windows were set in a wall so deep that this soon passed. On the west side were six windows also, but about these was a porch ; so no light ever came from the west.

Thus in the dark they would laugh and talk with lowered voices. Jurgen came to these encounters well primed with wine, and in consequence, as he quite comprehended, talked like an angel, without confining himself exclusively to celestial topics. He was often delighted by his own brilliance, and it seemed to him a pity there was no one handy to take it down : so much of his talking was necessarily just a little over the head of any girl, however beautiful and adorable.

And Guenevere, he found, talked infinitely better at night. It was not altogether the wine which made him think that, either : the girl displayed a side she veiled in the daytime. A girl, far less a princess, is not supposed to know more than agrees with a man's notion of maidenly ignorance, she contended.

" Nobody ever told me anything about so many interesting matters. Why, I remember——" And Guenevere narrated a quaintly pathetic little story, here irrelevant, of what had befallen her some three or four years earlier. " My mother was living then : but she had never said a word about such things, and frightened as I was, I did not go to her."

Jurgen asked questions.

" Why, yes. There was nothing else to do. I cannot
talk freely with my maids and ladies even now. I cannot question them, that is : of course I can listen as they
talk among themselves. For me to do more would be
unbecoming in a princess. And I wonder quietly about
so many things ! " She educed instances. " After that I
used to notice the animals and the poultry. So I worked
out problems for myself, after a fashion. But nobody
ever told me anything directly."

" Yet I dare say that Thragnar—well, the Troll King,
being very wise, must have made zoology much clearer."

" Thragnar was a skilled enchanter," says a demure
voice in the dark; " and through the potency of his
abominable arts I can remember nothing whatever about
Thragnar."

Jurgen laughed, ruefully. Still, he was tolerably sure
about Thragnar now.

So they talked : and Jurgen marvelled, as millions of
men had done aforetime, and have done since, at the
girl's eagerness, now that barriers were down, to discuss
in considerable detail all such matters as etiquette had
previously compelled them to ignore. About her ladies
in waiting, for example, she afforded him some very
curious data : and concerning men in general she asked
innumerable questions that Jurgen found delicious.

Such innocence combined—upon the whole—with a
certain moral obtuseness, seemed inconceivable. For to
Jurgen it now appeared that Guenevere was behaving
with not quite the decorum which might fairly be
expected of a princess. Contrition, at least, one might
have looked for, over this hole and corner business :
whereas it worried him to note that Guenevere was
coming to accept affairs almost as a matter of course.
Certainly she did not seem to think at all of any
wickedness anywhere : the utmost she suggested was the
necessity of being very careful. And while she never

contradicted him in these private conversations, and submitted in everything to his judgment, her motive now appeared to be hardly more than a wish to please him. It was almost as though she were humouring him in his foolishness. And all this within six weeks! reflected Jurgen: and he nibbled his finger-nails, with a mental side-glance toward the opinions of King Gogyrvan Gawr.

But in daylight the Princess remained unchanged. In daylight Jurgen adored her, but with no feeling of intimacy. Very rarely did occasion serve for them to be actually alone in the daytime. Once or twice, though, he kissed her in open sunlight: and then her eyes were melting but wary, and the whole affair was rather flat. She did not repulse him: but she stayed a princess, appreciative of her station, and seemed not at all the invisible person who talked with him at night in the Hall of Judgment.

Presently, by common consent, they began to avoid each other by daylight. Indeed, the time of the Princess was now pre-occupied: for now had come into Glathion a ship with saffron-coloured sails, and having for its figure-head a dragon that was painted with thirty colours. Such was the ship which brought Messire Merlin Ambrosius and Dame Anaïtis, the Lady of the Lake, with a great retinue, to fetch young Guenevere to London, where she was to be married to King Arthur.

First there was a week of feasting and tourneys and high mirth of every kind. Now the trumpets blared, and upon a scaffolding that was gay with pennons and smart tapestries King Gogyrvan sat nodding and blinking in his brightest raiment, to judge who did the best: and into the field came joyously a press of dukes and earls and barons and many famous knights, to contend for honour and a trumpery chaplet of pearls.

Jurgen shrugged, and honoured custom. The Duke of Logreus acquitted himself with credit in the opening tournament, unhorsing Sir Dodinas le Sauvage, Earl Roth

of Meliot, Sir Epinogris, and Sir Hector de Maris : then
Earl Damas of Listenise smote like a whirlwind, and
Jurgen slid contentedly down the tail of his fine horse.
His part in the tournament was ended, and he was heartily
glad of it. He preferred to contemplate rather than share
in such festivities : and he now followed his bent with
a most exquisite misery, because he considered that never
had any other poet occupied a situation more picturesque.

By day he was the Duke of Logreus, which in itself
was a notable advance upon pawnbroking : after night-
fall he discounted the peculiar privileges of a king. It
was the secrecy, the deluding of everybody, which he
especially enjoyed : and in the thought of what a monstrous clever fellow was Jurgen, he almost lost sight of the
fact that he was miserable over the impending marriage
of the lady he loved.

Once or twice he caught the tail-end of a glance from
Gogyrvan's bright old eye. Jurgen by this time abhorred
Gogyrvan, as a person of abominably unjust dealings.

"To take no better care of his own daughter," Jurgen
considered, " is infamous. The man is neglecting his
duties as a father, and to do that is not fair."

CHAPTER XVI

DIVERS IMBROGLIOS OF KING SMOIT

OW it befell that for three nights in succession the Princess Guenevere was unable to converse with Jurgen in the Hall of Judgment. So upon one of these disengaged evenings Duke Jurgen held a carouse with Aribert and Orien, two of Gogyrvan's barons, who had just returned from Pengwaed-Gir, and had queer tales to narrate of the Trooping Fairies who garrison that place.

All three were seasoned topers, so Jurgen went to bed prepared for anything. Later he sat up in bed, and found it was much as he had suspected. The room was haunted, and at the foot of his couch were two ghosts : one an impudent-looking leering phantom, in a suit of old-fashioned armour, and the other a beautiful pale lady, in the customary flowing white draperies.

" Good-morning to you both," says Jurgen, " and sorry am I that I cannot truthfully observe I am glad to see you. Though you are welcome enough if you can manage to haunt the room quietly." Then, seeing that both phantoms looked puzzled, Jurgen proceeded to explain. " Last year, when I was travelling upon business in Westphalia, it was my grief to spend a night in the haunted castle of Neuedesberg, for I could not get any sleep at all in that place. There was a ghost in charge who persisted in rattling very large iron chains and in groaning dismally throughout the night. Then toward morning he took the form of a monstrous cat, and climbed upon the foot of

JURGEN bowed as gracefully as was possible
in his circumstances

my bed : and there he squatted yowling until daybreak. And as I am ignorant of German, I was not able to convey to him any idea of my disapproval of his conduct. Now I trust that as compatriots, or as I might say with more exactness, as former compatriots, you will appreciate that such behaviour is out of all reason."

"Messire," says the male ghost, and he oozed to his full height, "you are guilty of impertinence in harbouring such a suspicion. I can only hope it proceeds from ignorance."

"For I am sure," put in the lady, "that I always disliked cats, and we never had them about the castle."

"And you must pardon my frankness, messire," continued the male ghost, "but you cannot have moved widely in noble company if you are indeed unable to distinguish between members of the feline species and of the reigning family of Glathion."

"Well, I have seen dowager queens who justified some such confusion," observed Jurgen. "Still, I entreat the forgiveness of both of you, for I had no idea that I was addressing royalty."

"I was King Smoit," explained the male phantom, "and this was my ninth wife, Queen Sylvia Tereu."

Jurgen bowed as gracefully, he flattered himself, as was possible in his circumstances. It is not easy to bow gracefully while sitting erect in bed.

"Often and over again have I heard of you, King Smoit," says Jurgen. "You were the grandfather of Gogyrvan Gawr, and you murdered your ninth wife, and your eighth wife, and your fifth wife, and your third wife too : and you went under the title of the Black King, for you were reputed the wickedest monarch that ever reigned in Glathion and the Red Islands."

It seemed to Jurgen that King Smoit evinced embarrassment, but it is hard to be quite certain when a ghost is blushing. "Perhaps I was spoken of in some

such terms," says Smoit, " for the neighbours were cen-
sorious gossips, and I was not lucky in my marriages.
And I regret, I bitterly regret, to confess that, in a
moment of extreme yet not quite unprovoked excitement,
I assassinated the lady whom you now behold."

" And I am sure, through no fault of mine," says Sylvia
Tereu.

" Certainly, my dear, you resisted with all your might.
I only wish that you had been a larger and a brawnier
woman. But you, messire, can now perceive, I suppose,
the folly of expecting a high King of Glathion, and the
queen that he took delight in, to sit upon your bed and
howl ? "

So then, upon reflection, Jurgen admitted he had never
had that experience ; nor, he handsomely added, could he
recall any similar incident among his friends.

" The notion is certainly preposterous," went on King
Smoit, and very grimly he smiled. " We are drawn hither
by quite other intentions. In fact, we wish to ask of
you, as a member of the family, your assistance in a
delicate affair."

" I would be delighted," Jurgen stated, " to aid you
in any possible way. But why do you call me a member of
the family ? "

" Now, to deal frankly," says Smoit, with a grin, " I am
not claiming any alliance with the Duke of Logreus——"

" Sometimes," says Jurgen, " one prefers to travel
incognito. As a king, you ought to understand that."

" —My interest is rather in the grandson of Steinvor.
Now you will remember your grandmother Steinvor as,
I do not doubt, a charming old lady. But I remember
Steinvor, the wife of Ludwig, as one of the loveliest
girls that a king's eyes ever lighted on."

" Oh, sir," says Jurgen, horrified, " and what is this
you are telling me ? "

" Merely that I had always an affectionate nature,"
replied King Smoit, " and that I was a fine upstanding

young king in those days. And one of the results of my
being these things was your father, whom men called
Coth the son of Ludwig. But I can assure you Ludwig
had done nothing to deserve it."

"Well, well!" said Jurgen: "all this is very scanda-
lous: and very upsetting, too, it is to have a brand-new
grandfather foisted upon you at this hour of the morning.
Still, it happened a great while ago: and if Ludwig did
not fret over it, I see no reason why I should do so. And
besides, King Smoit, it may be that you are not telling
me the truth."

"If you doubt my confession, messire my grandson,
you have only to look into the next mirror. It is precisely on this account that we have ventured to dispel
your slumbers. For to me you bear a striking resemblance.
You have the family face."

Now Jurgen considered the lineaments of King Smoit
of Glathion. "Really," said Jurgen, "of course it is very
flattering to be told that your appearance is regal. I do
not at all know what to say in reply to the implied compliment, without seeming uncivil. I would never for a
moment question that you were much admired in your
day, sir, and no doubt very justly so. None the less—
well, my nose, now, from such glimpses of it as mirrors
have hitherto afforded, does not appear to be a snub-
nose."

"Ah, but appearances are proverbially deceitful,"
observed King Smoit.

"And about the left-hand corner," protested Queen
Sylvia Tereu, "I detect a distinct resemblance."

"Now I may seem unduly obtuse," said Jurgen, "for
I am a little obtuse. It is a habit with me, a very bad
habit formed in early infancy, and I have never been able
to break myself of it. And so I have not any notion at
what you two are aiming."

Replied the ghost of King Smoit: "I will explain.
Just sixty-three years ago to-night I murdered my ninth

wife in circumstances of peculiar brutality, as you with rather questionable taste have mentioned."

Then Jurgen was somewhat abashed, and felt that it did not become him, who had so recently cut off the head of his own wife, to assume the airs of a precisian. " Of course," says Jurgen, more broad-mindedly, " these little family differences are always apt to occur in married life."

" So be it ! Though, by the so-and-sos of Ursula's eleven thousand travelling companions, there was a time wherein I would not have brooked such criticism. Ah, well, that time is overpast, and I am a bloodless thing that the wind sweeps at the wind's will through lands in which but yesterday King Smoit was dreaded. So I let that which has been be."

" Well, that seems reasonable," said Jurgen, " and to be a trifle rhetorical is the privilege of grandfathers. Therefore I entreat you, sir, to continue."

" Two years afterward I followed the Emperor Locrine in his expedition against the Suevetii, an evil and luxurious people who worship Gozarin peculiarly, by means of little boats. I must tell you, grandson, that was a goodly raid, conducted by a band of tidy fighters in a land of wealth and of fine women. But alack, as the saying is, in our return from Osnach my loved general Locrine was captured by that arch-fiend Duke Corineus of Cornwall : and I, among many others who had followed the Emperor, paid for our merry larcenies and throat-cuttings a very bitter price. Corineus was not at all broad-minded, not what you would call a man of the world. So it was in a noisome dungeon that I was incarcerated, —I, Smoit of Glathion, who conquered Enisgarth and Sargyll in open battle and fearlessly married the heiress of Camwy ! But I spare you the unpleasant details. It suffices to say that I was dissatisfied with my quarters. Yet fain to leave them as I became, there was but one way. It involved the slaying of my gaoler, a step which was, I confess, to me distasteful. I was getting on in life, and had grown tired of killing people. Yet, to mature deliberation, the life of a graceless varlet, void of all gentleness and with no bowels of compassion, and deaf to suggestions of bribery, appeared of no over-whelming importance."

" I can readily imagine, grandfather, that you were not deeply interested in either the nature or the anatomy of your gaoler. So you did what was unavoidable."

" Yes, I treacherously slew him, and escaped in an impenetrable disguise to Glathion, where not long after-ward I died. My dying just then was most annoying, for I was on the point of being married, and she was a remarkably attractive girl,—King Tyrnog's daughter, from Craintnor way. She would have been my thirteenth wife. And not a week before the ceremony I tripped and fell down my own castle steps, and broke my neck. It was an humiliating end for one who had been a warrior of considerable repute. Upon my word, it made me think there might be something, after all, in those old superstitions about thirteen being an unlucky number. But what was I saying?—oh, yes! It is also unlucky to be careless about one's murders. You will readily under-stand that for one or two such affairs I am condemned yearly to haunt the scene of my crime on its anniversary : such an arrangement is fair enough, and I make no com-plaint, though of course it does rather break into the evening. But it happened that I treacherously slew my gaoler with a large cobble-stone on the fifteenth of June. Now the unfortunate part, the really awkward feature, was that this was to an hour the anniversary of the death of my ninth wife."

" And you murdering insignificant strangers on such a day !" said Queen Sylvia. " You climbing out of gaol windows figged out as a lady abbess, on an anniversary you ought to have kept on your knees in unavailing re-pentance ! But you were a hard man, Smoit, and it was little loving courtesy you showed your wife at a time when she might reasonably look to be remembered, and that is a fact."

"My dear, I admit it was heedless of me. I could not possibly say more. At any rate, grandson, I discovered after my decease that such heedlessness entailed my haunting on every fifteenth of June at three in the morning two separate places."

"Well, but that was justice," says Jurgen.

"It may have been justice," Smoit admitted: "but my point is that it happened to be impossible. However, I was aided by my great-great-grandfather Penpingon Vreichvras ap Mylwald Glasanief. He too had the family face; and in every way resembled me so closely that he impersonated me to everyone's entire satisfaction; and with my wife's assistance re-enacted my disastrous crime upon the scene of its occurrence, June after June."

"Indeed," said Queen Sylvia, "he handled his sword infinitely better than you, my dear. It was a thrilling pleasure to be murdered by Penpingon Vreichvras ap Mylwald Glasanief, and I shall always regret him."

"For you must understand, grandson, that the term of King Penpingon Vreichvras ap Mylwald Glasanief's stay in Purgatory has now run out, and he has recently gone to Heaven. That was pleasant for him, I dare say, so I do not complain. Still, it leaves me with no one to take my place. Angels, as you will readily understand, are not permitted to perpetrate murders, even in the way of kindness. It might be thought to establish a dangerous precedent."

"All this," said Jurgen, "seems regrettable, but not strikingly explicit. I have a heart and a half to serve you, sir, with not seven-eighths of a notion as to what you want of me. Come, put a name to it!"

"You have, as I have said, the family face. You are, in fact, the living counterpart of Smoit of Glathion. So I beseech you, messire my grandson, for this one night to impersonate my ghost, and with the assistance of Queen Sylvia Tereu to see that at three o'clock the White Turret is haunted to everyone's satisfaction. Otherwise," said Smoit, gloomily, " the consequences will be deplorable."

" But I have had no experience at haunting," Jurgen confessed. " It is a pursuit in which I do not pretend to competence : and I do not even know just how one goes about it."

" That matter is simple, although mysterious preliminaries will be, of course, necessitated, in order to convert a living person into a ghost——"

" The usual preliminaries, sir, are out of the question : and I must positively decline to be stabbed or poisoned or anything of that kind, even to humour my grandfather."

Both Smoit and Sylvia protested that any such radical step would be superfluous, since Jurgen's ghostship was to be transient. In fact, all Jurgen would have to do would be to drain the embossed goblet which Sylvia Tereu held out to him, with Druidical invocations.

And for a moment Jurgen hesitated. The whole business seemed rather improbable. Still, the ties of kin are strong, and it is not often one gets the chance to aid, however slightly, one's long-dead grandfather : besides, the potion smelt very invitingly.

" Well," says Jurgen, " I am willing to taste any drink once." Then Jurgen drank.

The flavour was excellent. Yet the drink seemed not to affect Jurgen, at first. Then he began to feel a trifle light-headed. Next he looked downward, and was surprised to notice there was nobody in his bed. Closer investigation revealed the shadowy outline of a human figure, through which the bedclothing had collapsed. This, he decided, was all that was left of Jurgen. And it gave him a queer sensation. Jurgen jumped like a startled horse, and so violently that he flew out of bed, and found himself floating imponderably about the room.

Now Jurgen recognised the feeling perfectly. He had often had it in his sleep, in dreams wherein he would bend his legs at the knees so that his feet came up behind him, and he would pass through the air without any effort. Then it seemed ridiculously simple, and he would wonder why he never thought of it before. And then he would reflect : " This is an excellent way of getting around. I will come to breakfast this way in the morning, and show Lisa how simple it is. How it will astonish her, to be sure, and how clever she will think me ! " And then Jurgen would wake up, and find that somehow he had forgotten the trick of it.

But just now this manner of locomotion was undeniably easy. So Jurgen floated around his bed once or twice, then to the ceiling, for practice. Through inexperience, he miscalculated the necessary force, and popped through into the room above, where he found himself hovering immediately over the Bishop of Merion. His eminence was not alone, but as both occupants of the apartment were asleep, Jurgen witnessed nothing unepiscopal. Now Jurgen rejoined his grandfather, and girded on charmed Caliburn, and demanded what must next be done.

" The assassination will take place in the White Turret, as usual. Queen Sylvia will instruct you in the details. You can invent most of the affair, however, as the Lady of the Lake, who occupies this room to-night, is very probably unacquainted with our terrible history."

Then King Smoit observed that it was high time he kept his appointment in Cornwall, and he melted into air, with an easy confidence that bespoke long practice; and Jurgen followed Queen Sylvia Tereu.

CHAPTER XVII

ABOUT A COCK THAT CROWED TOO SOON

NEXT the tale tells of how Jurgen and the ghost of Queen Sylvia Tereu came into the White Turret. The Lady of the Lake was in bed : she slept unaccompanied, as Jurgen noted with approval, for he wished to intrude upon no more tête-à-têtes. And Dame Anaïtis did not at first awake.

Now this was a gloomy and high-panelled apartment, with exactly the traditional amount of moonlight streaming through two windows. Any ghost, even an apprentice, could have acquitted himself with credit in such surroundings, and Jurgen thought he did extremely well. He was atavistically brutal, and to improvise the accompanying dialogue he did not find difficult. So everything went smoothly, and with such spirit that Anaïtis was presently wakened by Queen Sylvia's very moving wails for mercy, and sat erect in bed, as though a little startled. Then the Lady of the Lake leaned back among the pillows, and witnessed the remainder of the terrible scene with remarkable self-possession.

So it was that the tragedy swelled to its appalling climax, and subsided handsomely. With the aid of Caliburn, Jurgen had murdered his temporary wife. He had dragged her insensate body across the floor, by the hair of her head, and had carefully remembered first to put her comb in his pocket, as Queen Sylvia had requested, so that it would not be lost. He had given vent to several fiendish " Ha-ha's " and all the old high imprecations he remembered : and in short, everything had gone splendidly when he left the White Turret with a sense of self-approval and Queen Sylvia Tereu.

The two of them paused in the winding stairway ; and in the darkness, after he had restored her comb, the Queen was telling Jurgen how sorry she was to part with him.

" For it is back to the cold grave I must be going now, Messire Jurgen, and to the tall flames of Purgatory : and it may be that I shall not ever see you any more."

" I shall regret the circumstance, madame," says Jurgen, " for you are the loveliest person I have ever seen."

The Queen was pleased. " That is a delightfully boyish speech, and one can see it comes from the heart. I only wish that I could meet with such unsophisticated persons in my present abode. Instead, I am herded with battered sinners who have no heart, who are not frank and outspoken about anything, and I detest their affectations."

" Ah, then you are not happy with your husband, Sylvia ? I suspected as much."

" I see very little of Smoit. It is true he has eight other wives all resident in the same flame, and cannot well show any partiality. Two of his Queens, though, went straight to Heaven : and his eighth wife, Gudrun, we are compelled to fear, must have been an unrepentant sinner, for she has never reached Purgatory. But I always distrusted Gudrun, myself : otherwise I would never have suggested to Smoit that he have her strangled in order to make me his queen. You see, I thought it a fine thing to be a queen, in those days, Jurgen, when I was an artless slip of a girl. And Smoit was all honey and perfume and velvet in those days, Jurgen, and little did I suspect the cruel fate that was to befall me."

" Indeed, it is a sad thing, Sylvia, to be murdered by the hand which, so to speak, is sworn to keep an eye on your welfare, and which rightfully should serve you on its knees."

"It was not that I minded. Smoit killed me in a fit of jealousy, and jealousy is in its blundering way a compliment. No, a worse thing than that befell me, Jurgen, and embittered all my life in the flesh." And Sylvia began to weep.

"And what was that thing, Sylvia?"

Queen Sylvia whispered the terrible truth. "My husband did not understand me."

"Now, by Heaven," says Jurgen, "when a woman tells me that, even though the woman be dead, I know what it is she expects of me."

So Jurgen put his arm about the ghost of Queen Sylvia Tereu, and comforted her. Then, finding her quite willing to be comforted, Jurgen sat for a while upon the dark steps, with one arm still about Queen Sylvia. The effect of the potion had evidently worn off, because Jurgen found himself to be composed no longer of cool imponderable vapour, but of the warmest and hardest sort of flesh everywhere. But probably the effect of the wine which Jurgen had drunk earlier in the evening had not worn off : for now Jurgen began to talk wildishly in the dark, about the necessity of his, in some way, avenging the injury inflicted upon his nominal grandfather, Ludwig, and Jurgen drew his sword, charmed Caliburn.

"For, as you perceive," said Jurgen, "I carry such weapons as are sufficient for all ordinary encounters. And am I not to use them, to requite King Smoit for the injustice he did poor Ludwig? Why, certainly I must. It is my duty."

"Ah, but Smoit by this is back in Purgatory," Queen Sylvia protested. "And to draw your sword against a woman is cowardly."

"The avenging sword of Jurgen, my charming Sylvia, is the terror of envious men, but it is the comfort of all pretty women."

"It is undoubtedly a very large sword," said she: "oh, a magnificent sword, as I can perceive even in the dark. But Smoit, I repeat, is not here to measure weapons with you."

"Now your arguments irritate me, whereas an honest woman would see to it that all the legacies of her dead husband were duly satisfied——"

"Oh, oh! and what do you mean——?"

"Well, but certainly a grandson is—at one remove, I grant you—a sort of legacy."

"There is something in what you advance——"

"There is a great deal in what I advance, I can assure you. It is the most natural and most penetrating kind of logic; and I wish merely to discharge a duty——"

"But you upset me with that big sword of yours; you make me nervous, and I cannot argue so long as you are flourishing it about. Come now, put up your sword! Oh, what is anybody to do with you? Here is the sheath for your sword," says she.

At this point they were interrupted.

"Duke of Logreus," says the voice of Dame Anaïtis, "do you not think it would be better to retire, before such antics at the door of my bedroom give rise to a scandal?"

For Anaïtis had half-opened the door of her bedroom, and with a lamp in her hand, was peering out into the narrow stairway. Jurgen was a little embarrassed, for his apparent intimacy with a lady who had been dead for sixty-three years would be, he felt, a matter difficult to explain. So Jurgen rose to his feet, and hastily put up the weapon he had exhibited to Queen Sylvia, and decided to pass airily over the whole affair. And outside, a cock crowed, for it was now dawn.

"I bid you a good morning, Dame Anaïtis," said Jurgen. "But the stairways hereabouts are confusing, and I must have lost my way. I was going for a stroll. This is my distant relative Queen Sylvia Tereu, who kindly offered to accompany me. We were going out to gather mushrooms and to watch the sunrise, you conceive."

"Messire de Logreus, I think you had far better go back to bed."

"To the contrary, madame, it is my manifest duty to serve as Queen Sylvia's escort——"

"For all that, messire, I do not see any Queen Sylvia."

Jurgen looked about him. And certainly his grandfather's ninth wife was no longer visible. "Yes, she has vanished. But that was to be expected at cockcrow. Still, that cock crew just at the wrong moment," said Jurgen, ruefully. "It was not fair."

And Dame Anaïtis said: "Gogyrvan's cellar is well stocked: and you sat late with Urien and Aribert: and doubtless they also were lucky enough to discover a queen or two in Gogyrvan's cellar. No less, I think you are still a little drunk."

"Now answer me this, Dame Anaïtis: were you not visited by two ghosts to-night?"

"Why, that is as it may be," she replied: "but the White Turret is notoriously haunted, and it is few quiet nights I have passed there, for Gogyrvan's people were a bad lot."

"Upon my word," wonders Jurgen, "what manner of person is this Dame Anaïtis, who remains unstirred by such a brutal murder as I have committed, and makes no more of ghosts than I would of moths? I have heard she is an enchantress; I am sure she is a fine figure of a woman: and in short, here is a matter which would repay looking into, were not young Guenevere the mistress of my heart."

Aloud he said: "Perhaps then I am drunk, madame. None the less, I still think the cock crew just at the wrong moment."

"Some day you must explain the meaning of that,"

says she. "Meanwhile I am going back to bed, and I again advise you to do the same."

Then the door closed, the bolt fell, and Jurgen went away, still in considerable excitement.

"This Dame Anaïtis is an interesting personality," he reflected, "and it would be a pleasure, now, to demonstrate to her my grievance against the cock, did occasion serve. Well, things less likely than that have happened. Then, too, she came upon me when my sword was out, and in consequence knows I wield a respectable weapon. She may feel the need of a good swordsman some day, this handsome Lady of the Lake who has no husband. So let us cultivate patience. Meanwhile, it appears that I am of royal blood. Well, I fancy there is something in the scandal, for I detect in me a deal in common with this King Smoit. Twelve wives, though! no, that is too many. I would limit no man's liaisons, but twelve wives in lawful matrimony bespeaks an optimism unknown to me. No, I do not think I am drunk: but it is unquestionable that I am not walking very straight. Certainly, too, we did drink a great deal. So I had best go quietly back to bed, and say nothing more about to-night's doings."

As much he did. And this was the first time that Jurgen, who had been a pawnbroker, held any discourse with Dame Anaïtis, whom men called the Lady of the Lake.

CHAPTER XVIII

WHY MERLIN TALKED IN TWILIGHT

T was two days later that Jurgen was sent for by Merlin Ambrosius. The Duke of Logreus came to the magician in twilight, for the windows of this room were covered with sheets which shut out the full radiance of day. Everything in the room was thus visible in a diffused and tempered light that cast no shadows. In his hand Merlin held a small mirror, about three inches square, from which he raised his dark eyes puzzlingly.

" I have been talking to my fellow ambassador, Dame Anaïtis : and I have been wondering, Messire de Logreus, if you have ever reared white pigeons."

Jurgen looked at the little mirror. " There was a woman of the Léshy who not long ago showed me an employment to which one might put the blood of white pigeons. She too used such a mirror. I saw what followed, but I must tell you candidly that I understood nothing of the ins and outs of the affair."

Merlin nodded. " I suspected something of the sort. So I elected to talk with you in a room wherein, as you perceive, there are no shadows."

" Now, upon my word," says Jurgen, " but here at last is somebody who can see my attendant ! Why is it, pray, that no one else can do so ? "

" It was my own shadow which drew my notice to your follower. For I, too, have had a shadow given me. It was the gift of my father, of whom you have probably heard."

It was Jurgen's turn to nod. Everybody knew who had begotten Merlin Ambrosius, and sensible persons preferred not to talk of the matter. Then Merlin went on to speak of the traffic between Merlin and Merlin's shadow.

"Thus and thus," says Merlin, "I humour my shadow. And thus and thus my shadow serves me. There is give-and-take, such as is requisite everywhere."

"I understand," says Jurgen: "but has no other person ever perceived this shadow of yours?"

"Once only, when for a while my shadow deserted me," Merlin replied. "It was on a Sunday my shadow left me, so that I walked unattended in naked sunlight: for my shadow was embracing the church-steeple, where church-goers knelt beneath him. The church-goers were obscurely troubled without suspecting why, for they looked only at each other. The priest and I alone saw him quite clearly,—the priest because this thing was evil, and I because this thing was mine."

"Well, now I wonder what did the priest say to your bold shadow?"

"'But you must go away!'—and the priest spoke without any fear. Why is it they seem always without fear, those dull and calm-eyed priests? 'Such conduct is unseemly. For this is High God's house, and far-off peoples are admonished by its steadfast spire, pointing always heavenward, that the place is holy,' said the priest. And my shadow answered, 'But I only know that steeples are of phallic origin.' And my shadow wept, wept ludicrously, clinging to the steeple where church-goers knelt beneath him."

"Now, and indeed that must have been disconcerting, Messire Merlin. Still, as you got your shadow back again, there was no great harm done. But why is it that such attendants follow some men while other men are permitted to live in decent solitude? It does not seem quite fair."

" Perhaps I could explain it to you, friend, but certainly I shall not. You know too much as it is. For you appear in that bright garment of yours to have come from a land and a time which even I, who am a skilled magician, can only cloudily foresee, and cannot understand at all. What puzzles me, however——— " And Merlin's forefinger shot out. " How many feet had the first wearer of your shirt ? and were you ever an old man ? " says he.

" Well, four, and I was getting on," says Jurgen.

" And I did not guess ! But certainly that is it,—an old poet loaned at once a young man's body and the Centaur's shirt. Adères has loosed a new jest into the world, for her own reasons——— "

" But you have things backwards. It was Sereda whom I cajoled so nicely."

" Names that are given by men amount to very little in a case like this. The shadow which follows you I recognise—and revere—as the gift of Adères, a dreadful Mother of small Gods. No doubt she has a host of other names. And you cajoled her, you consider ! I would not willingly walk in the shirt of any person who considers that. But she will enlighten you, my friend, at her appointed time."

" Well, so that she deals justly——— " Jurgen said, and shrugged.

Now Merlin put aside the mirror. " Meanwhile it was another matter entirely that Dame Anaïtis and I discussed, and about which I wished to be speaking with you. Gogyrvan is sending to King Arthur, along with Gogyrvan's daughter, that Round Table which Uther Pendragon gave Gogyrvan, and a hundred knights to fill the sieges of this table. Gogyrvan, who, with due respect, possesses a deplorable sense of humour, has numbered you among these knights. Now it is rumoured the Princess is given to conversing a great deal with you in private, and Arthur has never approved of garrulity. So I warn you that for you to come with us to London would not be convenient."

"I hardly think so, either," said Jurgen, with appropriate melancholy; "for me to pursue the affair any further would only result in marring what otherwise will always be a perfect memory of divers very pleasant conversations."

"Old poet, you are well advised," said Merlin,— "especially now that the little princess whom we know is about to enter queenhood and become a symbol. I am sorry for her, for she will be worshipped as a revelation of Heaven's splendour, and being flesh and blood, she will not like it. And it is to no effect I have forewarned King Arthur, for that must happen which will always happen so long as wisdom is impotent against human stupidity. So wisdom can but make the best of it, and be content to face the facts of a great mystery."

Thereupon, Merlin arose, and lifted the tapestry behind him, so that Jurgen could see what hitherto this tapestry had screened.

* * *

"You have embarrassed me horribly," said Jurgen, "and I can feel that I am still blushing, about the ankles. Well, I was wrong: so let us say no more concerning it."

"I wished to show you," Merlin returned, "that I know what I am talking about. However, my present purpose is to put Guenevere out of your head: for in your heart I think she never was, old poet, who go so modestly in the Centaur's shirt. Come, tell me now! and does the thought of her approaching marriage really disturb you?"

"I am the unhappiest man that breathes," said Jurgen, with unction. "All night I lie awake in my tumbled bed, and think of the miserable day which is past, and of what is to happen in that equally miserable day whose dawn

I watch with a sick heart. And I cry aloud, in the immortal words of Apollonius Myronides——"

" Of whom ? " says Merlin.

" I allude to the author of the *Myrosis*," Jurgen explained, " whom so many persons rashly identify with Apollonius Herophileius."

" Oh yes, of course ! your quotation is very apt. Why, then your condition is sad but not incurable. For I am about to give you this token, with which, if you are bold enough, you will do thus and thus."

" But indeed this is a somewhat strange token, and the arms and legs, and even the head, of this little man are remarkably alike ! Well, and you tell me thus and thus. But how does it happen, Messire Merlin, that you have never used this token in the fashion you suggest to me ? "

" Because I was afraid. You forget I am only a magician, whose conjuring raises nothing more formidable than devils. But this is a bit of the Old Magic that is no longer understood, and I prefer not to meddle with it. You, to the contrary, are a poet, and the Old Magic was always favourable to poets."

" Well, I will think about it," says Jurgen, " if this will really put Dame Guenevere out of my head."

" Be assured it will do that," said Merlin. " For with reason does the *Dirghâgama* declare, ' The brightness of the glow-worm cannot be compared to that of a lamp.' "

" A very pleasant little work, the *Dirghâgama*," said Jurgen, tolerantly—" though superficial, of course."

Then Merlin Ambrosius gave Jurgen the token, and some advice.

So that night Jurgen told Guenevere he would not go in her train to London. He told her candidly that Merlin was suspicious of their intercourse.

" And therefore, in order to protect you and to protect your fame, my dearest dear," said Jurgen, " it is necessary that I sacrifice myself and everything I prize in life. I shall suffer very much : but my consolation will be that I have dealt fairly with you whom I love with an entire heart, and shall have preserved you through my misery."

But Guenevere did not appear to notice how noble this was of Jurgen. Instead, she wept very softly, in a heart-broken way that Jurgen found unbearable.

"For no man, whether emperor or peasant," says the Princess, "has ever been loved more dearly or faithfully or more wholly without any reserve or forethought than you, my dearest, have been loved by me. All that I had I have given you. All that I had you have taken, consuming it. So now you leave me with not anything more to give you, not even any anger or contempt, now that you turn me adrift, for there is nothing in me anywhere save love of you, who are unworthy."

"But I die many deaths," said Jurgen, "when you speak thus to me." And in point of fact, he did feel rather uncomfortable.

"I speak the truth, though. You have had all : and so you are a little weary, and perhaps a little afraid of what may happen if you do not break off with me."

"Now you misjudge me, darling——"

"No, I do not misjudge you, Jurgen. Instead, for the first time I judge both of us. You I forgive, because I love you, but myself I do not forgive, and I cannot ever forgive, for having been a spendthrift fool."

And Jurgen found such talking uncomfortable and tedious and very unfair to him. "For there is nothing I can do to help matters," says Jurgen. "Why, what could anybody possibly expect me to do about it ? And so why not be happy while we may ? It is not as though we had any time to waste."

For this was the last night but one before the day that was set for Guenevere's departure.

CHAPTER XIX

THE BROWN MAN WITH QUEER FEET

EARLY in the following morning Jurgen left Cameliard, travelling toward Carohaise, and went into the Druid forest there, and followed Merlin's instructions.

"Not that I for a moment believe in such nonsense," said Jurgen: "but it will be amusing to see what comes of this business, and it is unjust to deny even nonsense a fair trial."

So he presently observed a sun-browned brawny fellow, who sat upon the bank of a stream, dabbling his feet in the water, and making music with a pipe constructed of seven reeds of irregular lengths. To him Jurgen displayed, in such a manner as Merlin had prescribed, the token which Merlin had given. The man made a peculiar sign, and rose. Jurgen saw that this man's feet were unusual.

Jurgen bowed low, and he said, as Merlin had bidden: "Now praise be to thee, thou lord of the two truths! I have come to thee, O most wise, that I may learn thy secret. I would know thee, and would know the forty-two mighty ones who dwell with thee in the hall of the two truths, and who are nourished by evil-doers, and who partake of wicked blood each day of the reckoning before Wennofree. I would know thee for what thou art."

The brown man answered: "I am everything that was and that is to be. Never has any mortal been able to discover what I am."

Then this brown man conducted Jurgen to an open glen, at the heart of the forest.

" Merlin dared not come himself, because," observed the brown man, " Merlin is wise. But you are a poet. So you will presently forget that which you are about to see, or at worst you will tell pleasant lies about it, particularly to yourself."

" I do not know about that," says Jurgen, " but I am willing to taste any drink once. What are you about to show me ? "

The brown man answered : " All."

So it was near evening when they came out of the glen. It was dark now, for a storm had risen. The brown man was smiling, and Jurgen was in a flutter.

" It is not true," Jurgen protested. " What you have shown me is a pack of nonsense. It is the degraded lunacy of a so-called Realist. It is sorcery and pure childishness and abominable blasphemy. It is, in a word, something I do not choose to believe. You ought to be ashamed of yourself ! "

" Even so, you do believe me, Jurgen."

" I believe that you are an honest man and that I am your cousin : so there are two more lies for you."

The brown man said, still smiling : " Yes, you are certainly a poet, you who have borrowed the apparel of my cousin. For you come out of my glen, and from my candour, as sane as when you entered. That is not saying much, to be sure, in praise of a poet's sanity at any time. But Merlin would have died, and Merlin would have died without regret, if Merlin had seen what you have seen, because Merlin receives facts reasonably."

" Facts ! sanity ! and reason ! " Jurgen raged : " why, but what nonsense you are talking ! Were there a bit of truth in your silly puppetry this world of time and space and consciousness would be a bubble, a bubble which contained the sun and moon and the high stars, and still was but a bubble in fermenting swill ! I must go cleanse my mind of all this foulness. You would have me believe that men, that all men who have ever lived or shall ever live hereafter, that even I am of no importance ! Why, there would be no justice in any such arrangement, no justice anywhere ! "

" That vexed you, did it not ? It vexes me at times, even me, who under Koshchei's will alone am changeless."

" I do not know about your variability : but I stick to my opinion about your veracity," says Jurgen, for all that he was upon the verge of hysteria. " Yes, if lies could choke people that shaggy throat would certainly be sore."

Then the brown man stamped his foot, and the striking of his foot upon the moss made a new noise such as Jurgen had never heard : for the noise seemed to come multitudinously from every side, at first as though each leaf in the forest were tinily cachinnating ; and then this noise was swelled by the mirth of larger creatures, and echoes played with this noise, until there was a reverberation everywhere like that of thunder. The earth moved under their feet very much as a beast twitches its skin under the annoyance of flies. Another queer thing Jurgen noticed, and it was that the trees about the glen had writhed and arched their trunks, and so had bended, much as candles bend in very hot weather, to lay their topmost foliage at the feet of the brown man. And the brown man's appearance was changed as he stood there, terrible in a continuous brown glare from the low-hanging clouds, and with the forest making obeisance, and with shivering and laughter everywhere.

" Make answer, you who chatter about justice ! how if I slew you now," says the brown man,—" I being what I am ? "

" Slay me, then ! " says Jurgen, with shut eyes, for he did not at all like the appearance of things. " Yes, you can kill me if you choose, but it is beyond your power to make me believe that there is no justice anywhere, and that I am unimportant. For I would have you know I

am a monstrous clever fellow.   As for you, you are either
a delusion or a god or a degraded Realist.   But whatever
you are, you have lied to me, and I know that you have
lied, and I will not believe in the insignificance of Jurgen."

Chillingly came the whisper of the brown man : " Poor
fool !   O shuddering, stiff-necked fool ! and have you not
just seen that which you may not ever quite forget ? "

" None the less, I think there is something in me which
will endure.   I am fettered by cowardice, I am enfeebled
by disastrous memories ; and I am maimed by old follies.
Still, I seem to detect in myself something which is
permanent and rather fine.   Underneath everything, and
in spite of everything, I really do seem to detect that
something.   What rôle that something is to enact after
the death of my body, and upon what stage, I cannot guess.
When fortune knocks I shall open the door.   Meanwhile
I tell you candidly, you brown man, there is something
in Jurgen far too admirable for any intelligent arbiter ever
to fling into the dust-heap.   I am, if nothing else, a
monstrous clever fellow : and I think I shall endure,
somehow.   Yes, cap in hand goes through the land, as the
saying is : and I believe I can contrive some trick to cheat
oblivion when the need arises," says Jurgen, trembling,
and gulping, and with his eyes shut tight, but even so,
with his mind quite made up about it.   " Of course you
may be right ; and certainly I cannot go so far as to say
you are wrong : but still, at the same time——"

" Now, but before a fool's opinion of himself," the
brown man cried, " the Gods are powerless.   Oh, yes, and
envious, too ! "

And when Jurgen very cautiously opened his eyes the
brown man had left him physically unharmed.   But the
state of Jurgen's nervous system was deplorable.

CHAPTER XX

EFFICACY OF PRAYER

JURGEN went in a tremble to the Cathedral of the Sacred Thorn in Cameliard. All night Jurgen prayed there, not in repentance, but in terror. For his dead he prayed, that they should not have been blotted out in nothingness, for the dead among his kindred whom he had loved in boyhood, and for these only. About the men and women whom he had known since then he did not seem to care, or not at least so vitally. But he put up a sort of prayer for Dame Lisa— " wherever my dear wife may be, and, O God, grant that I may come to her at last, and be forgiven ! " he wailed, and wondered if he really meant it.

He had forgotten about Guenevere. And nobody knows what were that night the thoughts of the young Princess, nor if she offered any prayers, in the deserted Hall of Judgment.

In the morning a sprinkling of persons came to early mass. Jurgen attended with fervour, and started doorward with the others. Just before him a merchant stopped to get a pebble from his shoe, and the merchant's wife went forward to the holy-water font.

" Madame, permit me," said a handsome young esquire, and offered her holy water.

" At eleven," said the merchant's wife, in low tones. " He will be out all day."

" My dear," says her husband, as he rejoined her, " and who was the young gentleman ? "

"Why, I do not know, darling. I never saw him before."

"He was certainly very civil. I wish there were more like him. And a fine-looking young fellow, too!"

"Was he? I did not notice," said the merchant's wife, indifferently.

And Jurgen saw and heard and regarded the departing trio ruefully. It seemed to him incredible the world should be going on just as it went before he ventured into the Druid forest.

He paused before a crucifix, and he knelt and looked up wistfully. "If one could only know," says Jurgen, "what really happened in Judea! How immensely would matters be simplified, if anyone but knew the truth about You, Man upon the Cross!"

Now the Bishop of Merion passed him, coming from celebration of the early mass. "My Lord Bishop," says Jurgen, simply, "can you tell me the truth about this Christ?"

"Why, indeed, Messire de Logreus," replied the Bishop, "one cannot but sympathise with Pilate in thinking that the truth about Him is very hard to get at, even nowadays. Was He Melchisedek, or Shem, or Adam? or was He verily the Logos? and in that event, what sort of a something was the Logos? Granted He was a god, were the Arians or the Sabellians in the right? had He existed always, co-substantial with the Father and the Holy Spirit, or was He a creation of the Father, a kind of Israelitic Zagreus? Was He the husband of Acharamoth, that degraded Sophia, as the Valentinians aver? or the son of Pantherus, as say the Jews? or Kalakau, as contends Basilidês? or was it, as the Docetês taught, only a tinted cloud in the shape of a man that went from Jordan to Golgotha? Or were the Merinthians right? These are a few of the questions, Messire de Logreus, which naturally arise. And not all of them are to be settled out of hand."

Thus speaking, the gallant prelate bowed, then raised three fingers in benediction, and so quitted Jurgen, who was still kneeling before the crucifix.

" Ah, ah ! " says Jurgen, to himself, " but what a variety of interesting problems are, in point of fact, suggested by religion. And what delectable exercise would the settling of these problems, once for all, afford the mind of a monstrous clever fellow ! Come now, it might be well for me to enter the priesthood. It may be that I have a call."

But people were shouting in the street. So Jurgen rose and dusted his knees. And as Jurgen came out of the Cathedral of the Sacred Thorn the cavalcade was passing that bore away Dame Guenevere to the arms and throne of her appointed husband. Jurgen stood upon the Cathedral porch, his mind in part pre-occupied by theology, but still not failing to observe how beautiful was this young princess, as she rode by on her white palfrey, green-garbed and crowned and a-glitter with jewels. She was smiling as she passed him, bowing her small tenderly-coloured young countenance this way and that way, to the shouting people, and not seeing Jurgen at all.

Thus she went to her bridal, that Guenevere who was the symbol of all beauty and purity to the chivalrous people of Glathion. The mob worshipped her ; and they spoke as though it were an angel who passed.

" Our beautiful young Princess ! "

" Ah, there is none like her anywhere ! "

" And never a harsh word for anyone, they say—— ! "

" Oh, but she is the most admirable of ladies—— ! "

" And so brave too, that lovely smiling child who is leaving her home for ever ! "

" And so very, very pretty ! "

"—So generous ! "

" King Arthur will be hard put to it to deserve her ! "

Said Jurgen : " Now it is droll that to these truths I have but to add another truth in order to have large

paving-stones flung at her ! and to have myself tumultu-
ously torn into fragments, by those unpleasantly sweaty
persons who, thank Heaven, are no longer jostling me ! "

For the Cathedral porch had suddenly emptied, because
as the procession passed heralds were scattering silver
among the spectators.

" Arthur will have a very lovely queen," says a soft
lazy voice.

And Jurgen turned and saw that beside him was Dame
Anaïtis, whom people called the Lady of the Lake.

" Yes, he is greatly to be envied," says Jurgen, politely.
" But do you not ride with them to London ? "

" Why, no," says the Lady of the Lake, " because my
part in this bridal was done when I mixed the stirrup-cup
of which the Princess and young Lancelot drank this
morning.   He is the son of King Ban of Benwick, that
tall young fellow in blue armour.   I am partial to Lancelot, for I reared him, at the bottom of a lake that belongs to me, and I consider he does me credit.   I also
believe that Madame Guenevere by this time agrees with
me.   And so, my part being done to serve my creator,
I am off for Cocaigne."

" And what is this Cocaigne ? "

" It is an island wherein I rule."

" I did not know you were a queen, madame."

" Why, indeed there are a many things unknown to
you, Messire de Logreus, in a world where nobody gets
any assuredness of knowledge about anything.   For it
is a world wherein all men that live have but a little
while to live, and none knows his fate thereafter.   So
that a man possesses nothing certainly save a brief loan
of his own body : and yet the body of man is capable of
much curious pleasure."

" I believe," said Jurgen, as his thoughts shuddered
away from what he had seen and heard in the Druid
forest, " that you speak wisdom."

" Then in Cocaigne we are all wise : for that is our

religion But of what are you thinking, Duke of Logreus ? "

" I was thinking," says Jurgen, " that your eyes are unlike the eyes of any other woman that I have ever seen."

Smilingly the dark woman asked him wherein they differed, and smilingly he said he did not know. They were looking at each other warily. In each glance an experienced gamester acknowledged a worthy opponent.

" Why, then you must come with me into Cocaigne," says Anaïtis, " and see if you cannot discover wherein lies that difference. For it is not a matter I would care to leave unsettled."

" Well, that seems only just to you," says Jurgen. " Yes, certainly I must deal fairly with you."

Then they left the Cathedral of the Sacred Thorn, walking together. The folk who went toward London were now well out of sight and hearing, which possibly accounts for the fact that Jurgen was now in no wise thinking of Guenevere. So it was that Guenevere rode out of Jurgen's life for a while : and as she rode she talked with Lancelot.

CHAPTER XXI

HOW ANAÏTIS VOYAGED

OW the tale tells that Jurgen and this Lady of the Lake came presently to the wharves of Cameliard, and went aboard the ship which had brought Anaïtis and Merlin into Glathion. This ship was now to every appearance deserted: yet all its saffron-coloured sails were spread, as though in readiness for the ship's departure.

"The crew are scrambling, it may be, for the largesse, and fighting over Gogyrvan's silver pieces," says Anaïtis, "but I think they will not be long in returning. So we will sit here upon the prow, and await their leisure."

"But already the vessel moves," says Jurgen, "and I hear behind us the rattling of silver chains and the flapping of shifted saffron-coloured sails."

"They are roguish fellows," says Anaïtis, smiling. "Evidently, they hid from us, pretending there was nobody aboard. Now they think to give us a surprise when the ship sets out to sea as though it were of itself. But we will disappoint these merry rascals, by seeming to notice nothing unusual."

So Jurgen sat with Anaïtis in the two tall chairs that were in the prow of the vessel, under a canopy of crimson stuff embroidered with gold dragons, and just back of the ship's figurehead, which was a dragon painted with thirty colours: and the ship moved out of the harbour, and so into the open sea. Thus they passed Enisgarth.

"And it is a queer crew that serve you, Anaïtis, who

So JURGEN sat with ANAÏTIS‥

are Queen of Cocaigne : for I can hear them talking, far back of us, and their language is all a cheeping and a twittering, as though the mice and the bats were holding conference."

" Why, you must understand that these are outlanders who speak a dialect of their own, and are not like any other people you have ever seen."

" Indeed, now, that is very probable, for I have seen none of your crew. Sometimes it is as though small flickerings passed over the deck, and that is all."

" It is but the heat waves rising from the deck, for the day is warmer than you would think, sitting here under this canopy. And besides, what call have you and I to be bothering over the pranks of common mariners, so long as they do their proper duty ? "

" I was thinking, O woman with unusual eyes, that these are hardly common mariners."

" And I was thinking, Duke Jurgen, that I would tell you a tale of the Old Gods, to make the time speed more pleasantly as we sit here untroubled as a god and a goddess."

Now they had passed Camwy : and Anaïtis began to narrate the history of Anistar and Calmoora and of the unusual concessions they granted each other, and of how Calmoora contented her five lovers : and Jurgen found the tale perturbing.

While Anaïtis talked the sky grew dark, as though the sun were ashamed and veiled his shame with clouds : and they went forward in a grey twilight which deepened steadily over a tranquil sea. So they passed the lights of Sargyll, most remote of the Red Islands, while Anaïtis talked of Procris and King Minos and Pasiphaë. As colour went out of the air new colours entered into the sea, which now assumed the varied gleams of water that has long been stagnant. And a silence brooded over the sea, so that there was no noise anywhere except the sound of the voice of Anaïtis, saying, " All men that live have

but a little while to live, and none knows his fate thereafter. So that a man possesses nothing certainly save
a brief loan of his own body; and yet the body of man
is capable of much curious pleasure."

They came thus to a low-lying naked beach, where
there was no sign of habitation. Anaïtis said this was
the land they were seeking, and they went ashore.

"Even now," says Jurgen, "I have seen none of the
crew who brought us hither."

And the beautiful dark woman shrugged, and marvelled why he need perpetually be bothering over the
doings of common sailors.

They went forward across the beach, through sand
hills, to a moor, seeing no one, and walking in a grey fog.
They passed many grey fat sluggish worms and some
curious grey reptiles such as Jurgen had never imagined
to exist, but Anaïtis said these need not trouble
them.

"So there is no call to be fingering your charmed
sword as we walk here, Duke Jurgen, for these great
worms do not ever harm the living."

"For whom, then, do they lie here in wait, in this grey
fog, wherethrough the green lights flutter, and wherethrough I hear at times a thin and far-off wailing?"

"What is that to you, Duke Jurgen, since you and I are
still in the warm flesh? Surely there was never a man
who asked more idle questions."

"Yet this is an uncomfortable twilight."

"To the contrary, you should rejoice that it is a fog
too heavy to be penetrated by the Moon."

"But what have I to do with the Moon?"

"Nothing, as yet. And that is as well for you, Duke
Jurgen, since it is authentically reported you have derided
the day which is sacred to the Moon. Now the Moon
does not love derision, as I well know, for in part I
serve the Moon."

"Eh?" says Jurgen: and he began to reflect.

So they came to a wall that was high and grey, and to the door which was in the wall.

"You must knock two or three times," says Anaïtis, "to get into Cocaigne."

Jurgen observed the bronze knocker upon the door, and he grinned in order to hide his embarrassment.

"It is a quaint fancy," said he, "and the two constituents of it appear to have been modelled from life."

"They were copied very exactly from Adam and Eve," says Anaïtis, "who were the first persons to open this gateway."

"Why, then," says Jurgen, "there is no earthly doubt that men degenerate, since here under my hand is the proof of it."

With that he knocked, and the door opened, and the two of them entered.

CHAPTER XXII

AS TO A VEIL THEY BROKE

O it was that Jurgen came into Cocaigne, wherein is the bedchamber of Time. And Time, they report, came in with Jurgen, since Jurgen was mortal: and Time, they say, rejoiced in this respite from the slow toil of dilapidating cities stone by stone, and with his eyes tired by the finicky work of etching in wrinkles, went happily into his bedchamber, and fell asleep just after sunset on this fine evening in late June : so that the weather remained fair and changeless, with no glaring sun rays anywhere, and with one large star shining alone in clear daylight. This was the star of Venus Mechanitis, and Jurgen later derived considerable amusement from noting how this star was trundled about the dome of heaven by a largish beetle, named Khepre. And the trees everywhere kept their first fresh foliage, and the birds were about their indolent evening songs, all during Jurgen's stay in Cocaigne, for Time had gone to sleep at the pleasantest hour of the year's most pleasant season. So tells the tale.

And Jurgen's shadow also went in with Jurgen, but in Cocaigne as in Glathion, nobody save Jurgen seemed to notice this curious shadow which now followed Jurgen everywhere.

In Cocaigne Queen Anaïtis had a palace, where domes and pinnacles beyond numbering glimmered with a soft whiteness above the top of an old twilit forest, wherein the vegetation was unlike that which is nourished by ordinary earth. There was to be seen in these woods, for instance, a sort of moss which made Jurgen shudder. So Anaïtis and Jurgen came through narrow paths, like murmuring green caverns, into a courtyard walled and paved with yellow marble, wherein was nothing save the dimly coloured statue of a god with ten heads and thirty-four arms : he was represented as very much engrossed by a woman, and with his unoccupied hands was holding yet other women.

"It is Jigsbyed," said Anaïtis.

Said Jurgen : "I do not criticise. Nevertheless, I think this Jigsbyed is carrying matters to extremes."

Then they passed the statue of Tangaro Loloquong, and afterward the statue of Legba. Jurgen stroked his chin, and his colour heightened. "Now certainly, Queen Anaïtis," he said, "you have unusual taste in sculpture."

Thence Jurgen came with Anaïtis into a white room, with copper plaques upon the walls, and there four girls were heating water in a brass tripod. They bathed Jurgen, giving him astonishing caresses meanwhile—with the tongue, the hair, the finger-nails, and the tips of the breasts,—and they anointed him with four oils, then dressed him again in his glittering shirt. Of Caliburn, said Anaïtis, there was no present need : so Jurgen's sword was hung upon the wall.

These girls brought silver bowls containing wine mixed with honey, and they brought pomegranates and eggs and barleycorn, and triangular red-coloured loaves, whereon they sprinkled sweet-smelling little seeds with formal gestures. Then Anaïtis and Jurgen broke their fast, eating together while the four girls served them.

"And now," says Jurgen, "and now, my dear, I would suggest that we enter into the pursuit of those curious pleasures of which you were. telling me."

"I am very willing," responded Anaïtis, "since there is no one of these pleasures but is purchased by some diversion of man's nature. Yet first, as I need hardly inform you, there is a ceremonial to be observed."

" And what, pray, is this ceremonial ? "

" Why, we call it the Breaking of the Veil." And Queen Anaïtis explained what they must do.

" Well," says Jurgen, " I am willing to taste any drink once."

So Anaïtis led Jurgen into a sort of chapel, adorned with very unchurchlike paintings. There were four shrines, dedicated severally to St. Cosmo, to St. Damianus, to St. Guignole of Brest, and to St. Foutin de Varailles. In this chapel were a hooded man, clothed in long garments that were striped with white and yellow, and two naked children, both girls. One of the children carried a censer : the other held in one hand a vividly blue pitcher half filled with water, and in her left hand a cellar of salt.

First of all, the hooded man made Jurgen ready. " Behold the lance," said the hooded man, " which must serve you in this adventure."

" I accept the adventure," Jurgen replied, " because I believe the weapon to be trustworthy."

Said the hooded man : " So be it ! but as you are, so once was I."

Meanwhile Duke Jurgen held the lance erect, shaking it with his right hand. This lance was large, and the tip of it was red with blood.

" Behold," said Jurgen, " I am a man born of a woman incomprehensibly. Now I, who am miraculous, am found worthy to perform a miracle, and to create that which I may not comprehend."

Anaïtis took salt and water from the child, and mingled these. " Let the salt of earth enable the thin fluid to assume the virtue of the teeming sea ! "

Then, kneeling, she touched the lance, and began to stroke it lovingly. To Jurgen she said : " Now may you be fervent of soul and body ! May the endless Serpent be your crown, and the fertile flame of the sun your strength ! "

Said the hooded man, again : " So be it ! " His voice was high and bleating, because of that which had been done to him.

" That therefore which we cannot understand we also invoke," said Jurgen. " By the power of the lifted lance "—and now with his left hand he took the hand of Anaïtis,—" I, being a man born of a woman incomprehensibly, now seize upon that which alone I desire with my whole being. I lead you toward the east. I upraise you above the earth and all the things of earth."

Then Jurgen raised Queen Anaïtis so that she sat upon the altar, and that which was there before tumbled to the ground. Anaïtis placed together the tips of her thumbs and of her fingers, so that her hands made an open triangle ; and waited thus. Upon her head was a network of red coral, with branches radiating downward : her gauzy tunic had twenty-two openings, so as to admit all imaginable caresses, and was of two colours, being shot with black and crimson curiously mingled : her dark eyes glittered and her breath came fast.

Now the hooded man and the two naked girls performed their share in the ceremonial, which part it is not essential to record. But Jurgen was rather shocked by it.

None the less, Jurgen said : " O cord that binds the circling of the stars ! O cup which holds all time, all colour, and all thought ! O soul of space ! not unto any image of thee do we attain unless thy image show in what we are about to do. Therefore by every plant which scatters its seed and by the moist warm garden which receives and nourishes it, by the comminglement of bloodshed with pleasure, by the joy that mimics anguish with sighs and shudderings, and by the contentment which mimics death,—by all these do we invoke thee. O thou, continuous one, whose will these children attend, and whom I now adore in this fair-coloured and soft woman's body, it is thou whom I honour, not any woman, in doing what seems good to me : and it is thou who art about to speak, and not she."

Then Anaïtis said : " Yea, for I speak with the tongue of every woman, and I shine in the eyes of every woman, when the lance is lifted. To serve me is better than all else. When you invoke me with a heart wherein is kindled the serpent flame, if but for a moment, you will understand the delights of my garden, what joy unwordable pulsates therein, and how potent is the sole desire which uses all of a man. To serve me you will then be eager to surrender whatever else is in your life : and other pleasures you will take with your left hand, not thinking of them entirely : for I am the desire which uses all of a man, and so wastes nothing. And I accept you, I yearn toward you, I who am daughter and somewhat more than daughter to the Sun. I who am all pleasure, all ruin, and a drunkenness of the inmost sense, desire you."

Now Jurgen held his lance erect before Anaïtis. " O secret of all things, hidden in the being of all which lives, now that the lance is exalted I do not dread thee : for thou art in me, and I am thou. I am the flame that burns in every beating heart and in the core of the farthest star. I too am life and the giver of life, and in me too is death. Wherein art thou better than I ? I am alone : my will is justice : and there comes no other god where I am."

Said the hooded man behind Jurgen : " So be it ! but as you are, so once was I."

The two naked children stood one at each side of Anaïtis, and waited there trembling. These girls, as Jurgen afterward learned, were Alecto and Tisiphonê, two of the Eumenidês. And now Jurgen shifted the red point of the lance, so that it rested in the open triangle made by the fingers of Anaïtis.

" I am life and the giver of life," cried Jurgen. " Thou

that art one, that makest use of all! I who am a man born of woman, I in my station honour thee in honouring this desire which uses all of a man. Make open therefore the way of creation, encourage the flaming dust which is in our hearts, and aid us in that flame's perpetuation! For is not that thy law?"

Anaïtis answered: "There is no law in Cocaigne save, Do that which seems good to you."

Then said the naked children: "Perhaps it is the law, but certainly it is not justice. Yet we are little and quite helpless. So presently we must be made as you are: for now you two are no longer two, and your flesh is not shared merely with each other. For your flesh becomes our flesh, and your sins our sins: and we have no choice."

Jurgen lifted Anaïtis from the altar, and they went into the chancel and searched for the adytum. There seemed to be no doors anywhere in the chancel: but presently Jurgen found an opening screened by a pink veil. Jurgen thrust with his lance and broke this veil. He heard the sound of one brief wailing cry: it was followed by soft laughter. So Jurgen came into the adytum.

Black candles were burning in this place, and sulphur too was burning there, before a scarlet cross, of which the top was a circle, and whereon was nailed a living toad. And other curious matters Jurgen likewise noticed.

He laughed, and turned to Anaïtis: now that the candles were behind him, she was standing in his shadow. "Well, well! but you are a little old-fashioned, with all these equivocal mummeries. And I did not know that civilised persons any longer retained sufficient credulity to wring a thrill from god-baiting. Still, women must be humoured, bless them! and at last, I take it, we have quite fairly fulfilled the ceremonial requisite to the pursuit of curious pleasures."

Queen Anaïtis was very beautiful, even under his be-dimming shadow. Triumphant too was the proud face beneath that curious coral network, and yet this woman's face was sad.

"Dear fool," she said, "it was not wise, when you sang of the Léshy, to put an affront upon Monday. But you have forgotten that. And now you laugh because that which we have done you do not understand: and equally that which I am you do not understand."

"No matter what you may be, my dear, I am sure that you will presently tell me all about it. For I assume that you mean to deal fairly with me."

"I shall do that which becomes me, Duke Jurgen——"

"That is it, my dear, precisely! You intend to be true to yourself, whatever happens. The aspiration does you infinite honour, and I shall try to help you. Now I have noticed that every woman is most truly herself," says Jurgen, oracularly, "in the dark."

Then Jurgen looked at her for a moment, with twink-ling eyes: then Anaïtis, standing in his shadow, smiled with glowing eyes: then Jurgen blew out those black candles: and then it was quite dark.

CHAPTER XXIII

SHORTCOMINGS OF PRINCE JURGEN

NOW the happenings just recorded befell on the eve of the Nativity of St. John the Baptist: and thereafter Jurgen abode in Cocaigne, and complied with the customs of that country.

In the palace of Queen Anaïtis, all manner of pastimes were practised without any cessation. Jurgen, who considered himself to be somewhat of an authority upon such contrivances, was soon astounded by his own innocence. For Anaïtis showed him whatever was being done in Cocaigne, to this side and to that side, under the direction of Anaïtis, whom Jurgen found to be a nature myth of doubtful origin connected with the Moon; and who, in consequence, ruled not merely in Cocaigne but furtively swayed the tides of life everywhere the Moon keeps any power over tides. It was the mission of Anaïtis to divert and turn aside and deflect: in this the jealous Moon abetted her because sunlight makes for straightforwardness. So Anaïtis and the Moon were staunch allies. These mysteries of their private relations, however, as revealed to Jurgen, are not very nicely repeatable.

"But you dishonoured the Moon, Prince Jurgen, denying praise to the day of the Moon. Or so, at least, I have heard."

"I remember doing nothing of the sort. But I remember considering it unjust to devote one paltry day to the Moon's majesty. For night is sacred to the

Moon, each night that ever was the friend of lovers,—
night, the renewer and begetter of all life."

"Why, indeed, there is something in that argument,"
says Anaïtis, dubiously.

"'Something,' do you say? Why, but to my way of
thinking it proves the Moon is precisely seven times
more honourable than any of the Léshy. It is merely,
my dear, a question of arithmetic."

"Was it for that reason you did not praise Pandelis
and her Mondays with the other Léshy?"

"Why, to be sure," said Jurgen, glibly. "I did not
find it at all praiseworthy that such an insignificant
Léshy as Pandelis should name her day after the Moon :
to me it seemed blasphemy." Then Jurgen coughed,
and looked sidewise at his shadow. "Had it been
Sereda, now, the case would have been different, and
the Moon might well have appreciated the delicate
compliment."

Anaïtis appeared relieved. "I shall report your explanation. Candidly, there were ill things in store for
you, Prince Jurgen, because your language was misunder-
stood. But that which you now say puts quite a different
complexion upon matters."

Jurgen laughed, not understanding the mystery, but
confident he could always say whatever was required of
him.

"Now let us see a little more of Cocaigne!" cries
Jurgen.

For Jurgen was greatly interested by the pursuits of
Cocaigne, and for a week or ten days participated therein
industriously. Anaïtis, who reported the Moon's honour
to be satisfied, now spared no effort to divert him, and
they investigated innumerable pastimes together.

"For all men that live have but a little while to live,"
said Anaïtis, "and none knows his fate thereafter. So
that a man possesses nothing certainly save a brief loan
of his body : and yet the body of man is capable of much

curious pleasure. As thus and thus," says Anaïtis. And she revealed devices to her Prince Consort.

For Jurgen found that unknowingly he had in due and proper form espoused Queen Anaïtis, by participating in the Breaking of the Veil, which is the marriage ceremony of Cocaigne. His earlier relations with Dame Lisa had, of course, no legal standing in Cocaigne, where the Church is not Christian and the Law is, Do that which seems good to you.

"Well, when in Rome," said Jurgen, "one must be romantic. But certainly this proves that nobody ever knows when he is being entrapped into respectability : and never did a fine young fellow marry a high queen with less premeditation."

"Ah, my dear," says Anaïtis, "you were controlled by the finger of Fate."

"I do not altogether like that figure of speech. It makes one seem too trivial, to be controlled by a mere finger. No, it is not quite complimentary to call what prompted me a finger."

"By the long arm of coincidence, then."

"Much more appropriate, my love," says Jurgen, complacently : "it sounds more dignified, and does not wound my self-esteem."

Now this Anaïtis who was Queen of Cocaigne was a delicious tall dark woman, thinnish, and lovely, and very restless. From the first her new Prince Consort was puzzled by her fervours, and presently was fretted by them. He humbly failed to understand how anyone could be so frantic over Jurgen. It seemed unreasonable. And in her more affectionate moments this nature myth positively frightened him : for transports such as these could not but rouse discomfortable reminiscences of the female spider, who ends such recreations by devouring her partner.

"Thus to be loved is very flattering," he would reflect, "and I again am Jurgen, asking odds of none. But even so, I am mortal. She ought to remember that, in common fairness."

Then the jealousy of Anaïtis, while equally flattering, was equally out of reason. She suspected everybody, seemed assured that every bosom cherished a mad passion for Jurgen, and that not for a moment could he be trusted. Well, as Jurgen frankly conceded, his conduct toward Stella, that ill-starred yogini of Indawadi, had in point of fact displayed, when viewed from an especial and quite unconscionable point of view, an aspect which, when isolated by persons judging hastily, might, just possibly, appear to approach remotely, in one or two respects, to temporary forgetfulness of Anaïtis, if indeed there were people anywhere so mentally deficient as to find such forgetfulness conceivable.

But the main thing, the really important feature, which Anaïtis could not be made to understand, was that she had interrupted her consort in what was, in effect, a philosophical experiment, necessarily attempted in the dark The muntrus requisite to the sacti sodhana were always performed in darkness : everybody knew that. For the rest, this Stella had asserted so-and-so ; in simple equity she was entitled to a chance to prove her allegations if she could : so Jurgen had proceeded to deal fairly with her. Besides, why keep talking about this Stella, after a vengeance so spectacular and thorough as that to which Anaïtis had out of hand resorted ? why keep reverting to a topic which was repugnant to Jurgen and visibly upset the dearest nature myth in all legend ? Was it quite fair to anyone concerned ? That was the sensible way in which Jurgen put it.

Still, he became honestly fond of Anaïtis. Barring her eccentricities when roused to passion, she was a generous and kindly creature, although in Jurgen's opinion somewhat narrow-minded.

"My love," he would say to her, "you appear positively unable to keep away from virtuous persons ! You are always seeking out the people who endeavour to be upright and straightforward, and you are perpetually laying plans to divert these people. Ah, but why bother about them? What need have you to wear yourself out, and to devote your entire time to such proselytising, when you might be so much more agreeably employed? You should learn, in justice to yourself as well as to others, to be tolerant of all things, and to acknowledge that in a being of man's mingled nature a strain of respectability is apt to develop every now and then, whatever you might prefer."

But Anaïtis had high notions as to her mission, and merely told him that he ought not to speak with levity of such matters. "I would be much happier staying at home with you and the children," she would say, "but I feel that it is my duty——"

"And your duty to whom, in heaven's name?"

"Please do not employ such distasteful expressions, Jurgen. It is my duty to the power I serve, my very manifest duty to my creator. But you have no sense of religion, I am afraid; and the reflection is often a considerable grief to me."

"Ah, but, my dear, you are quite certain as to who made you, and for what purpose you were made. You nature myths were created in the Mythopœic age by the perversity of old heathen nations : and you serve your creator religiously. That is quite as it should be. But I have no such authentic information as to my origin and mission in life, I appear at all events to have no natural talent for being diverted, I do not take to it wholeheartedly, and these are facts we have to face." Now Jurgen put his arm around her. "My dear Anaïtis, you must not think it mere selfishness on my part. I was born with a something lacking that is requisite for anyone who aspires to be as thoroughly misled as most people : and you will have to love me in spite of it."

"I almost wish I had never seen you as I saw you in

that corridor, Jurgen. For I felt drawn toward you then and there. I almost wish I had never seen you at all. I cannot help being fond of you : and yet you laugh at the things I know to be required of me, and sometimes you make me laugh, too."

"But, darling, are you not just the least, littlest, tiniest, very weest trifle bigoted? For instance, I can see that you think I ought to evince more interest in your striking dances, and your strange pleasures, and your surprising caresses, and all your other elaborate diversions. And I do think they do you credit, great credit, and I admire your inventiveness no less than your industry——."

"You have no sense of reverence, Jurgen; you seem to have no sense at all of what is due to one's creator. I suppose you cannot help that : but you might at least remember it troubles me to hear you talk so flippantly of my religion."

"But I do not talk flippantly——"

"Indeed you do, though. And it does not sound at all well, let me tell you."

"—Instead, I but point out that your creed necessitates, upon the whole, an ardour I lack. You, my pet, were created by perversity : and everyone knows it is the part of piety to worship one's creator in fashions acceptable to that creator. So, I do not criticise your religious connections, dear, and nobody admires these ceremonials of your faith more heartily than I do. I merely confess that to celebrate these rites so frequently requires a sustention of enthusiasm which is beyond me. In fine, I have not your fervent temperament, I am more sceptical. You may be right; and certainly I cannot go so far as to say you are wrong : but still, at the same time——! That is how I feel about it, my precious, and that is why I find, with constant repetition of these ceremonials, a certain lack of firmness developing in my responses : and finally, darling, that is all there is to it."

"I never in my whole incarnation had such a Prince

Consort! Sometimes I think you do not care a bit about me one way or the other, Jurgen."

"Ah, but I do care for you very much. And to prove it, come now, let us try some brand-new diversion, at sight of which the skies will be blackened and the earth will shudder or something of that sort, and then I will take the children fishing, as I promised."

"No, Jurgen, I do not feel like diverting you just now. You take all the solemnity out of it with your jeering. Besides, you are always with the children. Jurgen, I believe you are fonder of the children than you are of me. And when you are not with them you are locked up in the Library."

"Well, and was there ever such a treasury as the Library of Cocaigne? All the diversions that you nature myths have practised I find recorded there: and to read of your ingenious devices delights and maddens me. For it is eminently interesting to meditate upon strange pleasures, and to make verses about them is the most amiable of avocations: it is merely the pursuit of them that I would discourage, as disappointing and mussy. Besides, the Library is the only spot I have to myself in the palace, what with your fellow nature myths making the most of life all over the place."

"It is necessary, Jurgen, for one in my position to entertain more or less. And certainly I cannot close the doors against my own relatives."

"Such riffraff, though, my darling! Such odds and ends! I cannot congratulate you upon your kindred, for I do not get on at all with these patchwork combinations, that are one-third man and the other two-thirds a vulgar fraction of bull or hawk or goat or serpent or ape or jackal or what not. Priapos is the only male myth who comes here in anything like the semblance of a complete human being: and I had infinitely rather he stayed away, because even I who am Jurgen cannot but be envious of him."

"And why, pray?"

" Well, where I go reasonably equipped with Caliburn, Priapos carries a lance I envy——"

" Like all the Bacchic myths he usually carries a thyrsos, and it is a showy weapon, certainly ; but it is not of much use in actual conflict."

" My darling ! and how do you know ? "

" Why, Jurgen, how do women always know these things ?—by intuition, I suppose."

" You mean that you judge all affairs by feeling rather than reason ? Indeed, I dare say that is true of most women, and men are daily chafed and delighted, about equally, by your illogical method of putting things together. But to get back to the congenial task of criticising your kindred, your cousin Apis, for example, may be a very good sort of fellow : but, say what you will, it is ill-advised of him to be going about in public with a bull's head. It makes him needlessly conspicuous, if not actually ridiculous : and it puts me out when I try to talk to him."

" Now, Jurgen, pray remember that you speak of a very generally respected myth, and that you are being irreverent——"

" —And moreover, I take the liberty of repeating, my darling, that even though this Ba of Mendes is your cousin, it honestly does embarrass me to have to meet three-quarters of a goat socially——"

" But, Jurgen, I must as a matter of course invite prolific Ba to my feasts of the Sacæ——"

" Even so, my dear, in issuing invitations a hostess may fairly presuppose that her guests will not make beasts of themselves. I often wish that this mere bit of ordinary civility were more rigorously observed by Ba and Hortanes and Fricco and Vul and Baal-Peor, and by all your other cousins who come to visit you in such a zoologically muddled condition. It shows a certain lack of respect for you, my darling."

" Oh, but it is all in the family, Jurgen——"

" Besides, they have no conversation. They merely bellow—or twitter or bleat or low or gibber or purr, according to their respective incarnations,—about unspeakable mysteries and monstrous pleasures until I am driven to the verge of virtue by their imbecility."

" If you were more practical, Jurgen, you would realise that it speaks splendidly for anyone to be really interested in his vocation——"

" And your female relatives are just as annoying, with their eternal whispered enigmas, and their crescent moons, and their mystic roses that change colour and require continual gardening, and their pathetic belief that I have time to fool with them. And the entire pack practises symbolism until the house is positively littered with asherahs and combs and phalloses and linghams and yonis and arghas and pulleiars and talys, and I do not know what other idiotic toys that I am continually stepping on ! "

" Which of those minxes has been making up to you ? " says Anaïtis, her eyes snapping.

" Ah, ah ! now many of your female cousins are enticing enough——"

" I knew it ! Oh, but you need not think you deluded me—— ! "

" My darling, pray consider ! be reasonable about it ! Your feminine guests at present are Sekhmet in the form of a lioness, Io incarnated as a cow, Hekt, as a frog, Derceto as a sturgeon, and—ah, yes !—Thoueris as a hippopotamus. I leave it to your sense of justice, dear Anaïtis, if of ladies with such tastes in dress a lovely myth like you can reasonably be jealous."

" And I know perfectly well who it is ! It is that Ephesian hussy, and I had several times noticed her behaviour. Very well, oh, very well, indeed ! nevertheless, I shall have a plain word or two with her at once, and the sooner she gets out of my house the better, as I shall tell her quite frankly. And as for you, Jurgen—— ! "

" But, my dear Lisa——! "

" What do you call me? Lisa was never an epithet of mine. Why do you call me Lisa? "

" It was a slip of the tongue, my pet, an involuntary but not unnatural association of ideas. As for the Ephesian Diana, she reminds me of an animated pine-cone, with that eruption of breasts all over her, and I can assure you of your having no particular reason to be jealous of her. It was merely of the female myths in general I spoke. Of course they all make eyes at me : I cannot well help that, and you should have anticipated as much when you selected such an attractive Prince Consort. What do these poor enamoured creatures matter when to you my heart is ever faithful? "

" It is not your heart I am worrying over, Jurgen, for I believe you have none. Yes, you have quite succeeded in worrying me to distraction, if that is any comfort to you. However, let us not talk about it. For it is now necessary, absolutely imperative, that I go into Armenia to take part in the mourning for Tammouz : people would not understand it at all if I stayed away from such important orgies. And I shall get no benefit whatever from the trip, much as I need the change, because, without speaking of that famous heart of yours, you are always up to some double-dealing, and I shall not know into what mischief you may be thrusting yourself."

Jurgen laughed, and kissed her. " Be off, and attend to your religious duties, dear, by all means. And I promise you I will stay safe locked in the Library till you come back."

Thus Jurgen abode among the offspring of heathen perversity, and conformed to their customs. Death ends all things for all, they contended, and life is brief : for how few years do men endure, and how quickly is the most subtle and appalling nature myth explained away by the Philologists ! So the wise person, and equally the foreseeing nature myth, will take his glut of pleasure while there is yet time to take anything, and will waste none of his short lien upon desire and vigour by asking questions.

" Oh, but by all means ! " said Jurgen, and he docilely crowned himself with a rose garland, and drank his wine, and kissed his Anaïtis. Then, when the feast of the Sacæ was at full-tide, he would whisper to Anaïtis, " I will be back in a moment, darling," and she would frown fondly at him as he very quietly slipped from his ivory dining couch, and went, with the merest suspicion of a reel, into the Library. She knew that Jurgen had no intention of coming back : and she despaired of his ever taking the position in the social life of Cocaigne to which he was entitled no less by his rank as Prince Consort than by his personal abilities. For Anaïtis did not really think that, as went natural endowments, her Jurgen had much reason to envy even such a general favourite as Priapos, say, from what she knew of both.

So it was that Jurgen honoured custom. " Because these beastly nature myths may be right," said Jurgen ; " and certainly I cannot go so far as to say they are wrong : but still, at the same time—— ! "

For Jurgen was content to dismiss no riddle with a mere " I do not know." Jurgen was no more able to give up questioning the meaning of life than could a trout relinquish swimming : indeed, he lived submerged in a flood of curiosity and doubt, as his native element. That death ended all things might very well be the case : yet if the outcome proved otherwise, how much more pleasant it would be, for everyone concerned, to have aforetime established amicable relations with the over-lords of his second life, by having done whatever it was they expected of him here.

" Yes, I feel that something is expected of me," says Jurgen : " and without knowing what it is, I am tolerably sure, somehow, that it is not an indulgence in endless pleasure. Besides, I do not think death is going to end all for me. If only I could be quite certain my encounter with King Smoit, and with that charming little Sylvia Tereu, was not a dream ! As it is, plain reasoning assures me I am not indispensable to the universe : but with this reasoning, somehow, does not travel my belief. No, it is only fair to my own interests to go graveward a little more open-mindedly than do these nature myths, since I lack the requisite credulity to become a free-thinking materialist. To believe that we know nothing assuredly, and cannot ever know anything assuredly, is to take too much on faith."

And Jurgen paused to shake his sleek black head two or three times, very sagely.

"No, I cannot believe in nothingness being the destined end of all : that would be too futile a climax to content a dramatist clever enough to have invented Jurgen. No, it is just as I said to the brown man : I cannot believe in the annihilation of Jurgen by any really thrifty overlords ; so I shall see to it that Jurgen does nothing which he cannot more or less plausibly excuse, in case of supernal inquiries. That is far safer."

Now Jurgen was shaking his head again : and he sighed.

"For the pleasures of Cocaigne do not satisfy me. They are all well enough in their way ; and I admit the truism that in seeking bed and board two heads are better than one. Yes, Anaïtis makes me an excellent wife. Nevertheless, her diversions do not satisfy me, and gallantly to make the most of life is not enough. No, it is something else that I desire : and Anaïtis does not quite understand me."

CHAPTER XXIV

OF COMPROMISES IN COCAIGNE

HUS Jurgen abode for a little over two months in Cocaigne, and complied with the customs of that country. Nothing altered in Cocaigne : but in the world wherein Jurgen was reared, he knew, it would by this time be September, with the leaves flaring gloriously, and the birds flocking southward, and the hearts of Jurgen's fellows turning to not unpleasant regrets. But in Cocaigne there was no regret and no variability, but only an interminable flow of curious pleasures, illumined by the wandering star of Venus Mechanitis.

"Why is it, then, that I am not content ? " said Jurgen. "And what thing is this which I desire ? It seems to me there is some injustice being perpetrated upon Jurgen, somewhere."

Meanwhile he lived with Anaïtis the Sun's daughter very much as he had lived with Lisa, who was daughter to a pawnbroker. Anaïtis displayed upon the whole a milder temper : in part because she could confidently look forward to several centuries more of life before being explained away by the Philologists, and so had less need than Dame Lisa to worry over temporal matters ; and in part because there was less to ruin one's disposition in two months than in ten years of Jurgen's company. Anaïtis nagged and sulked for a while when her Prince Consort slackened in the pursuit of strange delights, as he did very soon, with frank confession that his tastes were simple and that these outlandish refinements bored him. Later Anaïtis seemed to despair of his ever becoming proficient in curious pleasures, and she permitted Jurgen to lead a comparatively normal life, with only an occasional and half-hearted remonstrance.

What puzzled Jurgen was that she did not seem to tire of him : and he would often wonder what this lovely myth, so skilled and potent in arts wherein he was the merest bungler, could find to care for in Jurgen. For now they lived together like any other humdrum married couple, and their occasional exchange of endearments was as much a matter of course as their meals, and hardly more exciting.

" Poor dear, I believe it is simply because I am a monstrous clever fellow. She distrusts my cleverness, she very often disapproves of it, and yet she values it as queer, as a sort of curiosity. Well, but who can deny that cleverness is truly a curiosity in Cocaigne ? "

So Anaïtis petted and pampered her Prince Consort, and took such open pride in his queerness as very nearly embarrassed him sometimes. She could not understand his attitude of polite amusement toward his associates and the events which befell him, and even toward his own doings and traits. Whatever happened, Jurgen shrugged, and, delicately avoiding actual laughter, evinced amusement. Anaïtis could not understand this at all, of course, since Asian myths are remarkably destitute of humour. To Jurgen in private she protested that he ought to be ashamed of his levity : but none the less, she would draw him out, when among the bestial and grim nature myths, and she would glow visibly with fond pride in Jurgen's queerness.

" She mothers me," reflected Jurgen. " Upon my word, I believe that in the end this is the only way in which females are capable of loving. And she is a dear and lovely creature, of whom I am sincerely fond. What is this thing, then, that I desire? Why do I feel life is not treating me quite justly?"

So the summer had passed; and Anaïtis travelled a great deal, being a popular myth in every land. Her sense of duty was so strong that she endeavoured to grace in person all the peculiar festivals held in her honour, and this, now the harvest season was at hand, left her with hardly a moment disengaged. Then, too, the mission of Anaïtis was to divert; and there were so many people whom she had personally to visit—so many notable ascetics who were advancing straight toward canonisation, and whom her underlings were unable to divert,—that Anaïtis was compelled to pass night after night in unwholesomely comfortless surroundings, in monasteries and in the cells and caves of hermits.

"You are wearing yourself out, my darling," Jurgen would say: "and does it not seem, after all, a game that is hardly worth the candle? I know that, for my part, before I would travel so many miles into a desert, and then climb a hundred-foot pillar, just to whisper diverting notions into an anchorite's very dirty ear, I would let the gaunt rascal go to Heaven. But you associate so much with saintly persons that you have contracted their incapacity for seeing the humorous side of things. Well, you are a dear, even so. Here is a kiss for you: and do you come back to your adoring husband as soon as you conveniently can without neglecting your duty."

"They report that this Stylites is very far gone in rectitude," said Anaïtis, absent-mindedly, as she prepared for the journey, "but I have hopes for him."

Then Anaïtis put purple powder on her hair, and hastily got together a few beguiling devices, and went into the Thebaid. Jurgen went back to the Library, and the *System of Worshipping a Girl*, and the unique manuscripts of Astyanassa and Elephantis and Sotadês, and the Dionysiac Formulæ, and the Chart of Postures,

and the *Litany of the Centre of Delight*, and the Spintrian
Treatises, and the *Thirty-two Gratifications*, and innumerable other volumes which he found instructive.

The Library was a vaulted chamber, having its walls
painted with the twelve Asan of Cyrenê; the ceiling
was frescoed with the arched body of a woman, whose
toes rested upon the cornice of the east wall, and whose
outstretched finger-tips touched the cornice of the
western wall. The clothing of this painted woman
was remarkable: and to Jurgen her face was not
unfamiliar.

"Who is that?" he inquired, of Anaïtis.

Looking a little troubled, Anaïtis told him this was
Æsred.

"Well, I have heard her called otherwise: and I
have seen her in quite other clothing."

"You have seen Æsred?"

"Yes, with a kitchen towel about her head, and otherwise unostentatiously apparelled—but very becomingly, I
can assure you!" Here Jurgen glanced sidewise at his
shadow, and he cleared his throat. "Oh, and a most
charming and a most estimable old lady I found this
Æsred to be, I can assure you also."

"I would prefer to know nothing about it," said
Anaïtis, hastily, "I would prefer, for both our sakes,
that you say no more of Æsred."

Jurgen shrugged.

Now in the Library of Cocaigne was garnered a record
of all that the nature myths had invented in the way of
pleasure. And here, with no companion save his queer
shadow, and with Æsred arched above and bleakly
regarding him, Jurgen spent most of his time, rather
agreeably, in investigating and meditating upon the more
curious of these recreations. The painted Asan were, in
all conscience, food for wonder: but over and above these
dozen surprising pastimes, the books of Anaïtis revealed
to Jurgen, without disguise or reticence, every other far-

fetched frolic of heathenry. Hitherto unheard-of forms
of diversion were unveiled to him, and every recreation
which ingenuity had been able to contrive, for the gratifying of the most subtle and the most strong-stomached
tastes. No possible sort of amusement would seem to
have been omitted, in running the quaint gamut of refinements upon nature which Anaïtis and her cousins had at
odd moments invented, to satiate their desire for some
more suave or more strange or more sanguinary pleasure.
Yet the deeper Jurgen investigated, and the longer he
meditated, the more certain it seemed to him that all such
employment was a peculiarly unimaginative pursuit of
happiness.

"I am willing to taste any drink once. So I must give
diversion a fair trial. But I am afraid these are the
games of mental childhood. Well, that reminds me I
promised the children to play with them for a while
before supper."

So he came out, and presently, brave in the shirt of
Nessus, and mimicked in every action by that incongruous
shadow, Prince Jurgen was playing tag with the three
little Eumenidês, the daughters of Anaïtis by her former
marriage with Acheron, the King of Midnight.

Anaïtis and the dark potentate had parted by mutual
consent. "Acheron meant well," she would say, with a
forgiving sigh, "and that in the Moon's absence he
occasionally diverted travellers, I do not deny. But he
did not understand me."

And Jurgen agreed that this tragedy sometimes befell
even the unapproachably diverting.

The three Eumenidês at this period were half-grown
girls, whom their mother was carefully tutoring to drive
guilty persons mad by the stings of conscience : and very
quaint it was to see the young Furies at practice in the
schoolroom, black-robed, and waving lighted torches,
and crowned each with her garland of pet serpents.
They became attached to Jurgen, who was always fond

of children, and who had frequently regretted that Dame Lisa had borne him none.

" It is enough to get the poor dear a name for eccentricity," he had been used to say.

So Jurgen now made much of his step-children : and indeed he found their innocent prattle quite as intelligent, in essentials, as the talk of the full-grown nature myths who infested the palace of Anaïtis. And the four of them—Jurgen, and critical Alecto, and grave Tisiphonê, and fairy-like little Megæra,—would take long walks, and play with their dolls (though Alecto was a trifle condescending toward dolls), and romp together in the eternal evening of Cocaigne ; and discuss what sort of dresses and trinkets Mother would probably bring them when she came back from Ecbatana or Lesbos, and would generally enjoy themselves.

Rather pathetically earnest and unimaginative little lasses, Jurgen found the young Eumenidês : they inherited much of their mother's narrow-mindedness, if not their father's brooding and gloomy tendencies ; but in them narrow-mindedness showed merely as amusing. And Jurgen loved them, and would often reflect what a pity it was that these dear little girls were destined, when they reached maturity, to spend the rest of their lives in haunting criminals and adulterers and parricides and, generally, such persons as must inevitably tarnish the girls' outlook upon life, and lead them to see too much of the worst side of human nature.

So Jurgen was content enough. But still he was not actually happy, not even among the endless pleasures of Cocaigne.

" And what is this thing that I desire ? " he would ask himself, again and again.

And still he did not know : he merely felt he was not getting justice : and a dim sense of this would trouble him even while he was playing with the Eumenidês.

CHAPTER XXV

CANTRAPS OF THE MASTER PHILOLOGIST

UT now, as has been recorded, it was September, and Jurgen could see that Anaïtis too was worrying over something. She kept it from him as long as possible : first said it was nothing at all, then said he would know it soon enough, then wept a little over the possibility that he would probably be very glad to hear it, and eventually told him. For in becoming the consort of a nature myth connected with the Moon Jurgen had of course exposed himself to the danger of being converted into a solar legend by the Philologists, and in that event would be compelled to leave Cocaigne with the Equinox, to enter into autumnal exploits elsewhere. And Anaïtis was quite heart-broken over the prospect of losing Jurgen.

"For I have never had such a Prince Consort in Cocaigne, so maddening, and so helpless, and so clever; and the girls are so fond of you, although they have not been able to get on at all with so many of their step-fathers ! And I know that you are flippant and heartless, but you have quite spoiled me for other men. No, Jurgen, there is no need to argue, for I have experimented with at least a dozen lovers lately, when I was travelling, and they bored me insufferably. They had, as you put it, dear, no conversation : and you are the only young man I have found in all these ages who could talk interestingly."

"There is a reason for that, since like you, Anaïtis, I am not so youthful as I appear."

"I do not care a straw about appearances," wept
Anaïtis, "but I know that I love you, and that you must
be leaving me with the Equinox unless you can settle
matters with the Master Philologist."

"Well, my pet," says Jurgen, "the Jews got into
Jericho by trying."

He armed, and girded himself with Caliburn, drank a
couple of bottles of wine, put on the shirt of Nessus over
all, and then went to seek this thaumaturgist.

Anaïtis showed him the way to an unpretentious residence, where a week's washing was drying and flapping
in the side yard. Jurgen knocked boldly, and after an
interval the door was opened by the Master Philologist
himself.

"You must pardon this informality," he said, blinking
through his great spectacles, which had dust on them :
"but time was by ill luck arrested hereabouts on a Thurs-
day evening, and so the maid is out indefinitely. I would
suggest, therefore, that the lady wait outside upon the
porch. For the neighbours to see her go in would not be
respectable."

"Do you know what I have come for?" says Jurgen,
blustering, and splendid in his glittering shirt and his
gleaming armour. "For I warn you I am justice."

"I think you are lying, and I am sure you are making
an unnecessary noise. In any event, justice is a word,
and I control all words."

"You will discover very soon, sir, that actions speak
louder than words."

"I believe that is so," said the Master Philologist, still
blinking, "just as the Jewish mob spoke louder than He
Whom they crucified. But the Word endures."

"You are a quibbler!"

"You are my guest. So I advise you, in pure friendliness, not to impugn the power of my words."

Said Jurgen, scornfully: "But is justice, then, a
word?"

" Oh, yes, it is one of the most useful. It is the Spanish *justicia*, the Portuguese *justiça*, the Italian *giustizia*, all from the Latin *justus*. Oh, yes, indeed, but justice is one of my best connected words, and one of the best trained also, I can assure you."

" Aha, and to what degraded uses do you put this poor enslaved intimidated justice ? "

" There is but one intelligent use," said the Master Philologist, unruffled, " for anybody to make of words. I will explain it to you, if you will come in out of this treacherous draught. One never knows what a cold may lead to."

Then the door closed upon them, and Anaïtis waited outside, in some trepidation.

Presently Jurgen came out of that unpretentious residence, and so back to Anaïtis, discomfited. Jurgen flung down his magic sword, charmed Caliburn.

" This, Anaïtis, I perceive to be an outmoded weapon. There is no weapon like words, no armour against words, and with words the Master Philologist has conquered me. It is not at all equitable : but the man showed me a huge book wherein were the names of everything in the world, and justice was not among them. It develops that, instead, justice is merely a common noun, vaguely denoting an ethical idea of conduct proper to the circumstances, whether of individuals or communities. It is, you observe, just a grammarian's notion."

" But what has he decided about you, Jurgen ? "

" Alas, dear Anaïtis, he has decided, in spite of all that I could do, to derive Jurgen from *jargon*, indicating a confused chattering such as birds give forth at sunrise : thus ruthlessly does the Master Philologist convert me into a solar legend. So the affair is settled, and we must part, my darling."

Anaïtis took up the sword. " But this is valuable, since the man who wields it is the mightiest of warriors."

" It is a rush, a rotten twig, a broomstraw, against the

insidious weapons of the Master Philologist. But keep it if you like, my dear, and give it to your next Prince Consort. I am ashamed to have trifled with such toys," says Jurgen, in fretted disgust. " And besides, the Master Philologist assures me I shall mount far higher through the aid of this."

" But what is on that bit of parchment ? "

" Thirty-two of the Master Philologist's own words that I begged of him. See, my dear, he made this cantrap for me with his own hand and ink." And Jurgen read from the parchment, impressively : " ' At the death of Adrian the Fifth, Pedro Juliani, who should be named John the Twentieth, was through an error in the reckoning elevated to the papal chair as John the Twenty-first.' "

Said Anaïtis, blankly : " And is that all ? "

" Why, yes : and surely thirty-two whole words should be enough for the most exacting."

" But is it magic ? are you certain it is authentic magic ? "

" I have learned that there is always magic in words."

" Now, if you ask my opinion, Jurgen, your cantrap is nonsense, and can never be of any earthly use to anybody. Without boasting, dear, I have handled a great deal of black magic in my day, but I never encountered a spell at all like this."

" None the less, my darling, it is evidently a cantrap, for else the Master Philologist would never have given it to me."

" But how are you to use it, pray ? "

" Why, as need directs," said Jurgen, and he put the parchment into the pocket of his glittering shirt. " Yes, I repeat, there is always something to be done with words, and here are thirty-two authentic words from the Master Philologist himself, not to speak of three commas and a full-stop. Oh, I shall certainly go far with this."

" We women have firmer faith in the sword," replied

Anaïtis. " At all events, you and I cannot remain upon this thaumaturgist's porch indefinitely."

So Anaïtis put up Caliburn, and carried it from the thaumaturgist's unpretentious residence to her fine palace in the old twilit wood : and afterward, as everybody knows, she gave this sword to King Arthur, who with its aid rose to be hailed as one of the Nine Worthies of the World. So did the husband of Guenevere win for himself eternal fame with that which Jurgen flung away.

CHAPTER XXVI

IN TIME'S HOUR-GLASS

 " WELL, well ! " said Jurgen, when he had taken off all that foolish ironmongery, and had made himself comfortable in his shirt; " well, beyond doubt, the situation is awkward. I was content enough in Cocaigne, and it is unfair that I should be thus ousted. Still, a sensible person will manage to be content anywhere. But whither, pray, am I expected to go ? "

" Into whatever land you may elect, my dear," said Anaïtis, fondly. " That much at least I can manage for you : and the interpretation of your legend can be arranged afterward."

" But I grow tired of all the countries I have ever seen, dear Anaïtis, and in my time I have visited nearly all the lands that are known to men."

" That too can be arranged : and you can go instead into one of the countries which are desired by men. Indeed there are a number of such realms which no man has ever visited except in dreams, so that your choice is wide."

" But how am I to make a choice without having seen any of these countries ? It is not fair to be expecting me to do anything of the sort."

" Why, I will show them to you," Anaïtis replied.

The two of them then went together into a small blue chamber, the walls of which were ornamented with gold stars placed helter-skelter. The room was entirely empty save for an hour-glass near twice the height of a man.

"It is Time's own glass," said Anaïtis, "which was left in my keeping when Time went to sleep."

Anaïtis opened a little door of carved crystal that was in the lower half of the hour-glass, just above the fallen sands. With her finger-tips she touched the sand that was in Time's hour-glass, and in the sand she drew a triangle with equal sides, she who was strangely gifted and perverse. Then she drew just such another figure so that the tip of it penetrated the first triangle. The sand began to smoulder there, and vapours rose into the upper part of the hour-glass, and Jurgen saw that all the sand in Time's hour-glass was kindled by a magic generated by the contact of these two triangles. And in the vapours a picture formed.

"I see a land of woods and rivers, Anaïtis. A very old fellow, regally crowned, lies asleep under an ash-tree, guarded by a watchman who has more arms and hands than Jigsbyed."

"It is Atlantis you behold, and the sleeping of ancient Time—Time, to whom this glass belongs,—while Briareus watches."

"Time sleeps quite naked, Anaïtis, and, though it is a delicate matter to talk about, I notice he has met with a deplorable accident."

"So that Time begets nothing any more, Jurgen, the while he brings about old happenings over and over, and changes the name of what is ancient, in order to persuade himself he has a new plaything. There is really no more tedious and wearing old dotard anywhere, I can assure you. But Atlantis is only the western province of Cocaigne. Now do you look again, Jurgen!"

"Now I behold a flowering plain and three steep hills, with a castle upon each hill. There are woods wherein the foliage is crimson : shining birds with white bodies and purple heads feed upon the clusters of golden berries that grow everywhere : and people go about in green clothes, with gold chains about their necks, and with broad bands of gold upon their arms, and all these people have untroubled faces."

"That is Inislocha : and to the south is Inis Daleb, and to the north Inis Ercandra. And there is sweet music to be listening to eternally, could we but hear the birds of Rhiannon, and there is the best of wine to drink, and there delight is common. For thither comes nothing hard nor rough, and no grief, nor any regret, nor sickness, nor age, nor death, for this is the Land of Women, a land of many-coloured hospitality."

"Why, then, it is no different from Cocaigne. And into no realm where pleasure is endless will I ever venture again of my own free will, for I find that I do not enjoy pleasure."

Then Anaïtis showed him Ogygia, and Tryphême, and Sudarsana, and the Fortunate Islands, and Æaea, and Caer-Is, and Invallis, and the Hesperides, and Meropis, and Planasia, and Uttarra, and Avalon, and Tir-nam-Beo, and Thelême, and a number of other lands to enter which men have desired : and Jurgen groaned.

"I am ashamed of my fellows," says he : "for it appears their notion of felicity is to dwell eternally in a glorified brothel. I do not think that as a self-respecting young Prince I would care to inhabit any of these earthly paradises, for were there nothing else, I would always be looking for an invasion by the police."

"There remains, then, but one other realm, which I have not shown you, in part because it is an obscure little place, and in part because, for a reason that I have, I shall not assist you to go thither. Still, there is Leukê, where Queen Helen rules : and Leukê it is that you behold."

"But Leukê seems like any other country in autumn, and appears to be reasonably free from the fantastic animals and overgrown flowers which made the other paradises look childish. Come now, there is an attractive simplicity about Leukê. I might put up with Leukê if the local by-laws allowed me a rational amount of discomfort."

" Discomfort you would have full measure. For the heart of no man remains untroubled after he has once viewed Queen Helen and the beauty that is hers. It is for that reason, Jurgen, I shall not help you to go into Leukê : for in Leukê you would forget me, having seen Queen Helen."

" Why, what nonsense you are talking, my darling ! I will wager she cannot hold a candle to you."

" See for yourself ! " said Anaïtis, sadly.

Now through the rolling vapours came confusedly a gleaming and a surging glitter of all the loveliest colours of heaven and earth : and these took order presently, and Jurgen saw before him in the hour-glass that young Dorothy who was not Heitman Michael's wife. And long and wistfully he looked at her, and the blinding tears came to his eyes for no reason at all, and for the while he could not speak.

Then Jurgen yawned, and said, " But certainly this is not the Helen who was famed for beauty."

" I can assure you that it is," said Anaïtis : " and that it is she who rules in Leukê, whither I do not intend you shall go."

" Why, but, my darling ! this is preposterous. The girl is nothing to look at twice, one way or the other. She is not actually ugly, I suppose, if one happens to admire that washed-out blonde type, as of course some people do. But to call her beautiful is out of reason ; and that I must protest in simple justice."

" Do you really think so ? " says Anaïtis, brightening.

" I most assuredly do. Why, you remember what Calpurnius Bassus says about all blondes ? "

" No, I believe not. What did he say, dear ? "

" I would only spoil the splendid passage by quoting it

inaccurately from memory. But he was quite right, and his opinion is mine in every particular. So if that is the best Leukê can offer, I heartily agree with you I had best go into some other country."

" I suppose you already have your eyes upon some minx or other ? "

" Well, my love, those girls in the Hesperides were strikingly like you, with even more wonderful hair than yours : and the girl Aillê whom we saw in Tir-nam-Beo likewise resembled you remarkably, except that I thought she had the better figure. So I believe in either of those countries I could be content enough, after a while. Since part from you I must," said Jurgen, tenderly, " I intend, in common fairness to myself, to find a companion as like you as possible. You conceive I can pretend it is you at first : and then as I grow fonder of her for her own sake, you will gradually be put out of my mind without my incurring any intolerable anguish."

Anaïtis was not pleased. " So you are already hankering after those huzzies ! And you think them better looking than I am ! And you tell me so to my face ! "

" My darling, you cannot deny we have been married all of three whole months : and nobody can maintain an infatuation for any woman that long, in the teeth of having nothing refused him. Infatuation is largely a matter of curiosity, and both of these emotions die when they are fed."

" Jurgen," said Anaïtis, with conviction, " you are lying to me about something. I can see it in your eyes."

" There is no deceiving a woman's intuition. Yes, I was not speaking quite honestly when I pretended I had as lief go into the Hesperides as to Tir-nam-Beo : it was wrong of me, and I ask your pardon. I thought that by affecting indifference I could manage you better. But you saw through me at once, and very rightly became angry. So I fling my cards upon the table, I no longer beat about the bushes of equivocation. It is Aillê, the daughter of Cormac, whom I love, and who can blame me? Did you ever in your life behold a more enticing figure, Anaïtis?—certainly I never did. Besides, I noticed—but never mind about that! Still I could not help seeing them. And then such eyes! twin beacons that light my way to comfort for my not inconsiderable regret at losing you, my darling. Oh, yes, assuredly it is to Tir-nam-Beo I elect to go."

"Whither you go, my fine fellow, is a matter in which I have the choice, not you. And you are going to Leukê."

"My love, now do be reasonable! We both agreed that Leukê was not a bit suitable. Why, were there nothing else, in Leukê there are no attractive women."

"Have you no sense except book-sense! It is for that reason I am sending you to Leukê."

And thus speaking, Anaïtis set about a strong magic that hastened the coming of the Equinox. In the midst of her charming she wept a little, for she was fond of Jurgen.

And Jurgen preserved a hurt and angry face as well as he could : for at the sight of Queen Helen, who was so like young Dorothy la Désirée, he had ceased to care for Queen Anaïtis and her diverting ways, or to care for aught else in the world save only Queen Helen, the delight of gods and men. But Jurgen had learned that Anaïtis required management.

"For her own good," as he put it, "and in simple justice to the many admirable qualities which she possesses."

CHAPTER XXVII

VEXATIOUS ESTATE OF QUEEN HELEN

 "BUT how can I travel with the Equinox, with a fictitious thing, with a mere convention?" Jurgen had said. "To demand any such proceeding of me is preposterous."

"Is it any more preposterous than to travel with an imaginary creature like a centaur?" they had retorted. "Why, Prince Jurgen, we wonder how you, who have done that perfectly unheard-of thing, can have the effrontery to call anything else preposterous! Is there no reason at all in you? Why, conventions are respectable, and that is a deal more than can be said for a great many centaurs. Would you be throwing stones at respectability, Prince Jurgen? Why, we are unutterably astounded at your objection to any such well-known phenomenon as the Equinox!" And so on, and so on, and so on, said they.

And in fine, they kept at him until Jurgen was too confused to argue, and his head was in a whirl, and one thing seemed as preposterous as another : and he ceased to notice any especial improbability in his travelling with the Equinox, and so passed, without any further protest or argument about it, from Cocaigne to Leukê. But he would not have been thus readily flustered had Jurgen not been thinking all the while of Queen Helen and of the beauty that was hers.

So he inquired forthwith the way that one might quickliest come into the presence of Queen Helen.

" Why, you will find Queen Helen," he was told, " in her palace at Pseudopolis." His informant was a hamadryad, whom Jurgen encountered upon the outskirts of a forest overlooking the city from the west. Beyond broad sloping stretches of ripe corn, you saw Pseudopolis as a city builded of gold and ivory, now all a dazzling glitter under a hard-seeming sky that appeared unusually remote from earth.

" And is the Queen as fair as people report ? " asks Jurgen.

" Men say that she excels all other women," replied the Hamadryad, " as immeasurably as all we women perceive her husband to surpass all other men——"

" But, oh, dear me ! " says Jurgen.

"—Although, for one, I see nothing remarkable in Queen Helen's looks. And I cannot but think that a woman who has been so much talked about ought to be more careful in the way she dresses."

" So this Queen Helen is already provided with a husband ! " Jurgen was displeased, but saw no reason for despair. Then Jurgen inquired as to the Queen's husband, and learned that Achilles, the son of Peleus, was now wedded to Helen, the Swan's daughter, and that these two ruled in Pseudopolis.

" For they report," said the Hamadryad, " that in Adês' dreary kingdom Achilles remembered her beauty, and by this memory was heartened to break the bonds of Adês : so did Achilles, King of Men, and all his ancient comrades come forth resistlessly upon a second quest of this Helen, whom people call—and as I think, with considerable exaggeration—the wonder of this world. Then the Gods fulfilled the desire of Achilles, because, they said, the man who has once beheld Queen Helen will never any more regain contentment so long as his life lacks this wonder of the world. Personally, I would dislike to think that all men are so foolish."

" Men are not always rational, I grant you : but then,"

says Jurgen, slyly, "so many of their ancestresses are feminine."

"But an ancestress is always feminine. Nobody ever heard of a man being an ancestress. Men are ancestors. Why, whatever are you talking about?"

"Well, we were speaking, I believe, of Queen Helen's marriage."

"To be sure we were! And I was telling you about the Gods, when you made that droll mistake about ancestors. Everybody makes mistakes, sometimes, however, and foreigners are always apt to get words confused. I could see at once you were a foreigner——"

"Yes," said Jurgen, "but you were not telling me about myself but about the Gods."

"Why, you must know the ageing Gods desired tranquillity. So we will give her to Achilles, they said; and then, it may be, this King of Men will retain her so safely that his littler fellows will despair, and will cease to war for Helen: and so we shall not be bothered any longer by their wars and other foolishnesses. For this reason it was that the Gods gave Helen to Achilles, and sent the pair to reign in Leukê: though, for my part," concluded the Hamadryad, "I shall never cease to wonder what he saw in her—no, not if I live to be a thousand."

"I must," says Jurgen, "observe this monarch Achilles before the world is a day older. A king is all very well, of course, but no husband wears a crown so as to prevent the affixion of other head-gear."

And Jurgen went down into Pseudopolis, swaggering.

*
*   *

So in the evening, just after sunset, Jurgen returned to the Hamadryad: he walked now with the aid of the ashen staff which Thersitês had given Jurgen, and Jurgen was mirthless and rather humble.

"I have observed your King Achilles," Jurgen says, "and he is a better man than I. Queen Helen, as I confess with regret, is worthily mated."

" And what have you to say about her ? " inquires the Hamadryad.

" Why, there is nothing more to say than that she is worthily mated, and fit to be the wife of Achilles." For once, poor Jurgen was really miserable. " For I admire this man Achilles, I envy him, and I fear him," says Jurgen : " and it is not fair that he should have been created my superior."

" But is not Queen Helen the loveliest of ladies that you have ever seen ? "

" As to that——! " says Jurgen. He led the Hamadryad to a forest pool hard-by the oak-tree in which she resided. The dusky water lay unruffled, a natural mirror. " Look ! " said Jurgen, and he spoke with a downward waving of his staff.

The silence gathering in the woods was wonderful. Here the air was sweet and pure : and the little wind which went about the ilex boughs in search of night was a tender and peaceful wind, because it knew that the all-healing night was close at hand.

The Hamadryad replied, " But I see only my own face."

" It is the answer to your question, none the less. Now do you tell me your name, my dear, so that I may know who in reality is the loveliest of all the ladies I have ever seen."

The Hamadryad told him that her name was Chloris, and that she always looked a fright with her hair arranged as it was to-day, and that he was a strangely impudent fellow. So he in turn confessed to her he was King Jurgen of Eubonia, drawn from his remote king-dom by exaggerated reports as to the beauty of Queen Helen. Chloris agreed with him that rumour was in such matters invariably untrustworthy.

This led to further talk as twilight deepened : and the while that a little by a little this pretty girl was con-verted into a warm breathing shadow, hardly visible to the eye, the shadow of Jurgen departed from him, and he began to talk better and better. He had seen Queen Helen face to face, and other women now seemed unimportant. Whether or not he got into the graces of this Hamadryad did not greatly matter one way or the other: and in consequence Jurgen talked with such fluency, such apposite remarks and such tenderness as astounded him.

So he sat listening with delight to the seductive tongue of that monstrous clever fellow, Jurgen. For this plump brown-haired bright-eyed little creature, this Chloris, he was honestly sorry. Into the uneventful life of a hamadryad, here in this uncultured forest, could not possibly have entered much pleasurable excitement, and it seemed only right to inject a little. "Why, simply in justice to her," Jurgen reflected, "I must deal fairly."

Now it grew darker and darker under the trees, and in the dark nobody can see what happens. There were only two voices that talked, with lengthy pauses: and they spoke gravely of unimportant trifles, like children at play together.

"And how does a king come thus to be travelling without any retinue or even a sword about him?"

"Why, I travel with a staff, my dear, as you perceive: and it suffices me."

"Certainly it is large enough, in all conscience. Alas, young outlander, who call yourself a king! you carry the bludgeon of a highwayman, and I am afraid of it."

"My staff is a twig from Yggdrasill, the tree of universal life: Thersitês gave it me, and the sap that throbs therein arises from the Undar fountain, where the grave Norns make laws for men and fix their destinies."

"Thersitês is a scoffer, and his gifts are mockery. I would have none of them."

The two began to wrangle, not at all angrily, as to what Jurgen had best do with his prized staff. "Do you take it away from me, at any rate ! " says Chloris. So Jurgen hid his staff where Chloris could not possibly see it ; and he drew the Hamadryad close to him, and he laughed contentedly.

"Oh, oh ! O wretched King," cried Chloris, " I fear that you will be the death of me ! And you have no right to oppress me in this way, for I am not your subject."

" Rather shall you be my queen, dear Chloris, receiving all that I most prize."

" But you are too domineering : and I am afraid to be alone with you and your big staff ! Ah ! not without knowing what she talked about did my mother use to quote her Æolic saying, The king is cruel and takes joy in bloodshed ! "

" Presently you will not be afraid of me, nor will you be afraid of my staff. Custom is all. For this likewise is an Æolic saying, The taste of the first olive is unpleasant, but the second is good."

Now for a while was silence save for the small secretive rumours of the forest. One of the large green locusts which frequent the Island of Leukê began shrilling tentatively.

" Wait now, King Jurgen, for surely I hear footsteps, and one comes to trouble us."

" It is a wind in the tree-tops : or perhaps it is a god who envies me. I pause for neither."

" Ah, but speak reverently of the Gods ! For is not Love a god, and a jealous god that has wings with which to leave us ? "

" Then am I a god, for in my heart is love, and in every fibre of me is love, and from me now love emanates."

" But certainly I heard somebody approaching through the forest——"

" Well, and do you not perceive I have withdrawn my staff from its hiding-place ? "

" Ah, you have great faith in that staff of yours ! "

" I fear nobody when I brandish it."

Another locust had answered the first one. Now the two insects were in full dispute, suffusing the warm darkness with their pertinacious whirrings.

" King of Eubonia, it is certainly true, that which you told me about olives."

" Yes, for always love begets truthfulness."

" I pray it may beget between us utter truthfulness, and nothing else, King Jurgen."

" Not ' Jurgen ' now, but ' love.' "

" Indeed, they tell that even so, in such deep darkness, Love came to his sweetheart Psychê."

" Then why do you complain because I piously emulate the Gods, and offer unto Love the sincerest form of flattery ? " And Jurgen shook his staff at her.

" Ah, but you are strangely ready with your flattery ! and Love threatened Psychê with no such enormous staff."

" That is possible : for I am Jurgen. And I deal fairly with all women, and raise my staff against none save in the way of kindness."

So they talked nonsense, in utter darkness, while the locusts, and presently a score of locusts, disputed obstinately. Now Chloris and Jurgen were invisible, even to each other, as they talked under her oak-tree : but before them the fields shone mistily under a gold-dusted dome, for this night seemed builded of stars. And the white towers of Pseudopolis also could Jurgen see, as he laughed there and took his pleasure with Chloris. He reflected that very probably Achilles and Helen were laughing thus, and were not dissimilarly occupied, out yonder, in this night of wonder.

He sighed. But in a while Jurgen and the Hamadryad were speaking again, just as inconsequently, and the locusts were whirring just as obstinately. Later the moon rose, and they all slept.

And they all slept.

With the dawn Jurgen arose, and left this Hamadryad Chloris still asleep. He stood where he overlooked the city, and the shirt of Nessus glittered in the
level sun rays : and Jurgen thought of Queen Helen.
Then he sighed, and went back to Chloris, and wakened
her with the sort of salutation that appeared her just due.

CHAPTER XXVIII

OF COMPROMISES IN LEUKÊ

NOW the tale tells that ten days later Jurgen and his Hamadryad were duly married, in consonance with the law of the Wood: not for a moment did Chloris consider any violation of the proprieties, so they were married the first evening she could assemble her kindred.

"Still, Chloris, I already have two wives," says Jurgen, "and it is but fair to confess it."

"I thought it was only yesterday you arrived in Leukê."

"That is true: for I came with the Equinox, over the long sea."

"Then Jugatinus has not had time to marry you to anybody, and certainly he would never think of marrying you to two wives. Why do you talk such nonsense?"

"No, it is true, I was not married by Jugatinus."

"So there!" says Chloris, as if that settled matters. "Now you see for yourself."

"Why, yes, to be sure," says Jurgen, "that does put rather a different light upon it, now I think of it."

"It makes all the difference in the world."

"I would hardly go that far. Still, I perceive it makes a difference."

"Why, you talk as if everybody did not know that Jugatinus marries people!"

"No, dear, let us be fair! I did not say precisely that."

"—And as if everybody was not always married by Jugatinus!"

" Yes, here in Leukê, perhaps. But outside of Leukê, you understand, my darling ! "

" But nobody goes outside of Leukê. Nobody ever thinks of leaving Leukê. I never heard such nonsense."

" You mean, nobody ever leaves this island ? "

" Nobody that you ever hear of. Of course, there are Lares and Penates, with no social position, that the kings of Pseudopolis sometimes take a-voyaging——"

" Still, the people of other countries do get married."

" No, Jurgen," said Chloris, sadly, " it is a rule with Jugatinus never to leave the island ; and indeed I am sure he has never even considered such unheard-of conduct : so, of course, the people of other countries are not able to get married."

" Well, but, Chloris, in Eubonia——"

" Now if you do not mind, dear, I think we had better talk about something more pleasant. I do not blame you men of Eubonia, because all men are in such matters perfectly irresponsible. And perhaps it is not altogether the fault of the women, either, though I do think any really self-respecting woman would have the strength of character to keep out of such irregular relations, and that much I am compelled to say. So do not let us talk any more about these persons whom you describe as your wives. It is very nice of you, dear, to call them that, and I appreciate your delicacy. Still, I really do believe we had better talk about something else."

Jurgen deliberated. " Yet do you not think, Chloris, that in the absence of Jugatinus—and in, as I understand it, the unavoidable absence of Jugatinus,—somebody else might perform the ceremony ? "

" Oh, yes, if they wanted to. But it would not count. Nobody but Jugatinus can really marry people. And so of course nobody else does."

" What makes you sure of that ? "

" Why, because," said Chloris, triumphantly, " nobody ever heard of such a thing."

"You have voiced," said Jurgen, "an entire code of philosophy. Let us by all means go to Jugatinus and be married."

So they were married by Jugatinus, according to the ceremony with which the People of the Wood were always married by Jugatinus. First Virgo loosed the girdle of Chloris in such fashion as was customary; and Chloris, after sitting much longer than Jurgen liked in the lap of Mutinus (who was in the state that custom required of him) was led back to Jurgen by Domiducus in accordance with immemorial custom; Subigo did her customary part; then Praema grasped the bride's plump arms: and everything was perfectly regular.

Thereafter Jurgen disposed of his staff in the way Thersitês had directed: and thereafter Jurgen abode with Chloris upon the outskirts of the forest, and complied with the customs of Leukê. Her tree was a rather large oak, for Chloris was now in her two hundred and sixty-sixth year; and at first its commodious trunk sheltered them. But later Jurgen builded himself a little cabin thatched with birds' wings, and made himself more comfortable.

"It is well enough for you, my dear, in fact it is expected of you, to live in a tree-bole. But it makes me feel uncomfortably like a worm, and it needlessly emphasises the restrictions of married life. Besides, you do not want me under your feet all the time, nor I you. No, let us cultivate a judicious abstention from familiarity: such is one secret of an enduring, because endurable, marriage. But why is it, pray, that you have never married before, in all these years?"

She told him. At first Jurgen could not believe her, but presently Jurgen was convinced, through at least two of his senses, that what Chloris told him was true about hamadryads.

"Otherwise, you are not markedly unlike the women of Eubonia," said Jurgen.

And now Jurgen met many of the People of the Wood; but since the tree of Chloris stood upon the verge of the forest, he saw far more of the People of the Field, who dwelt between the forest and the city of Pseudopolis. These were the neighbours and the ordinary associates of Chloris and Jurgen; though once in a while, of course, there would be family gatherings in the forest. But Jurgen presently had found good reason to distrust the People of the Wood, and went to none of these gatherings.

"For in Eubonia," he said, "we are taught that your wife's relatives will never find fault with you to your face so long as you keep away from them. And more than that no sensible man expects."

Meanwhile, King Jurgen was perplexed by the People of the Field, who were his neighbours. They one and all did what they had always done. Thus Runcina saw to it that the Fields were weeded: Seia took care of the seed while it was buried in the earth: Nodosa arranged the knots and joints of the stalk: Volusia folded the blade around the corn: each had an immemorial duty. And there was hardly a day that somebody was not busied in the Fields, whether it was Occator harrowing, or Sator and Sarritor about their sowing and raking, or Stercutius manuring the ground: and Hippona was always bustling about in one place or another looking after the horses, or else Bubona would be there attending to the cattle. There was never any restfulness in the Fields.

"And why do you do these things year in and year out?" asked Jurgen.

"Why, King of Eubonia, we have always done these things," they said, in high astonishment.

"Yes, but why not stop occasionally?"

"Because in that event the work would stop. The corn would die, the cattle would perish, and the Fields would become jungles."

"But, as I understand it, this is not your corn, nor your cattle, nor your Fields. You derive no good from them. And there is nothing to prevent your ceasing this interminable labour, and living as do the People of the Wood, who perform no heavy work whatever."

"I should think not!" said Aristæus, and his teeth flashed in a smile that was very pleasant to see, as he strained at the olive-press. "Whoever heard of the People of the Wood doing anything useful!"

"Yes, but," says Jurgen, patiently, "do you think it is quite fair to yourselves to be always about some tedious and difficult labour when nobody compels you to do it? Why do you not sometimes take holiday?"

"King Jurgen," replied Fornax, looking up from the little furnace wherein she was parching corn, "you are talking nonsense. The People of the Field have never taken holiday. Nobody ever heard of such a thing."

"We should think not indeed!" said all the others, sagely.

"Ah, ah!" said Jurgen, "so that is your demolishing reason. Well, I shall inquire about this matter among the People of the Wood, for they may be more sensible."

Then as Jurgen was about to enter the forest, he encountered Terminus, perfumed with ointment, and crowned with a garland of roses, and standing stock still.

"Aha," said Jurgen, "so here is one of the People of the Wood about to go down into the Fields. But if I were you, my friend, I would keep away from any such foolish place."

"I never go down into the Fields," said Terminus.

"Oh, then, you are returning into the forest."

"But certainly not. Whoever heard of my going into the forest!"

"Indeed, now I look at you, you are merely standing here."

"I have always stood here," said Terminus.

"And do you never move?"

"No," said Terminus.

"And for what reason?"

"Because I have always stood here without moving," replied Terminus. "Why, for me to move would be a quite unheard-of thing."

So Jurgen left him, and went into the forest. And there Jurgen encountered a smiling young fellow, who rode upon the back of a large ram. This young man had his left fore-finger laid to his lips, and his right hand held an astonishing object to be thus publicly displayed.

"But, oh, dear me! now, really, sir——!" says Jurgen.

"Bah!" says the ram.

But the smiling young fellow said nothing at all as he passed Jurgen, because it is not the custom of Harpocrates to speak.

"Which would be well enough," reflected Jurgen, "if only his custom did not make for stiffness and the embarrassment of others."

Thereafter Jurgen came upon a considerable commotion in the bushes, where a satyr was at play with an oread.

"Oh, but this forest is not respectable!" said Jurgen. "Have you no ethics and morals, you People of the Wood? Have you no sense of responsibility whatever, thus to be frolicking on a working-day?"

"Why, no," responded the Satyr, "of course not. None of my people have such things: and so the natural vocation of all satyrs is that which you are now interrupting."

"Perhaps you speak the truth," said Jurgen. "Still, you ought to be ashamed of the fact that you are not lying."

"For a satyr to be ashamed of himself would be indeed an unheard-of thing! Now go away, you in the glittering shirt! for we are studying eudæmonism, and you are talking nonsense, and I am busy, and you annoy me," said the Satyr.

"Well, but in Cocaigne," said Jurgen, "this eudæ-monism was considered an indoor diversion."

"And did you ever hear of a satyr going indoors ? "

"Why, save us from all hurt and harm ! but what has that to do with it ? "

"Do not try to equivocate, you shining idiot ! For now you see for yourself you are talking nonsense. And I repeat that such unheard-of nonsense irritates me," said the Satyr.

The Oread said nothing at all. But she too looked annoyed, and Jurgen reflected that it was probably not the custom of oreads to be rescued from the eudæmonism of satyrs.

So Jurgen left them ; and yet deeper in the forest he found a bald-headed squat old man, with a big paunch and a flat red nose and very small bleared eyes. Now the old fellow was so helplessly drunk that he could not walk : instead, he sat upon the ground, and leaned against a tree-bole.

"This is a very disgusting state for you to be in so early in the morning," observed Jurgen.

"But Silenus is always drunk," the bald-headed man responded, with a dignified hiccough.

"So here is another one of you ! Well, and why are you always drunk, Silenus ? "

"Because Silenus is the wisest of the People of the Wood."

"Ah, ah ! but I apologise. For here at last is some-body with a plausible excuse for his daily employment. Now, then, Silenus, since you are so wise, come, tell me, is it really the best fate for a man to be drunk always ? "

"Not at all. Drunkenness is a joy reserved for the Gods : so do men partake of it impiously, and so are they very properly punished for their audacity. For men, it

is best of all never to be born; but, being born, to die
very quickly."

" Ah, yes ! but failing either ? "

" The third best thing for a man is to do that which
seems expected of him," replied Silenus.

" But that is the Law of Philistia : and with Philistia,
they inform me, Pseudopolis is at war."

Silenus meditated. Jurgen had discovered an uncomfortable thing about this old fellow, and it was that his
small bleared eyes did not blink nor the lids twitch at
all. His eyes moved, as through magic the eyes of a
painted statue might move horribly, under quite motionless red lids. Therefore it was uncomfortable when
these eyes moved toward you.

" Young fellow in the glittering shirt, I will tell you a
secret : and it is that the Philistines were created after
the image of Koshchei who made some things as they are.
Do you think upon that ! So the Philistines do that
which seems expected. And the people of Leukê were
created after the image of Koshchei who made yet other
things as they are : therefore do the people of Leukê do
that which is customary, adhering to classical tradition.
Do you think upon that also ! Then do you pick your
side in this war, remembering that you side with stupidity
either way. And when that happens which will happen,
do you remember how Silenus foretold to you precisely
what would happen, a long while before it happened,
because Silenus was so old and so wise and so very
disreputably drunk, and so very, very sleepy."

" Yes, certainly, Silenus : but how will this war end ? "

" Dullness will conquer dullness : and it will not
matter."

" Ah, yes ! but what will become, in all this fighting,
of Jurgen ? "

" That will not matter either," said Silenus, comfortably. " Nobody will bother about you." And with
that he closed his horrible bleared eyes and went to sleep.

So Jurgen left the old tippler, and started to leave the forest also. " For undoubtedly all the people in Leukê are resolute to do that which is customary," reflected Jurgen, " for the unarguable reason it is their custom, and has always been their custom. And they will desist from these practices when the cat eats acorns, but not before. So it is the part of wisdom to inquire no further into the matter. For after all, these people may be right ; and certainly I cannot go so far as to say they are wrong." Jurgen shrugged. " But still, at the same time——! "

Now in returning to his cabin Jurgen heard a frightful sort of yowling and screeching as of mad people.

" Hail, daughter of various-formed Protogonus, thou that takest joy in mountains and battles and in the beating of the drum ! Hail, thou deceitful saviour, mother of all gods, that comest now, pleased with long wanderings, to be propitious to us ! "

But the uproar was becoming so increasingly un-pleasant that Jurgen at this point withdrew into a thicket : and thence he witnessed the passing through the Woods of a notable procession. There were features connected with this procession sufficiently unusual to cause Jurgen to vow that the desiderated moment wherein he walked unhurt from the forest would mark the termination of his last visit thereto. Then amaze-ment tripped up the heels of terror : for now passed Mother Sereda, or, as Anaïtis had called her, Æsred. To-day, in place of a towel about her head, she wore a species of crown, shaped like a circlet of crumbling towers : she carried a large key, and her chariot was drawn by two lions. She was attended by howling persons, with shaved heads : and it was apparent that these persons had parted with possessions which Jurgen valued.

" This is undoubtedly," said he, " a most unwholesome forest."

Jurgen inquired about this procession later, and from Chloris he got information which surprised him.

" And these are the beings who I had thought were poetic ornaments of speech ! But what is the old lady doing in such high company ? "

He described Mother Sereda, and Chloris told him who this was. Now Jurgen shook his sleek black head.

" Behold another mystery ! Yet after all, it is no concern of mine if the old lady elects for an additional anagram. I should be the last person to criticise her, inasmuch as to me she has been more than generous. Well, I shall preserve her friendship by the infallible recipe of keeping out of her way. Oh, but I shall certainly keep out of her way now that I have perceived what is done to the men who serve her."

And after that Jurgen and Chloris lived very pleasantly together, though Jurgen began to find his Hamadryad a trifle unperceptive, if not actually obtuse.

" She does not understand me, and she does not always treat my superior wisdom quite respectfully. That is unfair, but it seems to be an unavoidable feature of married life. Besides, if any woman had ever understood me she would, in self-protection, have refused to marry me. In any case, Chloris is a dear brown plump delicious partridge of a darling : and cleverness in women is, after all, a virtue misplaced."

And Jurgen did not return into the Woods, nor did he go down into the city. Neither the People of the Field nor of the Wood, of course, ever went within city gates. " But I would think that you would like to see the fine sights of Pseudopolis," says Chloris,—" and that fine Queen of theirs," she added, almost as though she spoke without premeditation.

" Woman dear," says Jurgen, " I do not wish to appear boastful. But in Eubonia, now ! well, really some day we must return to my kingdom, and you shall inspect for yourself a dozen or two of my cities—Ziph and Eglington

and Poissieux and Gazden and Bäremburg, at all events.
And then you will concede with me that this little village
of Pseudopolis, while well enough in its way——!"
And Jurgen shrugged. "But as for saying more!"

"Sometimes," said Chloris, "I wonder if there is any
such place as your fine kingdom of Eubonia: for certainly it grows larger and more splendid every time you
talk of it."

"Now can it be," asks Jurgen, more hurt than angry,
"that you suspect me of uncandid dealing and, in short,
of being an impostor?"

"Why, what does it matter? You are Jurgen," she
answered, happily.

And the man was moved as she smiled at him across
the glowing queer embroidery-work at which Chloris
seemed to labour interminably: he was conscious of a
tenderness for her which was oddly remorseful: and it
appeared to him that if he had known lovelier women
he had certainly found nowhere anyone more lovable
than was this plump and busy and sunny-tempered little
wife of his.

"My dear, I do not care to see Queen Helen again,
and that is a fact. I am contented here, with a wife
befitting my station, suited to my endowments, and
infinitely excelling my deserts."

"And do you think of that tow-headed bean-pole
very often, King Jurgen?"

"That is unfair, and you wrong me, Chloris, with
these unmerited suspicions. It pains me to reflect, my
dear, that you esteem the tie between us so lightly you
can consider me capable of breaking it even in thought."

"To talk of fairness is all very well, but it is no answer
to a plain question."

Jurgen looked full at her; and he laughed. "You
women are so unscrupulously practical. My dear, I
have seen Queen Helen face to face. But it is you whom
I love as a man customarily loves a woman."

"That is not saying much."

"No: for I endeavour to speak in consonance with my importance. You forget that I have also seen Achilles."

"But you admired Achilles! You told me so yourself."

"I admired the perfections of Achilles, but I cordially dislike the man who possesses them. Therefore I shall keep away from both the King and Queen of Pseudopolis."

"Yet you will not go into the Woods, either, Jurgen——"

"Not after what I have witnessed there," said Jurgen, with an exaggerated shudder that was not very much exaggerated.

Now Chloris laughed, and quitted her queer embroidery in order to rumple up his hair. "And you find the People of the Field so insufferably stupid, and so uninterested by your Zorobasiuses and Ptolemopiters and so on, that you keep away from them also. O foolish man of mine, you are determined to be neither fish nor beast nor poultry: and nowhere will you ever consent to be happy."

"It was not I who determined my nature, Chloris: and as for being happy, I make no complaint. Indeed, I have nothing to complain of nowadays. So I am very well contented by my dear wife and by my manner of living in Leukê," said Jurgen, with a sigh.

CHAPTER XXIX

CONCERNING HORVENDILE'S NONSENSE

IT was on a bright and tranquil day in November, at the period which the People of the Field called the summer of Alcyonê, that Jurgen went down from the forest; and after skirting the moats of Pseudopolis, and avoiding a meeting with any of the town's dispiritingly glorious inhabitants, Jurgen came to the seashore.

Chloris had suggested his doing this, in order that she could have a chance to straighten things in his cabin while she was tidying her tree for the winter, and could so make one day's work serve for two. For the dryad of an oak-tree has large responsibilities, what with the care of so many dead leaves all winter, and the acorns being blown from their places and littering up the ground everywhere, and the bark cracking until it looks positively disreputable : and Jurgen was at any such work less a help than a hindrance. So Chloris gave him a parcel of lunch and a perfunctory kiss, and told him to go down to the seashore and get inspired and make up a pretty poem about her. " And do you be back in time for an early supper, Jurgen," says she, " but not a minute before."

Thus it befell that Jurgen reflectively ate his lunch in solitude, and regarded the Euxine. The sun was high, and the queer shadow that followed Jurgen was huddled into shapelessness.

" This is indeed an inspiring spectacle," Jurgen

reflected. " How puny seems the race of man, in contrast with this mighty sea, which now spreads before me like, as So-and-so has very strikingly observed, a something or other under such and such conditions ! " Then Jurgen shrugged. " Really, now I think of it, though, there is no call for me to be suffused with the traditional emotions. It looks like a great deal of water, and like nothing else in particular. And I cannot but consider the water is behaving rather futilely."

So he sat in drowsy contemplation of the sea. Far out a shadow would form on the water, like the shadow of a broadish plank, scudding shoreward, and lengthening and darkening as it approached. Presently it would be some hundred feet in length, and would assume a hard smooth darkness, like that of green stone : this was the underside of the wave. Then the top of it would curdle, the southern end of the wave would collapse, and with exceeding swiftness this white feathery falling would plunge and scamper and bluster northward, the full length of the wave. It would be neater and more workmanlike to have each wave tumble down as a whole. From the smacking and the splashing, what looked like boiling milk would thrust out over the brown sleek sands : and as the mess spread it would thin to a reticulated whiteness, like lace, and then to the appearance of smoke sprays clinging to the sands. Plainly the tide was coming in.

Or perhaps it was going out. Jurgen's notions as to such phenomena were vague. But, either way, the sea was stirring up a large commotion and a rather pleasant and invigorating odour.

And then all this would happen once more : and then it would happen yet again. It had happened a number of hundred of times since Jurgen first sat down to eat his lunch : and what was gained by it ? The sea was behaving stupidly. There was no sense in this continual sloshing and spanking and scrabbling and spluttering.

Thus Jurgen, as he nodded over the remnants of his lunch.

"Sheer waste of energy, I am compelled to call it," said Jurgen, aloud, just as he noticed there were two other men on this long beach.

One came from the north, one from the south, so that they met not far from where Jurgen was sitting : and by an incredible coincidence Jurgen had known both of these men in his first youth. So he hailed them, and they recognised him at once. One of these travellers was the Horvendile who had been secretary to Count Emmerick when Jurgen was a lad : and the other was Perion de la Forêt, that outlaw who had come to Belle-garde very long ago disguised as the Vicomte de Puysange. And all three of these old acquaintances had kept their youth surprisingly.

Now Horvendile and Perion marvelled at the fine shirt which Jurgen was wearing.

"Why, you must know," he said, modestly, " that I have lately become King of Eubonia, and must dress according to my station."

So they said they had always expected some such high honour to befall him, and then the three of them fell to talking. And Perion told how he had come through Pseudopolis, on his way to King Theodoret at Lacre Kai, and how in the market-place at Pseudopolis he had seen Queen Helen. "She is a very lovely lady," said Perion, " and I marvelled over her resemblance to Count Emmerick's fair sister, whom we all remember."

"I noticed that at once," said Horvendile, and he smiled strangely, " when I, too, passed through the city."

"Why, but nobody could fail to notice it," said Jurgen.

"It is not, of course, that I consider her to be as lovely as Dame Melicent," continued Perion, " since, as I have contended in all quarters of the world, there has never lived, and will never live, any woman so beautiful as Melicent. But you gentlemen appear surprised by what seems to me a very simple statement. Your air, in fine, is one that forces me to point out it is a statement I can permit nobody to deny." And Perion's honest eyes had narrowed unpleasantly, and his sun-browned countenance was uncomfortably stern.

"Dear sir," said Jurgen, hastily, "it was merely that it appeared to me the lady whom they call Queen Helen hereabouts is quite evidently Count Emmerick's sister Dorothy la Désirée."

"Whereas I recognised her at once," says Horvendile, "as Count Emmerick's third sister, La Beale Ettarre."

And now they stared at one another, for it was certain that these three sisters were not particularly alike.

"Putting aside any question of eyesight," observes Perion, "it is indisputable that the language of both of you is distorted. For one of you says this is Madame Dorothy, and the other says this is Madame Ettarre : whereas everybody knows that this Queen Helen, whomever she may resemble, cannot possibly be anybody else save Queen Helen."

"To you, who are always the same person," replied Jurgen, "that may sound reasonable. For my part, I am several people : and I detect no incongruity in other persons resembling me."

"There would be no incongruity anywhere," suggested Horvendile, "if Queen Helen were the woman whom we had loved in vain. For the woman whom when we were young we loved in vain is the one woman that we can never see quite clearly, whatever happens. So we might easily, I suppose, confuse her with some other woman."

"But Melicent is the lady whom I have loved in vain," said Perion, "and I care nothing whatever about Queen Helen. Why should I ? What do you mean now, Horvendile, by your hints that I have faltered in my constancy to Dame Melicent since I saw Queen Helen ? I do not like such hints."

"No less, it is Ettarre whom I love, and have loved not quite in vain, and have loved unfalteringly," says Horvendile, with his quiet smile : "and I am certain that it was Ettarre whom I beheld when I looked upon Queen Helen."

"I may confess," says Jurgen, clearing his throat, "that I have always regarded Madame Dorothy with peculiar respect and admiration. For the rest, I am married. Even so, I think that Madame Dorothy is Queen Helen."

Then they fell to debating this mystery. And presently Perion said the one way out was to leave the matter to Queen Helen. "She at all events must know who she is. So do one of you go back into the city, and embrace her knees as is the custom of this country when one implores a favour of the King or the Queen : and do you then ask her fairly."

"Not I," says Jurgen. "I am upon terms of some intimacy with a hamadryad just at present. I am content with my Hamadryad. And I intend never to venture into the presence of Queen Helen any more, in order to preserve my contentment."

"Why, but I cannot go," says Perion, "because Dame Melicent has a little mole upon her left cheek. And Queen Helen's cheek is flawless. You understand, of course, that I am certain this mole immeasurably enhances the beauty of Dame Melicent," he added, loyally. "None the less, I mean to hold no further traffic with Queen Helen."

"Now my reason for not going is this," said Horvendile :—"that if I attempted to embrace the knees of Ettarre, whom people hereabouts call Helen, she would instantly vanish. Other matters apart, I do not wish to bring any such misfortune upon the Island of Leukê."

"But that," said Perion, "is nonsense."

"Of course it is," said Horvendile. "That is probably why it happens."

So none of them would go. And each of them clung, none the less, to his own opinion about Queen Helen. And presently Perion said they were wasting both time and words. Then Perion bade the two farewell, and Perion continued southward, toward Lacre Kai. And as he went he sang a song in honour of Dame Melicent, whom he celebrated as Heart o' My Heart : and the two who heard him agreed that Perion de la Forêt was probably the worst poet in the world.

"Nevertheless, there goes a very chivalrous and worthy gentleman," said Horvendile, "intent to play out the remainder of his romance. I wonder if the Author gets much pleasure from these simple characters ? At least, they must be easy to handle."

"I cultivate a judicious amount of gallantry," says Jurgen : "I do not any longer aspire to be chivalrous. And indeed, Horvendile, it seems to me indisputable that each one of us is the hero in his own romance, and cannot understand any other person's romance, but mis-interprets everything therein, very much as we three have fallen out in the simple matter of a woman's face."

Now young Horvendile meditatively stroked his own curly and reddish hair, brushing it away from his ears with his left hand, as he sat there staring meditatively at nothing in particular.

"I would put it, Jurgen, that we three have met like characters out of three separate romances which the Author has composed in different styles."

"That also," Jurgen submitted, "would be nonsense."

"Ah, but perhaps the Author very often perpe-trates nonsense. Come, Jurgen, you who are King of Eubonia !" says Horvendile, with his wide-set eyes a-twinkle ; "what is there in you or me to attest that our Author has not composed our romances with his tongue in his cheek ? "

"Messire Horvendile, if you are attempting to joke

about Koshchei who made all things as they are, I warn you I do not consider that sort of humour very wholesome. Without being prudish, I believe in common sense: and I would vastly prefer to have you talk about something else."

Horvendile was still smiling. "You look some day to come to Koshchei, as you call the Author. That is easily said, and sounds excellently. Ah, but how will you recognise Koshchei? and how do you know you have not already passed by Koshchei in some street or meadow? Come now, King Jurgen," said Horvendile, and still his young face wore an impish smile; "come, tell me, how do you know that I am not Koshchei, who made all things as they are?"

"Be off with you!" says Jurgen; "you would never have had the wit to invent a Jurgen. Something else is troubling me: I have just recollected that the young Perion, who left us only a moment since, grew to be rich and grey-headed and famous, and took Dame Melicent from her pagan husband, and married her himself: and that all this happened long years ago. So our recent talk with young Perion seems very improbable."

"Why, but do you not remember, too, that I ran away in the night when Maugis d'Aigremont stormed Storisende, and was never heard of any more, and that all this, too, took place a long, long while ago? Yet we have met as three fine young fellows, here on the beach of fabulous Leukê. I put it to you fairly, King Jurgen: now, how could this conceivably have come about unless the Author sometimes composes nonsense?"

"Truly the way that you express it, Horvendile, the thing does seem a little strange; and I can think of no explanation rendering it plausible."

"Again, see now, King Jurgen of Eubonia, how you underrate the Author's ability. This is one of the romancer's most venerable devices that is being practised.

See for yourself!" And suddenly Horvendile pushed
Jurgen so that Jurgen tumbled over in the warm sand.

Then Jurgen arose, gaping and stretching himself.
"That was a very foolish dream I had, napping here in
the sun. For it was certainly a dream. Otherwise, they
would have left footprints, these young fellows who have
gone the way of youth so long ago. And it was a dream
that had no sense in it. But indeed it would be strange
if that were the whole point of it, and if living, too, were
such a dream, as that queer Horvendile would have me
think."

Jurgen snapped his fingers.

"Well, and what in common fairness could he or anyone else expect me to do about it? That is the answer
I fling at you, you, Horvendile, whom I made up in a
dream. And I disown you as the most futile of my inventions. So be off with you! and a good riddance, too,
for I never held with upsetting people."

Then Jurgen dusted himself, and trudged home to an
early supper with the Hamadryad who contented him.

CHAPTER XXX

ECONOMICS OF KING JURGEN

NOW Jurgen's curious dream put notions into the restless head of Jurgen. So mighty became his curiosity that he went shuddering into the abhorred Woods, and passed over Coalisnacoan (which is the Ferry of Dogs), and did all such detestable things as were necessary to placate Phobetor. Then Jurgen tricked Phobetor by an indescribable device, wherein surprising use was made of a cheese and three beetles and a gimlet, and so cheated Phobetor out of a grey magic. And that night while Pseudopolis slept King Jurgen came down into this city of gold and ivory.

Jurgen went with distaste among the broad-browed and great-limbed monarchs of Pseudopolis, for they reminded him of things that he had long ago put aside, and they made him feel unpleasantly ignoble and insignificant. That was his real reason for avoiding the city.

Now he passed between unlighted and silent palaces, walking in deserted streets where the moon made ominous shadows. Here was the house of Ajax Telamon who reigned in sea-girt Salamis, here that of god-like Philoctetês : much-counselling Odysseus dwelt just across the way, and the corner residence was fair-haired Agamemnon's : in the moonlight Jurgen easily made out these names engraved upon the bronze shield that hung beside each doorway. To every side of him slept the heroes of old song while Jurgen skulked under their windows.

He remembered how incuriously—not even scornfully
—these people had overlooked him on that disastrous
afternoon when he had ventured into Pseudopolis by
daylight.   And a spiteful little gust of rage possessed
him, and Jurgen shook his fist at the big silent palaces.

" Yah ! " he snarled : for he did not know at all what
it was that he desired to say to those great stupid heroes
who did not care what he said, but he knew that he hated
them.   Then Jurgen became aware of himself growling
there like a kicked cur who is afraid to bite, and he began
to laugh at this Jurgen.

" Your pardon, gentlemen of Greece," says he, with
a wide ceremonious bow, " and I think the information
I wished to convey was that I am a monstrous clever
fellow."

Jurgen went into the largest palace, and crept stealthily
by the bedroom of Achilles, King of Men, treading a-tip-
toe ; and so came at last into a little room panelled with
cedar-wood where slept Queen Helen.   She was smiling
in her sleep when he had lighted his lamp, with due
observance of the grey magic.   She was infinitely beautiful, this young Dorothy whom people hereabouts through
some odd error called Helen.

For Jurgen saw very well that this was Count Emmerick's sister Dorothy la Désirée, whom Jurgen had vainly
loved in the days when Jurgen was young alike in body
and heart.   Just once he had won back to her, in the
garden between dawn and sunrise : but he was then a
time-battered burgher whom Dorothy did not recognise.
Now he returned to her a king, less admirable it might
be than some of the many other kings without realms
who slept now in Pseudopolis, but still very fine in his
borrowed youth, and above all, armoured by a grey
magic : so that improbabilities were possible.   And
Jurgen's eyes were furtive, and he passed his tongue
across his upper lip from one corner to the other, and
his hand went out toward the robe of violet-coloured

wool which covered the sleeping girl, for he stood ready to awaken Dorothy la Désirée in the way he often awoke Chloris.

But a queer thought held him. Nothing, he recollected, had shown the power to hurt him very deeply since he had lost this young Dorothy. And to affairs which threatened to result unpleasantly, he had always managed to impart an agreeable turn, since then, by virtue of preserving a cool heart. What if by some misfortune he were to get back his real youth, and were to become again the flustered boy who blundered from stammering rapture to wild misery, and back again, at the least word or gesture of a gold-haired girl?

"Thank you, no!" says Jurgen. "The boy was more admirable than I, who am by way of being not wholly admirable. But then he had a wretched time of it, by and large. Thus it may be that my real youth lies sleeping here : and for no consideration would I re-awaken it."

And yet tears came into his eyes, for no reason at all. And it seemed to him that the sleeping woman, here at his disposal, was not the young Dorothy whom he had seen in the garden between dawn and sunrise, although the two were curiously alike ; and that of the two this woman here was, somehow, infinitely the lovelier. And—"Lady, if you indeed be the Swan's daughter, long and long ago there was a child that was ill. And his illness turned to a fever, and in his fever he arose from his bed one night, saying that he must set out for Troy, because of his love for Queen Helen. I was once that child. I remember how strange it seemed to me I should be talking such nonsense : I remember how the warm room smelt of drugs : and I remember how I pitied the trouble in my nurse's face, drawn and old in the yellow lamplight. For she loved me, and she did not understand : and she pleaded with me to be a good boy and not to worry my sleeping parents. But I perceive now that I was not talking nonsense."

He paused, considering the riddle : and his fingers fretted with the robe of violet-coloured wool beneath which lay Queen Helen.

" Yours is that beauty of which men know by fabulous report alone, and which they may not ever find, nor ever win to, quite. And for that beauty I have hungered always, even in childhood. Toward that beauty I have struggled always, but not quite whole-heartedly. That night forecast my life. I have hungered for you : and " —Jurgen smiled here—" and I have always stayed a passably good boy, lest I should beyond reason disturb my family. For to do that, I thought, would not be fair : and still I believe for me to have done that would have been unfair."

He grimaced at this point : for Jurgen was finding his scruples inconveniently numerous.

" And now I think that what I do to-night is not quite fair to Chloris. And I do not know what thing it is that I desire, and the will of Jurgen is a feather in the wind. But I know that I would like to love somebody as Chloris loves me, and as so many women have loved me. And I know that it is you who have prevented this, Queen Helen, at every moment of my life since the disastrous moment when I first seemed to find your loveliness in the face of Madame Dorothy. It is the memory of your beauty, as I then saw it mirrored in the face of a jill-flirt, which has enfeebled me for such honest love as other men give women : and I envy these other men. For Jurgen has loved nothing—not even you, not even Jurgen !—quite whole-heartedly. Well, what if I took vengeance now upon this thieving comeliness, upon this robber that strips life of joy and sorrow ? "

Jurgen stood at Queen Helen's bedside, watching her, for a long while. He had shifted into a less fanciful mood : and the shadow that followed him was ugly and hulking and wavering upon the cedarn wall of Queen Helen's sleeping-chamber.

"Mine is a magic which does not fail," old Phobetor had said, while his attendants raised his eyelids so that he could see King Jurgen.

Now Jurgen remembered this. And reflectively he drew back the robe of violet-coloured wool, a little way. The breast of Queen Helen lay bare. And she did not move at all, but she smiled in her sleep.

Never had Jurgen imagined that any woman could be so beautiful nor so desirable as this woman, or that he could ever know such rapture. So Jurgen paused.

"Because," said Jurgen now, "it may be this woman has some fault : it may be there is some fleck in her beauty somewhere. And sooner than know that, I would prefer to retain my unreasonable dreams, and this longing which is unfed and hopeless, and the memory of to-night. Besides, if she were perfect in everything, how could I live any longer, who would have no more to desire? No, I would be betraying my own interests, either way ; and injustice is always despicable."

So Jurgen sighed and gently replaced the robe of violet-coloured wool, and he returned to his Hamadryad.

"And now that I think of it, too," reflected Jurgen, "I am behaving rather nobly. Yes, it is questionless that I have to-night evinced a certain delicacy of feeling which merits appreciation, at all events by King Achilles."

CHAPTER XXXI

THE FALL OF PSEUDOPOLIS

SO Jurgen abode in Leukê, and complied with the customs of that country; and what with one thing and another, he and Chloris made the time pass pleasantly enough, until the winter solstice was at hand. Now Pseudopolis, as has been said, was at war with Philistia: so it befell that at this season Leukê was invaded by an army of Philistines, led by their Queen Dolores, a woman who was wise but not entirely reliable. They came from the coast, a terrible army insanely clad in such garments as had been commanded by Ageus, a god of theirs; and chaunting psalms in honour of their god Vel-Tyno, who had inspired this crusade: thus they swept down upon Pseudopolis, and encamped before the city.

These Philistines fought in this campaign by casting before them a more horrible form of Greek fire, which consumed whatever was not grey-coloured. For that colour alone was now favoured by their god Vel-Tyno. "And all other colours," his oracles had decreed, "are for evermore abominable, until I say otherwise."

So the forces of Philistia were marshalled in the plain before Pseudopolis, and Queen Dolores spoke to her troops. And smilingly she said :—

"Whenever you come to blows with the enemy he will be beaten. No mercy will be shown, no prisoners taken. As the Philistines under Libnah and Goliath and Gershon, and a many other tall captains, made for themselves a name which is still mighty in traditions and legend, even thus to-day may the name of Realist be so fixed in Pseudopolis, by your deeds to-day, that no one shall ever dare again even to look askance at a Philistine. Open the door for Realism, once for all!"

Meanwhile within the city Achilles, King of Men, addressed his army :—

"The eyes of all the world will be upon you, because you are in some especial sense the soldiers of Romance. Let it be your pride, therefore, to show all men everywhere, not only what good soldiers you are, but also what good men you are, keeping yourselves fit and straight in everything, and pure and clean through and through. Let us set ourselves a standard so high that it will be a glory to live up to it, and then let us live up to it, and add a new laurel to the crown of Pseudopolis. May the Gods of Old keep you and guide you!"

Then said Thersitês, in his beard : " Certainly Pelidês has learned from history with what weapon a strong man discomfits the Philistines."

But the other kings applauded, and the trumpet was sounded, and the battle was joined. And that day the forces of Philistia were everywhere triumphant. But they report a queer thing happened : and it was that when the Philistines shouted in their triumph, Achilles and all they who served him rose from the ground like gleaming clouds and passed above the heads of the Philistines, deriding them.

Thus was Pseudopolis left empty, so that the Philistines entered thereinto without any opposition. They defiled this city of blasphemous colours, then burned it as a sacrifice to their god Vel-Tyno, because the colour of ashes is grey.

Then the Philistines erected lithoi (which were not unlike may-poles), and began to celebrate their religious rites.

*   *   *   *   *   *

So it was reported: but Jurgen witnessed none of these events.

"Let them fight it out," said Jurgen: "it is not my affair. I agree with Silenus: dullness will conquer dullness, and it will not matter. But do you, woman dear, take shelter with your kindred in the unconquerable Woods, for there is no telling what damage the Philistines may do hereabouts."

"Will you go with me, Jurgen?"

"My dear, you know very well that it is impossible for me ever again to go into the Woods, after the trick I played upon Phobetor."

"And if only you had kept your head about that bean-pole of a Helen, in her yellow wig—for I have not a doubt that every strand of it is false, and at all events this is not a time to be arguing about it, Jurgen, —why, then you would never have meddled with Uncle Phobetor! It simply shows you!"

"Yes," said Jurgen.

"Still, I do not know. If you come with me into the Woods, Uncle Phobetor in his impetuous way will quite certainly turn you into a boar-pig, because he has always done that to the people who irritated him——"

"I seem to recognise that reason."

"—But give me time, and I can get around Uncle Phobetor, just as I have always done, and he will turn you back."

"No," says Jurgen, obstinately, "I do not wish to be turned into a boar-pig."

"Now, Jurgen, let us be sensible about this! Of course, it is a little humiliating. But I will take the very best of care of you, and feed you with my own acorns, and it will be a purely temporary arrangement. And to be a pig for a week or two, or even for a month, is infinitely better for a poet than being captured by the Philistines."

"How do I know that?" says Jurgen.

" —For it is not, after all, as if Uncle Phobetor's heart were not in the right place. It is just his way. And besides, you must remember what you did with that gimlet ! "

Said Jurgen : " All this is hardly to the purpose. You forget I have seen the hapless swine of Phobetor, and I know how he ameliorates the natural ferocity of his boar-pigs. No, I am Jurgen. So I remain. I will face the Philistines, and whatever they may possibly do to me, rather than suffer that which Phobetor will quite certainly do to me."

" Then I stay too," said Chloris.

" No, woman dear—— ! "

" But do you not understand ? " says Chloris, a little pale, as he saw now. " Since the life of a hamadryad is linked with the life of her tree, nobody can harm me so long as my tree lives : and if they cut down my tree I will die, wherever I may happen to be."

" I had forgotten that." He was really troubled now.

" —And you can see for yourself, Jurgen, it is quite out of the question for me to be carrying that great oak anywhere, and I wonder at your talking such nonsense."

" Indeed, my dear," says Jurgen, " we are very neatly trapped. Well, nobody can live longer in peace than his neighbour chooses. Nevertheless, it is not fair."

As he spoke the Philistines came forth from the burning city. Again the trumpet sounded, and the Philistines advanced in their order of battle.

CHAPTER XXXII

SUNDRY DEVICES OF THE PHILISTINES

EANWHILE the People of the Field had watched Pseudopolis burn, and had wondered what would befall them. They had not long to wonder, for next day the Fields were occupied, without any resistance by the inhabitants.

"The People of the Field," said they, "have never fought, and for them to begin now would be a very unheard-of thing indeed."

So the Fields were captured by the Philistines, and Chloris and Jurgen and all the People of the Field were judged summarily. They were declared to be obsolete illusions, whose merited doom was to be relegated to limbo. To Jurgen this appeared unreasonable.

"For I am no illusion," he asserted. "I am manifestly flesh and blood, and in addition, I am the high King of Eubonia, and no less. Why, in disputing these facts you contest circumstances that are so well known hereabouts as to rank among mathematical certainties. And that makes you look foolish, as I tell you for your own good."

This vexed the leaders of the Philistines, as it always vexes people to be told anything for their own good. "We would have you know," said they, "that we are not mathematicians; and that, moreover, we have no kings in Philistia, where all must do what seems to be expected of them, and have no other law."

"How then can you be the leaders of Philistia?"

"Why, it is expected that women and priests should behave unaccountably. Therefore all we who are women or priests do what we will in Philistia, and the men there obey us. And it is we, the priests of Philistia, who do not think you can possibly have any flesh and blood under a shirt which we recognise to be a conventional figure of speech. It does not stand to reason. And certainly you could not ever prove such a thing by mathematics; and to say so is nonsense."

"But I can prove it by mathematics, quite irrefutably. I can prove anything you require of me by whatever means you may prefer," said Jurgen, modestly, "for the simple reason that I am a monstrous clever fellow."

Then spoke the wise Queen Dolores, saying: "I have studied mathematics. I will question this young man, in my tent to-night, and in the morning I will report the truth as to his claims. Are you content to endure this interrogatory, my spruce young fellow who wear the shirt of a king?"

Jurgen looked full upon her: she was lovely as a hawk is lovely: and of all that Jurgen saw Jurgen approved. He assumed the rest to be in keeping: and deduced that Dolores was a fine woman.

"Madame and Queen," said Jurgen, "I am content. And I can promise to deal fairly with you."

So that evening Jurgen was conducted into the purple tent of Queen Dolores of Philistia. It was quite dark there, and Jurgen went in alone, and wondering what would happen next: but this scented darkness he found of excellent augury, if only because it prevented his shadow from following him.

"Now, you who claim to be flesh and blood, and King of Eubonia, too," says the voice of Queen Dolores, "what is this nonsense you were talking about proving any such claims by mathematics?"

"Well, but my mathematics," replied Jurgen, "are Praxagorean."

" What, do you mean Praxagoras of Cos ? "

" As if," scoffed Jurgen, " anybody had ever heard of any other Praxagoras ! "

" But he, as I recall, belonged to the medical school of the Dogmatici," observed the wise Queen Dolores, " and was particularly celebrated for his researches in anatomy. Was he, then, also a mathematician ? "

" The two are not incongruous, madame, as I would be delighted to demonstrate."

" Oh, nobody said that ! For, indeed, it does seem to me I have heard of this Praxagorean system of mathematics, though, I confess, I have never studied it."

" Our school, madame, postulates, first of all, that since the science of mathematics is an abstract science, it is best inculcated by some concrete example."

Said the Queen : " But that sounds rather complicated."

" It occasionally leads to complications," Jurgen admitted, " through a choice of the wrong example. But the axiom is no less true."

" Come, then, and sit next to me on this couch, if you can find it in the dark ; and do you explain to me what you mean."

" Why, madame, by a concrete example I mean one that is perceptible to any of the senses—as to sight or hearing, or touch——"

" Oh, oh ! " said the Queen, " now I perceive what you mean by a concrete example. And grasping this, I can understand that complications must of course arise from a choice of the wrong example."

" Well, then, madame, it is first necessary to implant in you, by the force of example, a lively sense of the peculiar character, and virtues and properties, of each of the numbers upon which is based the whole science of Praxagorean mathematics. For in order to convince you thoroughly, we must start far down, at the beginning of all things."

" I see," said the Queen, " or rather, in this darkness, I cannot see at all, but I perceive your point. Your opening interests me : and you may go on."

" Now ONE, or the monad," says Jurgen, " is the principle and the end of all : it reveals the sublime knot which binds together the chain of causes : it is the symbol of identity, of equality, of existence, of conservation, and of general harmony." And Jurgen emphasised these characteristics vigorously. " In brief, ONE is a symbol of the union of things : it introduces that generating virtue which is the cause of all combinations : and consequently ONE is a good principle."

" Ah, ah ! " said Queen Dolores, " I heartily admire a good principle. But what has become of your concrete example ? "

" It is ready for you, madame : there is but ONE Jurgen."

" Oh, I assure you, I am not yet convinced of that. Still, the audacity of your example will help me to remember ONE, whether or not you prove to be really unique."

" Now, Two, or the dyad, the origin of contrasts——"

Jurgen went on penetratingly to demonstrate that Two was a symbol of diversity and of restlessness and of disorder, ending in collapse and separation : and was accordingly an evil principle. Thus was the life of every man made wretched by the struggle between his Two components, his soul and his body ; and thus was the rapture of expectant parents considerably abated by the advent of TWINS.

THREE, or the triad, however, since everything was composed of three substances, contained the most sublime mysteries, which Jurgen duly communicated. We must remember, he pointed out, that Zeus carried a TRIPLE thunderbolt, and Poseidon a TRIDENT, whereas Adês was guarded by a dog with THREE heads : this in

addition to the omnipotent brothers themselves being a
TRIO.

Thus Jurgen continued to impart the Praxagorean
significance of each digit separately : and by and by
the Queen was declaring his flow of wisdom was super-
human.

" Ah, but, madame, not even the wisdom of a king is
without limit. EIGHT, I repeat, then, is appropriately
the number of the Beatitudes. And NINE, or the en-
nead, also, being the multiple of THREE, should be
regarded as sacred——"

The Queen attended docilely to his demonstration of
the peculiar properties of NINE. And when he had
ended she confessed that beyond doubt NINE should be
regarded as miraculous. But she repudiated his analogues
as to the muses, the lives of a cat, and how many tailors
made a man.

" Rather, I shall remember always," she declared,
" that King Jurgen of Eubonia is a NINE days' wonder."

" Well, madame," said Jurgen, with a sigh, " now
that we have reached NINE, I regret to say we have
exhausted the digits."

" Oh, what a pity ! " cried Queen Dolores. " Nevertheless, I will concede the only illustration I disputed ;
there is but ONE Jurgen : and certainly this Praxagorean
system of mathematics is a fascinating study." And
promptly she commenced to plan Jurgen's return with
her into Philistia, so that she might perfect herself in
the higher branches of mathematics. " For you must
teach me calculus and geometry and all other sciences
in which these digits are employed. We can arrange
some compromise with the priests. That is always
possible with the priests of Philistia, and indeed the
priests of Sesphra can be made to help anybody in anything. And as for your Hamadryad, I will attend to
her myself."

" But, no," says Jurgen, " I am ready enough in all

conscience to compromise elsewhere : but to compound with the forces of Philistia is the one thing I cannot do."

"Do you mean that, King Jurgen ? " The Queen was astounded.

"I mean it, my dear, as I mean nothing else. You are in many ways an admirable people, and you are in all ways a formidable people. So I admire, I dread, I avoid, and at the very last pinch I defy. For you are not my people, and willy-nilly my gorge rises against your laws, as equally insane and abhorrent. Mind you, though, I assert nothing. You may be right in attributing wisdom to these laws ; and certainly I cannot go so far as to say you are wrong : but still, at the same time——! That is the way I feel about it. So I, who compromise with everything else, can make no compromise with Philistia. No, my adored Dolores, it is not a virtue, rather it is an instinct with me, and I have no choice."

Even Dolores, who was Queen of all the Philistines, could perceive that this man spoke truthfully.

"I am sorry," says she, with real regret, "for you could be much run after in Philistia."

"Yes," said Jurgen, "as an instructor in mathematics."

"But, no, King Jurgen, not only in mathematics," said Dolores, reasonably. "There is poetry, for instance ! For they tell me you are a poet, and a great many of my people take poetry quite seriously, I believe. Of course, I do not have much time for reading myself. So you can be the Poet Laureate of Philistia, on any salary you like. And you can teach us all your ideas by writing beautiful poems about them. And you and I can be very happy together."

"Teach, teach ! there speaks Philistia, and very temptingly, too, through an adorable mouth, that would bribe me with praise and fine food and soft days for ever. It is a thing that happens rather often, though. And I can but repeat that art is not a branch of pedagogy ! "

" Really, I am heartily sorry. For apart from mathematics, I like you, King Jurgen, just as a person."

" I, too, am sorry, Dolores. For I confess to a weakness for the women of Philistia."

" Certainly you have given me no cause to suspect you of any weakness in that quarter," observed Dolores, " in the long while you have been alone with me, and have talked so wisely and have reasoned so deeply. I am afraid that after to-night I shall find all other men more or less superficial. Heigho! and I shall probably weep my eyes out to-morrow when you are relegated to limbo. For that is what the priests will do with you, King Jurgen, on one plea or another, if you do not conform to the laws of Philistia."

" And that one compromise I cannot make! Ah, but even now I have a plan wherewith to escape your priests : and failing that, I possess a cantrap to fall back upon in my hour of direst need. My private affairs are thus not yet in a hopeless or even in a dejected condition. This fact now urges me to observe that TEN, or the decade, is the measure of all, since it contains all the numeric relations and harmonies——"

So they continued their study of mathematics until it was time for Jurgen to appear again before his judges. And in the morning Queen Dolores sent word to her priests that she was too sleepy to attend their council, but that the man was indisputably flesh and blood, amply deserved to be a king, and as a mathematician had not his peer.

Now a court was held by the Philistines to decide whether or not King Jurgen should be relegated to limbo. And when the judges were prepared for judging there came into the court a great tumble-bug, rolling in front of him his loved and properly housed young ones. With the creature came pages, in black and white, bearing a sword, a staff and a lance.

This insect looked at Jurgen, and its pincers rose

erect in horror. The bug cried to the three judges,
" Now, by St. Anthony ! this Jurgen must forthwith
be relegated to limbo, for he is offensive and lewd and
lascivious and indecent."

" And how can that be ? " says Jurgen.

" You are offensive," the bug replied, " because this
page has a sword which I choose to say is not a sword.
You are lewd because that page has a lance which I
prefer to think is not a lance. You are lascivious because yonder page has a staff which I elect to declare
is not a staff. And finally, you are indecent for reasons
of which a description would be objectionable to me,
and which therefore I must decline to reveal to anybody."

" Well, that sounds logical," says Jurgen, " but still,
at the same time, it would be no worse for an admixture
of common sense. For you gentlemen can see for yourselves, by considering these pages fairly and as a whole,
that these pages bear a sword and a lance and a staff,
and nothing else whatever ; and that all the lewdness
is in the insectival mind of him who itches to be calling
these things by other names."

The judges said nothing as yet. But they that guarded
Jurgen, and all the other Philistines, stood to this side
and to that side with their eyes shut tight, and saying :
" We decline to look at the pages fairly and as a whole,
because to look might seem to imply a doubt of what
the tumble-bug has decreed. Besides, as long as the
tumble-bug has reasons which he declines to reveal, his
reasons stay unanswerable, and you are plainly a prurient
rascal who are making trouble for yourself."

" To the contrary," says Jurgen, " I am a poet, and
I make literature."

" But in Philistia to make literature and to make
trouble for yourself are synonyms," the tumble-bug explained. " I know, for already we of Philistia have been
pestered by three of these makers of literature. Yes,
there was Edgar, whom I starved and hunted until I

was tired of it : then I chased him up a back alley one night, and knocked out those annoying brains of his. And there was Walt, whom I chivvied and battered from place to place, and made a paralytic of him : and him, too, I labelled offensive and lewd and lascivious and indecent. Then later there was Mark, whom I frightened into disguising himself in a clown's suit, so that nobody might suspect him to be a maker of literature : indeed, I frightened him so that he hid away the greater part of what he had made until after he was dead, and I could not get at him. That was a disgusting trick to play on me, I consider. Still, these are the only three detected makers of literature that have ever infested Philistia, thanks be to goodness and my vigilance, but for both of which we might have been no more free from makers of literature than are the other countries."

" Now, but these three," cried Jurgen, " are the glory of Philistia : and of all that Philistia has produced it is these three alone, whom living ye made least of, that to-day are honoured wherever art is honoured, and where nobody bothers one way or the other about Philistia."

" What is art to me and my way of living ? " replied the tumble-bug, wearily. " I have no concern with art and letters and the other lewd idols of foreign nations. I have in charge the moral welfare of my young, whom I roll here before me, and trust with St. Anthony's aid to raise in time to be God-fearing tumble-bugs like me, delighting in what is proper to their nature. For the rest, I have never minded dead men being well-spoken of. No, no, my lad ; once, whatever I may do means nothing to you, and once you are really rotten, you will find the tumble-bug friendly enough. Meanwhile I am paid to protest that living persons are offensive and lewd and lascivious and indecent, and one must live."

Then the Philistines who stood to this side and to that side said in indignant unison : " And we, the reputable citizenry of Philistia, are not at all in sympathy with those who would take any protest against the tumble-bug as a justification of what they are pleased to call art. The harm done by the tumble-bug seems to us very slight, whereas the harm done by the self-styled artist may be very great."

Jurgen now looked more attentively at this queer creature : and he saw that the tumble-bug was malodorous, certainly, but at bottom honest and well-meaning ; and this seemed to Jurgen the saddest thing he had found among the Philistines. For the tumble-bug was sincere in his insane doings, and all Philistia honoured him sincerely, so that there was nowhere any hope for this people.

Therefore King Jurgen addressed himself, as his need was, to submit to the strange customs of the Philistines. " Now do you judge me fairly," cried Jurgen to his judges, " if there be any justice in this mad country. And if there be none, do you relegate me to limbo or to any other place, so long as in that place this tumble-bug is not omnipotent and sincere and insane."

And Jurgen waited.

These points being settled, the tumble-bug went away, smiling benevolently. " Morals, not art," he said, as he departed. The judges rose, and they bowed low as the bug passed : the judges conferred together, and Jurgen was decreed a backslider into the ways of undesirable error. His judges were the priests of Vel-Tyno and Sesphra and Ageus, who are the Gods of Philistia.

Then the priest of Ageus put on his spectacles and consulted the canonical law, and declared that this change in the indictment necessitated a severance of Jurgen from the others, in the infliction of punishment.

" For each, of course, must be relegated to the limbo of his fathers, as was foretold, in order that the prophecies may be fulfilled. Religion languishes when prophecies are not fulfilled. Now it appears that the forefathers of the flesh-and-blood prisoner were of a different faith from the progenitors of these obsolete illusions, and that his fathers foretold quite different things, and that their limbo was called Hell."

" It is little you know," says Jurgen, " of the religion of Eubonia."

" We have it written down in this great book," the priest of Vel-Tyno then told him,—" every word of it without blot or error."

" Then you will see that the King of Eubonia is the head of the church there, and changes all the prophecies at will. Learned Gowlais says so directly : and the judicious Stevegonius was forced to agree with him, however unwillingly, as you will instantly discover by consulting the third section of his widely famous nineteenth chapter."

" Both Gowlais and Stevegonius were probably notorious heretics," says the priest of Ageus. " I believe that was settled once for all at the Diet of Orthumar."

" Eh ! " says Jurgen. He did not like this priest. " Now I will wager, sirs," Jurgen continued, a trifle patronisingly, " that you gentlemen have not read Gowlais, or even Stevegonius, in the light of Vossler's commentaries. And that is why you underrate them."

" I at least have read every word that was ever written by any of these three," replied the priest of Sesphra— " and with, as I need hardly say, the liveliest abhorrence. And this Gowlais in particular, as I hasten to agree with my learned confrère, is a most notorious heretic——"

" Oh, sir," said Jurgen, horrified, " whatever are you telling me about Gowlais ? "

" I tell you that I have been roused to indignation by his *Historia de Bello Veneris*——"

" You surprise me : still——"

" —Shocked by his *Pornoboscodidascolo*——"

" I can hardly believe it : even so, you must grant——"

" —And horrified by his *Liber de immortalitate Mentulæ*——"

" Well, conceding you that earlier work, sir, yet, at the same time——"

" —And have been disgusted by his *De modo coeundi*——"

" Ah, but, none the less——"

" —And have shuddered over the unspeakable enormities of his *Erotopægnion !* of his *Cinædica !* and especially of his *Epipedesis,* that most pestilential and abominable book, *quem sine horrore nemo potest legere*——"

" Still, you cannot deny——"

" —And have read also all the confutations of this detestable Gowlais : as those of Zanchius, Faventinus, Lelius Vincentius, Lagalla, Thomas Giaminus, and eight other admirable commentators——"

" You are very exact, sir : but——"

" —And that, in short, I have read every book you can imagine," says the priest of Sesphra.

The shoulders of Jurgen rose to his ears, and Jurgen silently flung out his hands, palms upward.

" For, I perceive," says Jurgen, to himself, " that this Realist is too circumstantial for me. None the less, he invents his facts : it is by citing books which never existed that he publicly confutes the Gowlais whom I invented privately : and that is not fair. Now there remains only one chance for Jurgen ; but luckily that chance is sure."

" Why are you fumbling in your pocket ? " asks the old priest of Ageus, fidgeting and peering.

" Aha, you may well ask ! " cried Jurgen. He unfolded the cantrap which had been given him by the Master Philologist, and which Jurgen had treasured against the time when more was needed than a glib tongue. " O most unrighteous judges," says Jurgen, sternly, " now hear and tremble ! ' At the death of Adrian the Fifth, Pedro Juliani, who should be named John the Twentieth, was through an error in the reckoning elevated to the papal chair as John the Twenty-first!'"

"Hah, and what have we to do with that?" inquired the priest of Vel-Tyno, with raised eyebrows. "Why are you telling us of these irrelevant matters?"

"Because I thought it would interest you," said Jurgen. "It was a fact that appeared to me rather amusing. So I thought I would mention it."

"Then you have very queer ideas of amusement," they told him. And Jurgen perceived that either he had not employed his cantrap correctly or else that its magic was unappreciated by the leaders of Philistia.

CHAPTER XXXIII

FAREWELL TO CHLORIS

NOW the Philistines led out their prisoners, and made ready to inflict the doom which was decreed. And they permitted the young King of Eubonia to speak with Chloris.

"Farewell to you now, Jurgen!" says Chloris, weeping softly. "It is little I care what foolish words these priests of Philistia may utter against me. But the big-armed axemen are felling my tree yonder, to get them timber to make a bedstead for the Queen of Philistia : for that is what this Queen Dolores ordered them to do the first thing this morning."

And Jurgen raised his hands. "You women!" he said. "What man would ever have thought of that?"

"So when my tree is felled I must depart into a sombre land wherein there is no laughter at all; and where the puzzled dead go wandering futilely through fields of scentless asphodel, and through tall sullen groves of myrtle,—the puzzled quiet dead, who may not even weep as I do now, but can only wonder what it is that they regret. And I too must taste of Lethê, and forget all I have loved."

"You should give thanks to the imagination of your forefathers, my dear, that your doom is no worse. For I am going into a more barbaric limbo, into the Hell of a people who thought entirely too much about flames and pitchforks," says Jurgen, ruefully. "I tell you it is the deuce and all, to come of morbid ancestry." And he kissed Chloris, upon the brow. " My dear, dear girl," he said, with a gulp, " as long as you remember me, do so with charity."

" Jurgen "—and she clung close to him—" you were not ever unkind, not even for a moment. Jurgen, you have not ever spoken one harsh word to me or any other person, in all the while we were together. O Jurgen, whom I have loved as you could love nobody, it was not much those other women had left me to worship ! "

" Indeed, it is a pity that you loved me, Chloris, for I was not worthy." And for the instant Jurgen meant it.

" If any other person said that, Jurgen, I would be very angry. And even to hear you say it troubles me, because there was never a hamadryad between two hills that had a husband one-half so clever-foolish as he made light of time and chance, with his sleek black head cocked to one side, and his mischievous brown eyes a-twinkle."

And Jurgen wondered that this should be the notion Chloris had of him, and that a gesture should be the thing she remembered about him : and he was doubly assured that no woman bothers to understand the man she elects to love and cosset and slave for.

" O woman dear," says Jurgen, " but I have loved you, and my heart is water now that you are taken from me : and to remember your ways and the joy I had in them will be a big and grinding sorrow in the long time to come. Oh, not with any heroic love have I loved you, nor with any madness and high dreams, nor with much talking either ; but with a love befitting my condition, with a quiet and cordial love."

" And must you be trying, while I die, to get your grieving for me into the right words ? " she asks him, smiling very sadly. " No matter : you are Jurgen, and I have loved you. And I am glad that I shall know nothing about it when in the long time to come you will be telling so many other women about what was said by Zorobasius and Ptolemopiter, and when you will be

posturing and romancing for their delight.   For presently
I shall have tasted Lethê : and presently I shall have forgotten you, King Jurgen, and all the joy I had in you,
and all the pride, and all the love I had for you, King
Jurgen, who loved me as much as you were able."

"Why, and will there be any love-making, do you
think, in Hell ? " he asks her, with a doleful smile.

"There will be love-making," she replied, "wherever
you go, King Jurgen.   And there will be women to
listen.   And at the last there will be a bean-pole of a
woman, in a wig."

"I am sorry——" he said.   "And yet I have loved
you, Chloris."

"That is my comfort now.   And presently there will
be Lethê.   I put the greater faith in Lethê.   And still,
I cannot help but love you, Jurgen, in whom I have no
faith at all."

He said again : "I am not worthy."

They kissed.   Then each of them was conveyed to an
appropriate doom.

And tears were in the eyes of Jurgen, who was not
used to weep : and he thought not at all of what was to
befall him, but only of this and that small trivial thing
which would have pleased his Chloris had Jurgen done
it, and which for one reason or another Jurgen had left
undone.

"I was not ever unkind to her, says she ! ah, but I
might have been so much kinder.   And now I shall not
ever see her any more, nor ever any more may I awaken
delight and admiration in those bright tender eyes which
saw no fault in me ! Well, but it is a comfort surely
that she does not know how I devoted the last night she
was to live to teaching mathematics."

And then Jurgen wondered how he would be despatched into the Hell of his fathers ? And when the
Philistines showed him what manner they proposed to
inflict their sentence he wondered at his own obtuseness.

" For I might have surmised this would be the way of it," said Jurgen. " And yet as always there is a simplicity in the methods of the Philistines which is unimaginable by really clever fellows. And as always, too, these methods are unfair to us clever fellows. Well, I am willing to taste any drink once : but this is a very horrible device, none the less ; and I wonder if I have the pluck to endure it ? "

Then as he stood considering this matter, a man-at-arms came hurrying. He brought with him three great rolled parchments, with seals and ribbons and everything in order : and these were Jurgen's pardon and Jurgen's nomination as Poet Laureate of Philistia and Jurgen's appointment as Mathematician Royal.

The man-at-arms brought also a letter from Queen Dolores, and this Jurgen read with a frown.

" Do you consider now what fun it would be to hood-wink everybody by pretending to conform to our laws ! " said this letter, and it said nothing more : Dolores was really a wise woman. Yet there was a postscript. " For we could be so happy ! " said the postscript.

And Jurgen looked toward the Woods, where men were sawing up a great oak-tree. And Jurgen gave a fine laugh, and with fine deliberateness he tore up the Queen's letter into little strips. Then statelily he took the parchments, and found they were so tough he could not tear them. This was uncommonly awkward, for Jurgen's ill-advised attempt to tear the parchments impaired the dignity of his magnanimous self-sacrifice : he even suspected one of the guards of smiling. So there was nothing for it but presently to give up that futile tugging and jerking, and to compromise by crumpling these parchments.

" This is my answer," said Jurgen, heroically, and with some admiration of himself, but still a little dashed by the uncalled-for toughness of the parchments.

Then Jurgen cried farewell to fallen Leukê ; and

scornfully he cried farewell to the Philistines and to their devices. Then he submitted to their devices. Thus it was, without making any special protest about it, that Jurgen was relegated to limbo, and was despatched to the Hell of his fathers, two days before Christmas.

CHAPTER XXXIV

HOW EMPEROR JURGEN FARED INFERNALLY

OW the tale tells how the devils of Hell were in one of their churches celebrating Christmas in such manner as the devils observe that day; and how Jurgen came through the trapdoor in the vestry-room; and how he saw and wondered over the creatures which inhabited this place. For to him after the Christmas services came all such devils as his fathers had foretold, and in not a hair or scale or talon did they differ from the worst that anybody had been able to imagine.

"Anatomy is hereabouts even more inconsequent than in Cocaigne," was Jurgen's first reflection. But the first thing the devils did was to search Jurgen very carefully, in order to make sure he was not bringing any water into Hell.

"Now, who may you be, that come to us alive, in a fine shirt of which we never saw the like before?" asked Dithican. He had the head of a tiger, but otherwise the appearance of a large bird, with shining feathers and four feet: his neck was yellow, his body green, and his feet black.

"It would not be treating honestly with you to deny that I am the Emperor of Noumaria," said Jurgen, somewhat advancing his estate.

Now spoke Amaimon, in the form of a thick suet-coloured worm going upright upon his tail, which shone like the tail of a glowworm. He had no feet, but under his chops were two short hands, and upon his back were bristles such as grow upon hedgehogs.

" But we are rather overrun with emperors," said Amaimon, doubtfully, " and their crimes are a great trouble to us. Were you a very wicked ruler ? "

" Never since I became an emperor," replied Jurgen, " have any of my subjects uttered one word of complaint against me. So it stands to reason I have nothing very serious with which to reproach myself."

" Your conscience, then, does not demand that you be punished ? "

" My conscience, gentlemen, is too well-bred to insist on anything."

" You do not even wish to be tortured ? "

" Well, I admit I had expected something of the sort. But none the less, I will not make a point of it," said Jurgen, handsomely. " No, I shall be quite satisfied even though you do not torture me at all."

And then the mob of devils made a great to-do over Jurgen.

" For it is exceedingly good to have at least one unpretentious and undictatorial human being in Hell. Nobody as a rule drops in on us save inordinately proud and conscientious ghosts, whose self-conceit is intolerable, and whose demands are outrageous."

" How can that be ? "

" Why, we have to punish them. Of course they are not properly punished until they are convinced that what is happening to them is just and adequate. And you have no notion what elaborate tortures they insist their exceeding wickedness has merited, as though that which they did or left undone could possibly matter to anybody. And to contrive these torments quite tires us out."

" But wherefore is this place called the Hell of my fathers ? "

" Because your forefathers builded it in dreams," they

told him, " out of the pride which led them to believe that what they did was of sufficient importance to merit punishment. Or so at least we have heard : but if you want the truth of the matter you must go to our Grandfather at Barathum."

" I shall go to him, then. And do my own grandfathers, and all the forefathers that I had in the old time, inhabit this grey place ? "

" All such as are born with what they call a conscience come hither," the devils said. " Do you think you could persuade them to go elsewhere ? For in that event, we would be deeply obliged to you. Their self-conceit is pitiful : but it is also a nuisance, because it prevents our getting any rest."

" Perhaps I can help you to obtain justice, and certainly to attempt to secure justice for you is my imperial duty. But who governs this country ? "

They told him how Hell was divided into principalities that had for governors Lucifer and Beelzebub and Belial and Ascheroth and Phlegeton : but that over all these was Grandfather Satan, who lived in the Black House at Barathum.

" Well, I prefer," says Jurgen, " to deal directly with your principal, especially if he can explain the polity of this insane and murky country. Do some of you conduct me to him in such state as becomes an emperor ! "

So Cannagosta fetched a wheelbarrow, and Jurgen got into it, and Cannagosta trundled him away. Cannagosta was something like an ox, but rather more like a cat, and his hair was curly.

And as they came through Chorasma, a very uncomfortable place where the damned abide in torment, whom should Jurgen see but his own father, Coth, the son of Smoit and Steinvor, standing there chewing his long moustaches in the midst of an especially tall flame.

" Do you stop now for a moment ! " says Jurgen, to his escort.

"Oh, but this is the most vexatious person in all Hell!" cried Cannagosta; "and a person whom there is absolutely no pleasing!"

"Nobody knows that better than I," says Jurgen.

And Jurgen civilly bade his father good-day, but Coth did not recognise this spruce young Emperor of Noumaria, who went about Hell in a wheelbarrow.

"You do not know me, then?" says Jurgen.

"How should I know you when I never saw you before?" replied Coth, irritably.

And Jurgen did not argue the point: for he knew that he and his father could never agree about anything. So Jurgen kept silent for that time, and Cannagosta wheeled him through the grey twilight, descending always deeper and yet deeper into the lowlands of Hell, until they had come to Barathum.

And JURGEN civilly bade his father good day

CHAPTER XXXV

WHAT GRANDFATHER SATAN REPORTED

EXT the tale tells how three inferior devils made a loud music with bagpipes as Jurgen went into the Black House of Barathum, to talk with Grandfather Satan. Satan was like a man of sixty, or it might be sixty-two, in all things save that he was covered with grey fur, and had horns like those of a stag. He wore a breech-clout of very dark grey, and he sat in a chair of black marble, on a daïs: his bushy tail, which was like that of a squirrel, waved restlessly over his head as he looked at Jurgen, without speaking, and without turning his mind from an ancient thought. And his eyes were like light shining upon little pools of ink, for they had no whites to them.

"What is the meaning of this insane country?" says Jurgen, plunging at the heart of things. "There is no sense in it, and no fairness at all."

"Ah," replied Satan, in his curious hoarse voice, "you may well say that: and it is what I was telling my wife only last night."

"You have a wife, then!" says Jurgen, who was always interested in such matters. "Why, but to be sure! either as a Christian or as a married man, I should have comprehended this was Satan's due. And how do you get on with her?"

"Pretty well," says Grandfather Satan: "but she does not understand me."

"*Et tu, Brute!*" says Jurgen.

" And what does that mean ? "

" It is an expression connotating astonishment over an event without parallel. But everything in Hell seems rather strange, and the place is not at all as it was rumoured to be by the priests and the bishops and the cardinals that used to be exhorting me in my fine palace at Breschau."

" And where, did you say, is this palace ? "

" In Noumaria, where I am the Emperor Jurgen. And I need not insult you by explaining Breschau is my capital city, and is noted for its manufacture of linen and woollen cloth and gloves and cameos and brandy, though the majority of my subjects are engaged in cattle-breeding and agricultural pursuits."

" Of course not : for I have studied geography. And, Jurgen, it is often I have heard of you, though never of your being an emperor."

" Did I not say this place was not in touch with new ideas ? "

" Ah, but you must remember that thoughtful persons keep out of Hell. Besides, the war with Heaven prevents us from thinking of other matters. In any event, you, Emperor Jurgen, by what authority do you question Satan, in Satan's home ? "

" I have heard that word which the ass spoke with the cat," replied Jurgen ; for he recollected upon a sudden what Merlin had shown him.

Grandfather Satan nodded comprehendingly. " All honour be to Set and Bast ! and may their power increase. This, Emperor, is how my kingdom came about."

Then Satan, sitting erect and bleak in his tall marble chair, explained how he, and all the domain and all the infernal hierarchies he ruled, had been created extempore by Koshchei, to humour the pride of Jurgen's forefathers. " For they were exceedingly proud of their sins. And Koshchei happened to notice Earth once upon a time, with your forefathers walking about it exultant in the enormity of their sins and in the terrible punishments they expected in requital. Now Koshchei will do almost anything to humour pride, because to be proud is one of the two things that are impossible to Koshchei. So he was pleased, oh, very much pleased: and after he had had his laugh out, he created Hell extempore, and made it just such a place as your forefathers imagined it ought to be, in order to humour the pride of your forefathers."

" And why is pride impossible to Koshchei ? "

" Because he made things as they are; and day and night he contemplates things as they are, having nothing else to look at. How, then, can Koshchei be proud ? "

" I see. It is as if I were imprisoned in a cell wherein there was nothing, absolutely nothing, except my verses. I shudder to think of it ! But what is this other thing which is impossible to Koshchei ? "

" I do not know. It is something that does not enter into Hell."

" Well, I wish I too had never entered here, and now you must assist me to get out of this murky place."

" And why must I assist you ? "

" Because," said Jurgen, and he drew out the cantrap of the Master Philologist, " because at the death of Adrian the Fifth, Pedro Juliani, who should be named John the Twentieth, was through an error in the reckoning elevated to the papal chair as John the Twenty-first. Do you not find my reason sufficient ? "

" No," said Grandfather Satan, after thinking it over, " I cannot say that I do. But, then, popes go to Heaven. It is considered to look better, all around, and particularly by my countrymen, inasmuch as many popes have been suspected of pro-Celestialism. So we admit none of them into Hell, in order to be on the safe side, now that we are at war. In consequence, I am no judge of popes and their affairs, nor do I pretend to be."

And Jurgen perceived that again he had employed his cantrap incorrectly or else that it was impotent to rescue people from Satan. "But who would have thought," he reflected, "that Grandfather Satan was such a simple old creature?"

"How long, then, must I remain here?" asks Jurgen, after a dejected pause.

"I do not know," replied Satan. "It must depend entirely upon what your father thinks about it——"

"But what has he to do with it?"

"—Since I and all else that is here are your father's absurd notions, as you have so frequently proved by logic. And it is hardly possible that such a clever fellow as you can be mistaken."

"Why, of course, that is not possible," says Jurgen. "Well, the matter is rather complicated. But I am willing to taste any drink once : and I shall manage to get justice somehow, even in this unreasonable place where my father's absurd notions are the truth."

So Jurgen left the Black House of Barathum : and Jurgen also left Grandfather Satan, erect and bleak in his tall marble chair, and with his eyes gleaming in the dim light, as he sat there restively swishing his soft bushy tail, and not ever turning his mind from an ancient thought.

CHAPTER XXXVI

WHY COTH WAS CONTRADICTED

HEN Jurgen went back to Chorasma, where Coth, the son of Smoit and Steinvor, stood conscientiously in the midst of the largest and hottest flame he had been able to imagine, and rebuked the out-worn devils who were tormenting him, because the tortures they inflicted were not adequate to the wickedness of Coth.

And Jurgen cried to his father: "The lewd fiend Cannagosta told you I was the Emperor of Noumaria, and I do not deny it even now. But do you not perceive I am likewise your son Jurgen?"

"Why, so it is," said Coth, "now that I look at the rascal. And how, Jurgen, did you become an emperor?"

"Oh, sir, and is this a place wherein to talk about mere earthly dignities? I am surprised your mind should still run upon these empty vanities even here in torment."

"But it is inadequate torment, Jurgen, such as does not salve my conscience. There is no justice in this place, and no way of getting justice. For these shiftless devils do not take seriously that which I did, and they merely pretend to punish me, and so my conscience stays unsatisfied."

"Well, but, father, I have talked with them, and they seem to think your crimes do not amount to much, after all."

Coth flew into one of his familiar rages. "I would have you know that I killed eight men in cold blood,

and held five other men while they were being killed.
I estimate the sum of such iniquity as ten and a half
murders, and for these my conscience demands that I
be punished."

"Ah, but, sir, that was fifty years or more ago, and
these men would now be dead in any event, so you see
it does not matter now."

"I went astray with women, with I do not know how
many women."

Jurgen shook his head. "This is very shocking news
for a son to receive, and you can imagine my feelings.
None the less, sir, that also was fifty years ago, and
nobody is bothering over it now."

"You jackanapes, I tell you that I swore and stole
and forged and burned four houses and broke the Sabbath
and was guilty of mayhem and spoke disrespectfully to
my mother and worshipped a stone image in Porutsa. I
tell you I shattered the whole Decalogue, time and again.
I committed all the crimes that were ever heard of, and
invented six new ones."

"Yes, sir," said Jurgen: "but, still, what does it
matter if you did?"

"Oh, take away this son of mine!" cried Coth: "for
he is his mother all over again; and though I was the
vilest sinner that ever lived, I have not deserved to be
plagued twice with such silly questions. And I demand
that you loitering devils bring more fuel."

"Sir," said a panting little fiend, in the form of a tad-
pole with hairy arms and legs like a monkey's, as he ran
up with four bundles of faggots, "we are doing the very
best we can for your discomfort. But you damned have
no consideration for us, and do not remember that we are
on our feet day and night, waiting upon you," said the
little devil, whimpering, as with his pitchfork he raked
up the fire about Coth. "You do not even remember the
upset condition of the country, on account of the war
with Heaven, which makes it so hard for us to get you

all the inconveniences of life.   Instead, you lounge in
your flames, and complain about the service, and Grandfather Satan punishes us, and it is not fair."

"I think, myself," said Jurgen, "you should be gentler
with the boy.   And as for your crimes, sir, come, will
you not conquer this pride which you nickname conscience, and concede that after any man has been dead a
little while it does not matter at all what he did ?   Why,
about Bellegarde no one ever thinks of your throat-
cutting and Sabbath-breaking except when very old
people gossip over the fire, and your wickedness brightens
up the evening for them.   To the rest of us you are
just a stone in the churchyard which describes you as a
paragon of all the virtues.   And outside of Bellegarde,
sir, your name and deeds mean nothing now to anybody,
and no one anywhere remembers you.   So really your
wickedness is not bothering any person now save these
poor toiling devils : and I think that, in consequence,
you might consent to put up with such torments as
they can conveniently contrive, without complaining so
ill-temperedly about it."

"Ah, but my conscience, Jurgen ! that is the point."

"Oh, if you continue to talk about your conscience,
sir, you restrict the conversation to matters I do not
understand, and so cannot discuss.   But I dare say we
will find occasion to thresh out this, and all other matters,
by and by : and you and I will make the best of this
place, for now I will never leave you."

Coth began to weep : and he said that his sins in the
flesh had been too heinous for this comfort to be permitted him in the unendurable torment which he had
fairly earned, and hoped some day to come by.

"Do you care about me, one way or the other, then ? "
says Jurgen, quite astounded.

And from the midst of his flame Coth, the son of
Smoit, talked of the birth of Jurgen, and of the infant
that had been Jurgen, and of the child that had been

Jurgen. And a horrible, deep, unreasonable emotion moved in Jurgen as he listened to the man who had begotten him, and whose flesh was Jurgen's flesh, and whose thoughts had not ever been Jurgen's thoughts : and Jurgen did not like it. Then the voice of Coth was bitterly changed, as he talked of the young man that had been Jurgen, of the young man who was idle and rebellious and considerate of nothing save his own light desires ; and of the division which had arisen between Jurgen and Jurgen's father Coth spoke likewise : and Jurgen felt better now, but was still grieved to know how much his father had once loved him.

" It is lamentably true," says Jurgen, " that I was an idle and rebellious son. So I did not follow your teachings. I went astray, oh, very terribly astray. I even went astray, sir, I must tell you, with a nature myth connected with the Moon."

" Oh, hideous abomination of the heathen ! "

" And she considered, sir, that thereafter I was likely to become a solar legend."

" I should not wonder," said Coth, and he shook his bald and dome-shaped head despondently. " Ah, my son, it simply shows you what comes of these wild courses."

" And in that event, I would, of course, be released from sojourning in the underworld by the Spring Equinox. Do you not think so, sir ? " says Jurgen, very coaxingly, because he remembered that, according to Satan, whatever Coth believed would be the truth in Hell.

" I am sure," said Coth—" why, I am sure I do not know anything about such matters."

" Yes, but what do you think ? "

" I do not think about it at all."

" Yes, but—— "

" Jurgen, you have a very uncivil habit of arguing with people—— "

" Still, sir——"

" And I have spoken to you about it before——"

" Yet, father——"

" And I do not wish to have to speak to you about it again——"

" None the less, sir——"

" And when I say that I have no opinion——"

" But everybody has an opinion, father!" Jurgen shouted this, and felt it was quite like old times.

" How dare you speak to me in that tone of voice, sir?"

" But I only meant——"

" Do not lie to me, Jurgen! and stop interrupting me! For, as I was saying when you began to yell at your father as though you were addressing an unreasonable person, it is my opinion that I know nothing whatever about Equinoxes! and do not care to know anything about Equinoxes, I would have you understand! and that the less said as to such disreputable topics the better, as I tell you to your face!"

And Jurgen groaned. " Here is a pretty father! If you had thought so, it would have happened. But you imagine me in a place like this, and have not sufficient fairness, far less paternal affection, to imagine me out of it."

" I can only think of your well-merited affliction, you quarrelsome scoundrel! and of the host of light women with whom you have sinned! and the of doom which has befallen you in consequence!"

" Well, at worst," says Jurgen, " there are no women here. That ought to be a comfort to you."

" I think there are women here," snapped his father. " It is reputed that quite a number of women have had consciences. But these conscientious women are probably kept separate from us men, in some other part of Hell, for the reason that if they were admitted into Chorasma they would attempt to tidy the place and make it habitable. I know your mother would have been meddling out of hand."

"Oh, sir, and must you still be finding fault with mother?"

"Your mother, Jurgen, was in many ways an admirable woman. But," said Coth, "she did not understand me."

"Ah, well, that may have been the trouble. Still, all this you say about women being here is mere guess-work."

"It is not!" said Coth, "and I want none of your impudence, either. How many times must I tell you that?"

Jurgen scratched his ear reflectively. For he still remembered what Grandfather Satan had said, and Coth's irritation seemed promising. "Well, but the women here are all ugly, I wager."

"They are not!" said his father, angrily. "Why do you keep contradicting me?"

"Because you do not know what you are talking about," says Jurgen, egging him on. "How could there be any pretty women in this horrible place? For the soft flesh would be burned away from their little bones, and the loveliest of queens would be reduced to a horrid cinder."

"I think there are any number of vampires and succubi and such creatures, whom the flames do not injure at all, because these creatures are informed with an ardour that is unquenchable and is more hot than fire. And you understand perfectly what I mean, so there is no need for you to stand there goggling at me like a horrified abbess!"

"Oh, sir, but you know very well that I would have nothing to do with such unregenerate persons."

"I do not know anything of the sort. You are probably lying to me. You always lied to me. I think you are on your way to meet a vampire now."

" What, sir, a hideous creature with fangs and leathery wings ? "

" No, but a very poisonous and seductively beautiful creature."

" Come, now ! you do not really think she is beautiful ? "

" I do think so. How dare you tell me what I think and do not think ? "

" Ah, well, I shall have nothing to do with her."

" I think you will," said his father : " ah, but I think you will be up to your tricks with her before this hour is out. For do I not know what emperors are ? and do I not know you ? "

And Coth fell to talking of Jurgen's past, in the customary terms of a family squabble, such as are not very nicely repeatable elsewhere. And the fiends who had been tormenting Coth withdrew in embarrassment, and so long as Coth continued talking they kept out of earshot.

CHAPTER XXXVII

INVENTION OF THE LOVELY VAMPIRE

SO again Coth parted with his son in anger, and Jurgen returned again toward Barathum; and, whether or not it was a coincidence, Jurgen met precisely the vampire of whom he had inveigled his father into thinking. She was the most seductively beautiful creature that it would be possible for Jurgen's father or any other man to imagine : and her clothes were orange-coloured, for a reason sufficiently well known in Hell, and were embroidered everywhere with green fig-leaves.

"A good-morning to you, madame," says Jurgen, "and whither are you going ? "

"Why, to no place at all, good youth. For this is my vacation, granted yearly by the Law of Kalki——"

"And who is Kalki, madame ? "

"Nobody as yet : but he will come as a stallion. Meanwhile his Law precedes him, so that I am spending my vacation peacefully in Hell, with none of my ordinary annoyances to bother me."

"And what, madame, can they be ? "

"Why, you must understand that it is little rest a vampire gets on earth, with so many fine young fellows like yourself going about everywhere eager to be destroyed."

"But how, madame, did you happen to become a vampire if the life does not please you ? And what is it that they call you ? "

236

" My name, sir," replied the Vampire, sorrowfully, " is Florimel, because my nature no less than my person was as beautiful as the flowers of the field and as sweet as the honey which the bees (who furnish us with such admirable examples of industry) get out of these flowers. But a sad misfortune changed all this. For I chanced one day to fall ill and die (which, of course, might happen to anyone), and as my funeral was leaving the house the cat jumped over my coffin. That was a terrible misfortune to befall a poor dead girl so generally respected, and in wide demand as a seamstress; though, even then, the worst might have been averted had not my sister-in-law been of what they call a humane disposition and foolishly attached to the cat. So they did not kill it, and I, of course, became a vampire."

" Yes, I can understand that was inevitable. Still, it seems hardly fair. I pity you, my dear." And Jurgen sighed.

" I would prefer, sir, that you did not address me thus familiarly, since you and I have omitted the formality of an introduction; and in the absence of any joint acquaintances are unlikely ever to meet properly."

" I have no herald handy, for I travel incognito. However, I am that Jurgen who recently made himself Emperor of Noumaria, King of Eubonia, Prince of Cocaigne, and Duke of Logreus; and of whom you have doubtless heard."

" Why, to be sure! " says she, patting her hair straight. " And who would have anticipated meeting your highness in such a place! "

" One says ' majesty ' to an emperor, my dear. It is a detail, of course: but in my position one has to be a little exigent."

" I perfectly comprehend, your majesty; and indeed I might have divined your rank from your lovely clothes. I can but entreat you to overlook my unintentional breach of etiquette: and I make bold to add that a kind heart reveals the splendour of its graciousness through the interest which your majesty has just evinced in my disastrous history."

"Upon my word," thinks Jurgen, "but in this flow of words I seem to recognise my father's imagination when in anger."

Then Florimel told Jurgen of her horrible awakening in the grave, and of what had befallen her hands and feet there, the while that against her will she fed repugnantly, destroying first her kindred and then the neighbours. This done, she had arisen.

"For the cat still lived, and that troubled me. When I had put an end to this annoyance, I climbed into the church belfry, not alone, for one went with me of whom I prefer not to talk; and at midnight I sounded the bell so that all who heard it would sicken and die. And I wept all the while, because I knew that when everything had been destroyed which I had known in my first life in the flesh, I would be compelled to go into new lands, in search of the food which alone can nourish me, and I was always sincerely attached to my home. So it was, your majesty, that I for ever relinquished my sewing, and became a lovely peril, a flashing desolation, and an evil which smites by night, in spite of my abhorrence of irregular hours : and what I do I dislike extremely, for it is a sad fate to become a vampire, and still to sympathise with your victims, and particularly with their poor mothers."

So Jurgen comforted Florimel, and he put his arm around her.

"Come, come!" he said, "but I will see that your vacation passes pleasantly. And I intend to deal fairly with you, too."

Then he glanced sidewise at his shadow, and whispered a suggestion which caused Florimel to sigh.

"By the terms of my doom," said she, "at no time during the nine lives of the cat can I refuse. Still, it is a comfort you are the Emperor of Noumaria and have a kind heart."

" Oh, and a many other possessions, my dear ! and I again assure you that I intend to deal fairly with you."

So Florimel conducted Jurgen through the changeless twilight of Barathum, like that of a grey winter afternoon, to a quiet cleft by the Sea of Blood, which she had fitted out very cosily in imitation of her girlhood home; and she lighted a candle, and made him welcome to her cleft. And when Jurgen was about to enter it he saw that his shadow was following him into the Vampire's home.

" Let us extinguish this candle ! " says Jurgen, " for I have seen so many flames to-day that my eyes are tired."

So Florimel extinguished the candle, with a good-will that delighted Jurgen. And now they were in utter darkness, and in the dark nobody can see what is happening. But that Florimel now trusted Jurgen and his Noumarian claims was evinced by her very first remark.

" I was in the beginning suspicious of your majesty," said Florimel, " because I had always heard that every emperor carried a magnificent sceptre, and you then displayed nothing of the sort. But now, somehow, I do not doubt you any longer. And of what is your majesty thinking ? "

" Why, I was reflecting, my dear," says Jurgen, " that my father imagines things very satisfactorily."

CHAPTER XXXVIII

AS TO APPLAUDED PRECEDENTS

FTERWARD Jurgen abode in Hell, and complied with the customs of that country. And the tale tells that a week or it might be ten days after his meeting with Florimel, Jurgen married her, without being at all hindered by his having three other wives. For the devils, he found, esteemed polygamy, and ranked it above mere skill at torturing the damned, through a literal interpretation of the saying that it is better to marry than to burn.

" And formerly," they told Jurgen, " you could hardly come across a marriage anywhere that was not hall-marked ' made in Heaven ' : but since we have been at war with Heaven we have quite taken away that trade from our enemies. So you may marry here as much as you like."

" Why, then," says Jurgen, " I shall marry in haste, and repeat at leisure. But can one obtain a divorce here ? "

" Oh, no," said they. " We trafficked in them for a while, but we found that all persons who obtained divorces through our industry promptly thanked Heaven they were free at last. In the face of such ingratitude we gave over that profitless trade, and now there is a manufactory, for specialties in men's clothing, upon the old statutory grounds."

" But these makeshifts are unsatisfactory, and I wish to know, in confidence, what do you do in Hell when there is no longer any putting up with your wives."

The devils all blushed. " We would prefer not to tell you," said they, " for it might get to their ears."

" Now do I perceive," said Jurgen, " that Hell is pretty much like any other place."

So Jurgen and the lovely Vampire were duly married. First Jurgen's nails were trimmed, and the parings were given to Florimel. A broomstick was laid before them, and they stepped over it. Then Florimel said "Temon!" thrice, and nine times did Jurgen reply " Arigizator ! " Afterward the Emperor Jurgen and his bride were given a posset of dudaïm and eruca, and the devils modestly withdrew.

Thereafter Jurgen abode in Hell, and complied with the customs of that country, and was tolerably content for a while. Now Jurgen shared with Florimel that quiet cleft which she had fitted out in imitation of her girlhood home : and they lived in the suburbs of Barathum, very respectably, by the shore of the sea. There was, of course, no water in Hell; indeed the importation of water was forbidden, under severe penalties, in view of its possible use for baptismal purposes : this sea was composed of the blood that had been shed by piety in furthering the kingdom of the Prince of Peace, and was reputed to be the largest ocean in existence. And it explained the nonsensical saying which Jurgen had so often heard, as to Hell's being paved with good intentions.

" For Epigenes of Rhodes is right, after all," said Jurgen, " in suggesting a misprint : and the word should be ' laved.' "

" Why, to be sure, your majesty," assented Florimel : " ah, but I always said your majesty had remarkable powers of penetration, quite apart from your majesty's scholarship."

For Florimel had this cajoling way of speaking. None the less, all vampires have their foibles, and are nourished by the vigour and youth of their lovers. So one morning

Florimel complained of being unwell, and attributed it to indigestion.

Jurgen stroked her head meditatively; then he opened his glittering shirt, and displayed what was plain enough to see.

"I am full of vigour and I am young," said Jurgen, "but my vigour and my youthfulness are of a peculiar sort, and are not wholesome. So let us have no more of your tricks, or you will quite spoil your vacation by being very ill indeed."

"But I had thought all emperors were human!" said Florimel, in a flutter of blushing penitence, exceedingly pretty to observe.

"Even so, sweetheart, all emperors are not Jurgens," he replied, magnificently. "Therefore you will find that not every emperor is justly styled the father of his people, or is qualified by nature to wield the sceptre of Noumaria. I trust this lesson will suffice."

"It will," said Florimel, with a wry face.

So thereafter they had no further trouble of this sort, and the wound on Jurgen's breast was soon healed.

And Jurgen kept away from the damned, of course, because he and Florimel were living respectably. They paid a visit to Jurgen's father, however, very shortly after they were married, because this was the proper thing to do. And Coth was civil enough, for Coth, and voiced a hope that Florimel might have a good influence upon Jurgen and make him worth his salt, but did not pretend to be optimistic. Yet this visit was never returned, because Coth considered his wickedness was too great for him to be spared a moment of torment, and so would not leave his flame.

"And really, your majesty," said Florimel, "I do not wish for an instant to have the appearance of criticising your majesty's relatives. But I do think that your majesty's father might have called upon us, at least once, particularly after I offered to have a fire made up for him to sit on any time he chose to come. I consider that your majesty's father assumes somewhat extravagant airs, in the lack of any definite proof as to his having been a bit more wicked than anybody else : and the child-like candour which has always been with me a leading characteristic prevents concealment of my opinion."

" Oh, it is just his conscience, dear."

" A conscience is all very well in its place, your majesty ; and I, for one, would never have been able to endure the interminable labour of seducing and assassin-ating so many fine young fellows if my conscience had not assured me that it was all the fault of my sister-in-law. But, even so, there is no sense in letting your conscience make a slave of you : and when conscience reduces your majesty's father to ignoring the rules of common civility and behaving like a candle-wick, I am sure that matters are being carried too far."

" And right you are, my dear. However, we do not lack for company. So come now, make yourself fine, and shake the black dog from your back, for we are spending the evening with the Asmodeuses."

" And will your majesty talk politics again ? "

" Oh, I suppose so. They appear to like it."

" I only wish that I did, your majesty," observed Florimel, and she yawned by anticipation.

For with the devils Jurgen got on garrulously. The religion of Hell is patriotism, and the government is an enlightened democracy. This contented the devils, and Jurgen had learned long ago never to fall out with either of these codes, without which, as the devils were fond of observing, Hell would not be what it is.

They were, to Jurgen's finding, simple-minded fiends who allowed themselves to be deplorably overworked by the importunate dead. They got no rest because of the damned, who were such persons as had been saddled with a conscience, and who in consequence demanded inter-minable torments. And at the time of Jurgen's coming into Hell political affairs were in a very bad way, because there was a considerable party among the younger devils who were for compounding the age-old war with Heaven, at almost any price, in order to get relief from this unceasing influx of conscientious dead persons in search of torment. For it was well known that when Satan submitted to be bound in chains there would be no more death: and the annoying immigration would thus be ended. So said the younger devils: and considered Grandfather Satan ought to sacrifice himself for the general welfare.

Then too they pointed out that Satan had been perforce their presiding magistrate ever since the settlement of Hell, because a change of administration is inexpedient in war-time: so that Satan must term after term be re-elected: and of course Satan had been voted absolute power in everything, since this too is customary in wartime. Well, and after the first few thousand years of this the younger devils began to whisper that such government was not ideal democracy.

But their more conservative elders were enraged by these effete and wild new notions, and dealt with their juniors somewhat severely, tearing them into bits and quite destroying them. The elder devils then proceeded to inflict even more startling punishments.

* * *

So Grandfather Satan was much vexed, because the laws were being violated everywhere: and a day or two after Jurgen's advent Satan issued a public appeal to his subjects, that the code of Hell should be better respected. But under a democratic government people do not like to be perpetually bothering about law and order, as one of the older and stronger devils pointed out to Jurgen.

Jurgen drew a serious face, and he stroked his chin. "Why, but look you," says Jurgen, "in deploring the mob spirit that has been manifesting itself sporadically throughout this country against the advocates of peace and submission to the commands of Heaven and other pro-Celestial propaganda,—and in warning loyal citizenship that such outbursts must be guarded against, as hurtful to the public welfare of Hell,—why, Grandfather Satan should bear in mind that the government, in large measure, holds the remedy of the evil in its own hands." And Jurgen looked very severely toward Satan.

"Come now," says Phlegeton, nodding his head, which was like that of a bear, except for his naked long red ears, inside each of which was a flame like that of a spirit-lamp : "come now, but this young emperor in the fine shirt speaks uncommonly well ! "

"So we spoke together in Pandemonium," said Belial, wistfully, "in the brave days when Pandemonium was newly built and we were all imps together."

"Yes, his talk is of the old school, than which there is none better. So pray continue, Emperor Jurgen," cried the elderly devils, "and let us know what you are talking about."

"Why, merely this," says Jurgen, and again he looked severely toward Satan : "I tell you that as long as sentimental weakness marks the prosecution of offences in violation of the laws necessitated by war-time conditions ; as long as deserved punishment for overt acts of pro-Celestialism is withheld ; as long as weak-kneed clemency condones even a suspicion of disloyal thinking : then just so long will a righteously incensed, if now and then misguided, patriotism take into its own hands vengeance upon the offenders."

"But, still——" said Grandfather Satan.

"Ineffectual administration of the law," continued Jurgen, sternly, "is the true defence of these outbursts : and far more justly deplorable than acts of mob violence is the policy of condonation that furnishes occasion for them. The patriotic people of Hell are not in a temper to be trifled with, now that they are at war. Conviction

for offences against the nation should not be hedged
about with technicalities devised for over-refined peace-
time jurisprudence. Why, there is no one of you, I am
sure, but has at his tongue's tip the immortal words of
Livonius as to this very topic : and so I shall not repeat
them. But I fancy you will agree with me that what
Livonius says is unanswerable."

So it was that Jurgen went on at a great rate, and
looking always very sternly at Grandfather Satan.

" Yes, yes ! " said Satan, wriggling uncomfortably, but
still not thinking of Jurgen entirely : " yes, all this is
excellent oratory, and not for a moment would I decry
the authority of Livonius. And your quotation is uncommonly apropos and all that sort of thing. But with
what are you charging me ? "

" With sentimental weakness," retorted Jurgen.   " Was
it not only yesterday one of the younger devils was
brought before you, upon the charge that he had said
the climate in Heaven was better than the climate here ?
And you, sir, Hell's chief magistrate—you it was who
actually asked him if he had ever uttered such a disloyal
heresy ! "

" Now, but what else was I to do ? " said Satan, fidgeting, and swishing his great bushy tail so that it rustled
against his horns, and still not really turning his mind
from that ancient thought.

" You should have remembered, sir, that a devil whose
patriotism is impugned is a devil to be punished; and
that there is no time to be prying into irrelevant questions
of his guilt or innocence. Otherwise, I take it, you will
never have any real democracy in Hell."

Now Jurgen looked very impressive, and the devils
were all cheering him.

" And so," says Jurgen, " your disgusted hearers were
wearied by such frivolous interrogatories, and took the
fellow out of your hands, and tore him into particularly
small bits. Now I warn you, Grandfather Satan, that it

is your duty as a democratic magistrate just so to deal with such offenders first of all, and to ask your silly questions afterward. For what does Rudigernus say outright upon this point ? and Zantipher Magnus, too ? Why, my dear sir, I ask you plainly, where in the entire history of international jurisprudence will you find any more explicit language than these two employ ? "

" Now certainly," says Satan, with his bleak smile, " you cite very respectable authority : and I shall take your reproof in good part. I will endeavour to be more strict in the future. And you must not blame my laxity too severely, Emperor Jurgen, for it is a long while since any man came living into Hell to instruct us how to manage matters in time of war. No doubt, precisely as you say, we do need a little more severity hereabouts, and would gain by adopting more human methods. Rudigernus, now ?—Yes, Rudigernus is rather unanswerable, and I concede it frankly So do you come home and have supper with me, Emperor Jurgen, and we will talk over these things."

Then Jurgen went off arm-in-arm with Grandfather Satan, and Jurgen's erudition and sturdy common sense were for evermore established among the older and more solid element in Hell. And Satan followed Jurgen's suggestions, and the threatened rebellion was satisfactorily discouraged, by tearing into very small fragments anybody who grumbled about anything. So that all the subjects of Satan went about smiling broadly all the time at the thought of what might befall them if they seemed dejected. Thus was Hell a happier looking place because of Jurgen's coming.

CHAPTER XXXIX

OF COMPROMISES IN HELL

NOW Grandfather Satan's wife was called Phyllis : and apart from having wings like a bat's, she was the loveliest little slip of devilishness that Jurgen had seen in a long while. Jurgen spent this night at the Black House of Barathum, and two more nights, or it might be three nights : and the details of what Jurgen used to do there, after supper, when he would walk alone in the Black House Gardens, among the artfully coloured cast-iron flowers and shrubbery, and would so come to the grated windows of Phyllis's room, and would stand there joking with her in the dark, are not requisite to this story.

Satan was very jealous of his wife, and kept one of her wings clipped and held her under lock and key, as the treasure that she was. But Jurgen was accustomed to say afterward that, while the gratings over the windows were very formidable, they only seemed somehow to enhance the piquancy of his commerce with Dame Phyllis. This queen, said Jurgen, he had found simply unexcelled at repartee.

Florimel considered the saying cryptic : just what precisely did his majesty mean ?

" Why, that in any and all circumstances Dame Phyllis knows how to take a joke, and to return as good as she receives."

" So your majesty has already informed me : and certainly jokes can be exchanged through a grating——"

JURGEN spent this night at the Black House of Barathum.

" Yes, that was what I meant. And Dame Phyllis appeared to appreciate my ready flow of humour. She informs me Grandfather Satan is of a cold dry temperament, with very little humour in him, so that they go for months without exchanging any pleasantries. Well, I am willing to taste any drink once : and for the rest, remembering that my host had very enormous and intimidating horns, I was at particular pains to deal fairly with my hostess. Though, indeed, it was more for the honour and the glory of the affair than anything else that I exchanged pleasantries with Satan's wife. For to do that, my dear, I felt was worthy of the Emperor Jurgen."

" Ah, I am afraid your majesty is a sad scapegrace," replied Florimel : " however, we all know that the sceptre of an emperor is respected everywhere."

" Indeed," says Jurgen, " I have often regretted that I did not bring with me my jewelled sceptre when I left Noumaria."

She shivered at some unspoken thought : it was not until some while afterward that Florimel told Jurgen of her humiliating misadventure with the absent-minded Sultan of Garçao's sceptre. Now she only replied that jewels might, conceivably, seem ostentatious and out of place.

Jurgen agreed to this truism : for of course they were living very quietly, and Jurgen was splendid enough for any reasonable wife's requirements, in his glittering shirt.

So Jurgen got on pleasantly with Florimel. But he never became as fond of her as he had been of Guenevere or Anaïtis, nor one-tenth as fond of her as he had been of Chloris. In the first place, he suspected that Florimel had been invented by his father, and Coth and Jurgen had never any tastes in common : and in the second place, Jurgen could not but see that Florimel thought a great deal of his being an emperor.

" It is my title she loves, not me," reflected Jurgen, sadly, " and her affection is less for that which is really integral to me than for imperial orbs and sceptres and such-like external trappings."

And Jurgen would come out of Florimel's cleft considerably dejected, and would sit alone by the Sea of Blood, and would meditate how inequitable it was that the mere title of emperor should thus shut him off from sincerity and candour.

"We who are called kings and emperors are men like other men: we are as rightly entitled as other persons to the solace of true love and affection: instead, we live in a continuous isolation, and women offer us all things save their hearts, and we are a lonely folk. No, I cannot believe that Florimel loves me for myself alone: it is my title which dazzles her. And I would that I had never made myself the Emperor of Noumaria: for this emperor goes about everywhere in a fabulous splendour, and is, very naturally, resistless in his semi-mythical magnificence. Ah, but these imperial gewgaws distract the thoughts of Florimel from the real Jurgen; so that the real Jurgen is a person whom she does not understand at all. And it is not fair."

Then, too, he had a sort of prejudice against the way in which Florimel spent her time in seducing and murdering young men. It was not possible, of course, actually to blame the girl, since she was the victim of circumstances, and had no choice about becoming a vampire, once the cat had jumped over her coffin. Still, Jurgen always felt, in his illogical masculine way, that her vocation was not nice. And equally in the illogical way of men, did he persist in coaxing Florimel to tell him of her vampiric transactions, in spite of his underlying feeling that he would prefer to have his wife engaged in some other trade: and the merry little creature would humour him willingly enough, with her purple eyes a-sparkle, and with her vivid lips curling prettily back, so as to show her tiny white sharp teeth quite plainly.

She was really very pretty thus, as she told him of

what happened in Copenhagen when young Count
Osmund went down into the blind beggar-woman's
cellar, and what they did with bits of him; and of how
one kind of serpent came to have a secret name, which,
when cried aloud in the night, with the appropriate
ceremony, will bring about delicious happenings; and
of what one can do with small unchristened children,
if only they do not kiss you, with their moist uncertain
little mouths, for then this thing is impossible; and of
what use she had made of young Sir Ganelon's skull,
when he was through with it, and she with him; and of
what the young priest Wulfnoth had said to the crocodiles
at the very last.

"Oh, yes, my life has its amusing side," said Florimel:
"and one likes to feel, of course, that one is not wholly
out of touch with things, and is even, in one's modest way,
contributing to the suppression of folly. But even so,
your majesty, the calls that are made upon one! the
things that young men expect of you, as the price of
their bodily and spiritual ruin! and the things their
relatives say about you! and, above all, the constant
strain, the irregular hours, and the continual effort to
live up to one's position! Oh, yes, your majesty, I was
far happier when I was a consumptive seamstress and
took pride in my buttonholes. But from a sister-in-
law who only has you in to tea occasionally as a matter
of duty, and who is prominent in church work, one may,
of course, expect anything. And that reminds me that
I really must tell your majesty about what happened
in the hay-loft, just after the abbot had finished undressing——"

So she would chatter away, while Jurgen listened and
smiled indulgently. For she certainly was very pretty.
And so they kept house in Hell contentedly enough until
Florimel's vacation was at an end: and then they parted,
without any tears but in perfect friendliness.

And Jurgen always remembered Florimel most

pleasantly, but not as a wife with whom he had ever been on terms of actual intimacy.

Now when this lovely Vampire had quitted him, the Emperor Jurgen, in spite of his general popularity and the deference accorded his political views, was not quite happy in Hell.

"It is a comfort, at any rate," said Jurgen, "to discover who originated the theory of democratic government. I have long wondered who started the notion that the way to get a wise decision on any conceivable question was to submit it to a popular vote. Now I know. Well, and the devils may be right in their doctrines; certainly I cannot go so far as to say they are wrong: but still, at the same time——!"

For instance, this interminable effort to make the universe safe for democracy, this continual warring against Heaven because Heaven clung to a tyrannical form of autocratic government, sounded both logical and magnanimous, and was, of course, the only method of insuring any general triumph for democracy: yet it seemed rather futile to Jurgen, since, as he knew now, there was certainly something in the Celestial system which made for military efficiency, so that Heaven usually won. Moreover, Jurgen could not get over the fact that Hell was just a notion of his ancestors with which Koshchei had happened to fall in: for Jurgen had never much patience with antiquated ideas, particularly when anyone put them into practice, as Koshchei had done.

"Why, this place appears to me a glaring anachronism," said Jurgen, brooding over the fires of Chorasma: "and its methods of tormenting conscientious people I cannot but consider very crude indeed. The devils are simple-minded and they mean well, as nobody would dream of denying, but that is just it: for hereabouts is needed some more pertinacious and efficiently disagreeable person——"

And that, of course, reminded him of Dame Lisa : and so it was the thoughts of Jurgen turned again to doing the manly thing. And he sighed, and went among the devils tentatively looking and inquiring for that intrepid fiend who in the form of a black gentleman had carried off Dame Lisa. But a queer happening befell, and it was that nowhere could Jurgen find the black gentleman, nor did any of the devils know anything about him.

"From what you tell us, Emperor Jurgen," said they all, "your wife was an acidulous shrew, and the sort of woman who believes that whatever she does is right."

"It was not a belief," says Jurgen : "it was a mania with the poor dear."

"By that fact, then, she is for ever debarred from entering Hell."

"You tell me news," says Jurgen, "which if generally known would lead many husbands into vicious living."

"But it is notorious that people are saved by faith. And there is no faith stronger than that of a bad-tempered woman in her own infallibility. Plainly, this wife of yours is the sort of person who cannot be tolerated by anybody short of the angels. We deduce that your Empress must be in Heaven."

"Well, that sounds reasonable. And so to Heaven I will go, and it may be that there I shall find justice."

"We would have you know," the fiends cried, bristling, "that in Hell we have all kinds of justice, since our government is an enlightened democracy."

"Just so," says Jurgen : "in an enlightened democracy one has all kinds of justice, and I would not dream of denying it. But you have not, you conceive, that lesser plague, my wife ; and it is she whom I must continue to look for."

"Oh, as you like," said they, "so long as you do not criticise the exigencies of war-time. But certainly we are sorry to see you going into a country where the be-nighted people put up with an autocrat Who was not

duly elected to His position. And why need you continue seeking your wife's society when it is so much
pleasanter living in Hell?"

And Jurgen shrugged. "One has to do the manly
thing sometimes."

So the fiends told him the way to Heaven's frontiers,
pitying him. "But the crossing of the frontier must
be your affair."

"I have a cantrap," said Jurgen; "and my stay in
Hell has taught me how to use it."

Then Jurgen followed his instructions, and went into
Meridie, and turned to the left when he had come to
the great puddle where the adders and toads are reared,
and so passed through the mists of Tartarus, with due
care of the wild lightning, and took the second turn to
his left—" always in seeking Heaven be guided by your
heart," had been the advice given him by devils,—
and thus avoiding the abode of Jemra, he crossed the
bridge over the Bottomless Pit and the solitary Narakas.
And Brachus, who kept the toll-gate on this bridge,
did that of which the fiends had forewarned Jurgen:
but for this, of course, there was no help.

CHAPTER XL

THE ASCENSION OF POPE JURGEN

THE tale tells how on the feast of the Annunciation Jurgen came to the high white walls which girdle Heaven. For Jurgen's forefathers had, of course, imagined that Hell stood directly contiguous to Heaven, so that the blessed could augment their felicity by gazing down upon the tortures of the damned. Now at this time a boy angel was looking over the parapet of Heaven's wall.

"And a good-day to you, my fine young fellow," says Jurgen. "But of what are you thinking so intently?" For just as Dives had done long years before, now Jurgen found that a man's voice carries perfectly between Hell and Heaven.

"Sir," replies the boy, "I was pitying the poor damned."

"Why, then, you must be Origen," says Jurgen, laughing.

"No, sir, my name is Jurgen."

"Heyday!" says Jurgen: "well, but this Jurgen has been a great many persons in my time. So very possibly you speak the truth."

"I am Jurgen, the son of Coth and Azra."

"Ah, ah! but so were all of them, my boy."

"Why, then, I am Jurgen, the grandson of Steinvor, and the grandchild whom she loved above her other grandchildren: and so I abide for ever in Heaven with all the other illusions of Steinvor. But who, messire, are you that go about Hell unscorched, in such a fine-looking shirt ? "

Jurgen reflected. Clearly it would never do to give his real name, and thus raise the question as to whether Jurgen was in Heaven or Hell. Then he recollected the cantrap of the Master Philologist, which Jurgen had twice employed incorrectly. And Jurgen cleared his throat, for he believed that he now understood the proper use of cantraps.

"Perhaps," says Jurgen, " I ought not to tell you who I am. But what is life without confidence in one another ? Besides, you appear a boy of remarkable discretion. So I will confide in you that I am Pope John the Twentieth, Heaven's regent upon Earth, now visiting this place upon Celestial business which I am not at liberty to divulge more particularly, for reasons that will at once occur to a young man of your unusual cleverness."

"Oh, but I say ! that is droll. Do you just wait a moment ! " cried the boy angel.

His bright face vanished, with a whisking of brown curls : and Jurgen carefully re-read the cantrap of the Master Philologist. " Yes, I have found, I think, the way to use such magic," observes Jurgen.

Presently the young angel re-appeared at the parapet. " I say, messire ! I looked on the Register—all popes are admitted here the moment they die, without inquiring into their private affairs, you know, so as to avoid any unfortunate scandal,—and we have twenty-three Pope Johns listed. And sure enough, the mansion prepared for John the Twentieth is vacant. He seems to be the only pope that is not in Heaven."

" Why, but of course not," says Jurgen, complacently, " inasmuch as you see me, who was once Bishop of Rome and servant to the servants of God, standing down here on this cinder-heap."

" Yes, but none of the others in your series appear to

place you. John the Nineteenth says he never heard of you, and not to bother him in the middle of a harp lesson——"

"He died before my accession, naturally."

"——And John the Twenty-first says he thinks they lost count somehow, and that there never was any Pope John the Twentieth. He says you must be an impostor."

"Ah, professional jealousy!" sighed Jurgen: "dear me, this is very sad, and gives one a poor opinion of human nature. Now, my boy, I put it to you fairly, how could there have been a twenty-first unless there had been a twentieth? And what becomes of the great principle of papal infallibility when a pope admits to a mistake in elementary arithmetic? Oh, but this is a very dangerous heresy, let me tell you, an Inquisition matter, a consistory business! Yet, luckily, upon his own contention, this Pedro Juliani——"

"And that was his name, too, for he told me! You evidently know all about it, messire," said the young angel, visibly impressed.

"Of course I know all about it. Well, I repeat, upon his own contention this man is non-existent, and so whatever he may say amounts to nothing. For he tells you there was never any Pope John the Twentieth: and either he is lying or he is telling you the truth. If he is lying, you, of course, ought not to believe him: yet, if he is telling you the truth, about there never having been any Pope John the Twentieth, why then, quite plainly, there was never any Pope John the Twenty-first, so that this man asserts his own non-existence; and thus is talking nonsense, and you, of course, ought not to believe in nonsense. Even did we grant his insane contention that he is nobody, you are too well brought up, I am sure, to dispute that nobody tells lies in Heaven: it follows that in this case nobody is lying; and so, of course, I must be telling the truth, and you have no choice save to believe me."

" Now, certainly that sounds all right," the younger Jurgen conceded : " though you explain it so quickly it is a little difficult to follow you."

" Ah, but furthermore, and over and above this, and as a tangible proof of the infallible particularity of every syllable of my assertion," observes the elder Jurgen, " if you will look in the garret of Heaven you will find the identical ladder upon which I descended hither, and which I directed them to lay aside until I was ready to come up again. Indeed, I was just about to ask you to fetch it, inasmuch as my business here is satisfactorily concluded."

Well, the boy agreed that the word of no pope, whether in Hell or Heaven, was tangible proof like a ladder : and again he was off. Jurgen waited, in tolerable confidence.

It was a matter of logic. Jacob's Ladder must from all accounts have been far too valuable to throw away after one night's use at Beth-El ; it would come in very handy on Judgment Day : and Jurgen's knowledge of Lisa enabled him to deduce that anything which was being kept because it would come in handy some day would inevitably be stored in the garret, in any establishment imaginable by women. " And it is notorious that Heaven is a delusion of old women. Why, the thing is a certainty," said Jurgen; "simply a mathematical certainty."

And events proved his logic correct : for presently the younger Jurgen came back with Jacob's Ladder, which was rather cobwebby and obsolete-looking after having been lain aside so long.

" So you see you were perfectly right," then said this younger Jurgen, as he lowered Jacob's Ladder into Hell. " Oh, Messire John, do hurry up and have it out with that old fellow who slandered you ! "

Thus it came about that Jurgen clambered merrily from Hell to Heaven upon a ladder of unalloyed, time-tested gold : and as he climbed the shirt of Nessus

THUS it came about that JURGEN clambered merrily from HELL to HEAVEN.

glittered handsomely in the light which shone from Heaven : and by this great light above him, as Jurgen mounted higher and yet higher, the shadow of Jurgen was lengthened beyond belief along the sheer white wall of Heaven, as though the shadow were reluctant and adhered tenaciously to Hell. Yet presently Jurgen leaped the ramparts : and then the shadow leaped too; and so his shadow came with Jurgen into Heaven, and huddled dispiritedly at Jurgen's feet.

"Well, well!" thinks Jurgen, "certainly there is no disputing the magic of the Master Philologist when it is correctly employed. For through its aid I am entering alive into Heaven, as only Enoch and Elijah have done before me : and moreover, if this boy is to be believed, one of the very handsomest of Heaven's many mansions awaits my occupancy. One could not ask more of any magician fairly. Aha, if only Lisa could see me now!"

That was his first thought. Afterward Jurgen tore up the cantrap and scattered its fragments as the Master Philologist had directed. Then Jurgen turned to the boy who aided Jurgen to get into Heaven.

"Come, youngster, and let us have a good look at you!"

And Jurgen talked with the boy that he had once been, and stood face to face with all that Jurgen had been and was not any longer. And this was the one happening which befell Jurgen that the writer of the tale lacked heart to tell of.

So Jurgen quitted the boy that he had been. But first had Jurgen learned that in this place his grandmother Steinvor (whom King Smoit had loved) abode and was happy in her notion of Heaven; and that about her were her notions of her children and of her grandchildren. Steinvor had never imagined her husband in Heaven, nor King Smoit either.

"That is a circumstance," says Jurgen, "which heartens me to hope one may find justice here. Yet I shall keep away from my grandmother, the Steinvor whom I knew and loved, and who loved me so blindly that this boy here is her notion of me. Yes, in mere fairness to her, I must keep away."

So he avoided that part of Heaven wherein were his grandmother's illusions: and this was counted for righteousness in Jurgen. That part of Heaven smelt of mignonette, and a starling was singing there.

CHAPTER XLI

OF COMPROMISES IN HEAVEN

JURGEN then went unhindered to where the God of Jurgen's grandmother sat upon a throne, beside a sea of crystal. A rainbow, made high and narrow like a window frame, so as to fit the throne, formed an archway in which He sat : at His feet burned seven lamps, and four remarkable winged creatures sat there chaunting softly, " Glory and honour and thanks to Him Who liveth for ever ! " In one hand of the God was a sceptre, and in the other a large book with seven red spots on it.

There were twelve smaller thrones, without rainbows, upon each side of the God of Jurgen's grandmother, in two semi-circles : upon these inferior thrones sat benignant-looking elderly angels, with long white hair, all crowned, and clothed in white robes, and having a harp in one hand, and in the other a gold flask, about pint size. And everywhere fluttered and glittered the multi-coloured wings of seraphs and cherubs, like magnified paroquets, as they went softly and gaily about the golden haze that brooded over Heaven, to a continuous sound of hushed organ music and a remote and undistinguishable singing.

Now the eyes of this God met the eyes of Jurgen : and Jurgen waited thus for a long while, and far longer, indeed, than Jurgen suspected.

" I fear You," Jurgen said, at last : " and, yes, I love You : and yet I cannot believe. Why could You not let me believe, where so many believed? Or else, why could You not let me deride, as the remainder derided so noisily? O God, why could You not let me have faith? for You gave me no faith in anything, not even in nothingness. It was not fair."

And in the highest court of Heaven, and in plain view of all the angels, Jurgen began to weep.

"I was not ever your God, Jurgen."

"Once very long ago," said Jurgen, "I had faith in You."

"No, for that boy is here with Me, as you yourself have seen. And to-day there is nothing remaining of him anywhere in the man that is Jurgen."

"God of my grandmother! God Whom I too loved in boyhood!" said Jurgen then: "why is it that I am denied a God? For I have searched: and nowhere can I find justice, and nowhere can I find anything to worship."

"What, Jurgen, and would you look for justice, of all places, in Heaven?"

"No," Jurgen said; "no, I perceive it cannot be considered here. Else You would sit alone."

"And for the rest, you have looked to find your God without, not looking within to see that which is truly worshipped in the thoughts of Jurgen. Had you done so, you would have seen, as plainly as I now see, that which alone you are able to worship. And your God is maimed: the dust of your journeying is thick upon him: your vanity is laid as a napkin upon his eyes: and in his heart is neither love nor hate, not even for his only worshipper."

"Do not deride him, You Who have so many worshippers! At least, he is a monstrous clever fellow," said Jurgen: and boldly he said it, in the highest court of Heaven, and before the pensive face of the God of Jurgen's grandmother.

"Ah, very probably. I do not meet with many clever

people. And as for My numerous worshippers, you forget how often you have demonstrated that I was the delusion of an old woman."

" Well, and was there ever a flaw in my logic ? "

" I was not listening to you, Jurgen. You must know that logic does not much concern us, inasmuch as nothing is logical hereabouts."

And now the four winged creatures ceased their chaunting, and the organ music became a far-off murmuring. And there was silence in Heaven. And the God of Jurgen's grandmother, too, was silent for a while, and the rainbow under which He sat put off its seven colours and burned with an unendurable white, tinged bluishly, while the God considered ancient things. Then in the silence this God began to speak.

Some years ago (said the God of Jurgen's grandmother) it was reported to Koshchei that scepticism was abroad in his universe, and that one walked therein who would be contented with no rational explanation. " Bring me this infidel," says Koshchei : so they brought to him in the void a little bent grey woman in an old grey shawl. " Now, tell me why you will not believe," says Koshchei, " in things as they are."

Then the decent little bent grey woman answered civilly; " I do not know, sir, who you may happen to be. But, since you ask me, everybody knows that things as they are must be regarded as temporary afflictions, and as trials through which we are righteously condemned to pass, in order to attain to eternal life with our loved ones in Heaven."

" Ah, yes," said Koshchei, who made things as they are; " ah, yes, to be sure ! and how did you learn of this ? "

" Why, every Sunday morning the priest discoursed to us about Heaven, and of how happy we would be there after death."

" Has this woman died, then ? " asked Koshchei.

" Yes, sir," they told him,—" recently. And she will believe nothing we explain to her, but demands to be taken to Heaven."

" Now, this is very vexing," Koshchei said, " and I cannot, of course, put up with such scepticism. That would never do. So why do you not convey her to this Heaven which she believes in, and thus put an end to the matter ? "

" But, sir," they told him, " there is no such place."

Then Koshchei reflected. " It is certainly strange that a place which does not exist should be a matter of public knowledge in another place. Where does this woman come from ? "

" From Earth," they told him.

" Where is that ? " he asked : and they explained to him as well as they could.

" Oh, yes, over that way," Koshchei interrupted. " I remember. Now—but what is your name, woman who wish to go to Heaven ? "

" Steinvor, sir : and if you please I am rather in a hurry to be with my children again. You see, I have not seen any of them for a long while."

" But stay," said Koshchei : " what is that which comes into this woman's eyes as she speaks of her children ? " They told him it was love.

" Did I create this love ? " says Koshchei, who made things as they are. And they told him, no : and that there were many sorts of love, but that this especial sort was an illusion which women had invented for themselves, and which they exhibited in all dealings with their children. And Koshchei sighed.

" Tell me about your children," Koshchei then said to Steinvor : " and look at me as you talk, so that I may see your eyes."

So Steinvor talked of her children : and Koshchei, who made all things, listened very attentively. Of Coth she told him, of her only son, confessing Coth was the

finest boy that ever lived,—" a little wild, sir, at first,
but then you know what boys are,"—and telling of how
well Coth had done in business and of how he had even
risen to be an alderman. Koshchei, who made all things,
seemed properly impressed. Then Steinvor talked of
her daughters, of Imperia and Lindamira and Christine :
of Imperia's beauty, and of Lindamira's bravery under
the mishaps of an unlucky marriage, and of Christine's
superlative housekeeping. " Fine women, sir, every one
of them, with children of their own ! and to me they
still seem such babies, bless them ! " And the decent
little bent grey woman laughed. " I have been very
lucky in my children, sir, and in my grandchildren too,"
she told Koshchei. " There is Jurgen, now, my Coth's
boy ! You may not believe it, sir, but there is a story
I must tell you about Jurgen——" So she ran on very
happily and proudly, while Koshchei, who made all
things, listened, and watched the eyes of Steinvor.

Then privately Koshchei asked, " Are these children
and grandchildren of Steinvor such as she reports ? "

" No, sir," they told him privately.

So as Steinvor talked Koshchei devised illusions in
accordance with that which Steinvor said, and created
such children and grandchildren as she described. Male
and female he created them standing behind Steinvor,
and all were beautiful and stainless : and Koshchei gave
life to these illusions.

Then Koshchei bade her turn about. She obeyed :
and Koshchei was forgotten.

Well, Koshchei sat there alone in the void, looking not
very happy, and looking puzzled, and drumming upon his
knee, and staring at the little bent grey woman, who
was busied with her children and grandchildren, and had
forgotten all about him. " But surely, Lindamira," he
hears Steinvor say, " we are not yet in Heaven."—" Ah,
my dear mother," replies her illusion of Lindamira, " to
be with you again is Heaven : and besides, it may be

that Heaven is like this, after all."—" My darling child, it is sweet of you to say that, and exactly like you to say that. But you know very well that Heaven is fully described in the Book of Revelations, in the Bible, as the glorious place that Heaven is. Whereas, as you can see for yourself, around us is nothing at all, and no person at all except that very civil gentleman to whom I was just talking; and who, between ourselves, seems woefully uninformed about the most ordinary matters."

"Bring Earth to me," says Koshchei. This was done, and Koshchei looked over the planet, and found a Bible. Koshchei opened the Bible, and read the Revelation of St. John the Divine, while Steinvor talked with her illusions. "I see," said Koshchei. "The idea is a little garish. Still——!" So he replaced the Bible, and bade them put Earth, too, in its proper place, for Koshchei dislikes wasting anything. Then Koshchei smiled and created Heaven about Steinvor and her illusions, and he made Heaven just such a place as was described in the book.

"And so, Jurgen, that was how it came about," ended the God of Jurgen's grandmother. "And Me also Koshchei created at that time, with the seraphim and the saints and all the blessed, very much as you see us: and, of course, he caused us to have been here always, since the beginning of time, because that, too, was in the book."

"But how could that be done?" says Jurgen, with brows puckering. "And in what way could Koshchei juggle so with time?"

"How should I know, since I am but the illusion of an old woman, as you have so frequently proved by logic? Let it suffice that whatever Koshchei wills, not only happens, but has already happened beyond the ancientest memory of man and his mother. How otherwise could he be Koshchei?"

"And all this," said Jurgen, virtuously, "for a woman who was not even faithful to her husband!"

" Oh, very probably ! " said the God : " at all events, it was done for a woman who loved. Koshchei will do almost anything to humour love, since love is one of the two things which are impossible to Koshchei."

" I have heard that pride is impossible to Koshchei——"

The God of Jurgen's grandmother raised His white eyebrows. " What is pride ? I do not think I ever heard of it before. Assuredly it is something that does not enter here."

" But why is love impossible to Koshchei ? "

" Because Koshchei made things as they are, and day and night he contemplates things as they are. How, then, can Koshchei love anything ? "

But Jurgen shook his sleek black head. " That I cannot understand at all. If I were imprisoned in a cell wherein was nothing except my verses I would not be happy, and certainly I would not be proud : but even so, I would love my verses. I am afraid that I fall in more readily with the ideas of Grandfather Satan than with Yours ; and without contradicting You, I cannot but wonder if what You reveal is true."

" And how should I know whether or not I speak the truth ? " the God asked of him, " since I am but the illusion of an old woman, as you have so frequently proved by logic."

" Well, well ! " said Jurgen. " You may be right in all matters, and certainly I cannot presume to say You are wrong : but still, at the same time——! No, even now I do not quite believe in You."

" Who could expect it of a clever fellow, who sees so clearly through the illusions of old women ? " the God asked, a little wearily.

And Jurgen answered :

" God of my grandmother, I cannot quite believe in You, and Your doings as they are recorded I find in-coherent and a little droll. But I am glad the affair has been so arranged that You may always now be real to brave and gentle persons who have believed in and

have worshipped and have loved You. To have disappointed them would have been unfair : and it is
right that before the faith they had in You not even
Koshchei who made things as they are was able to be
reasonable.

"God of my grandmother, I cannot quite believe in
You ; but remembering the sum of love and faith that
has been given You, I tremble. I think of the dear
people whose living was confident and glad because of
their faith in You : I think of them, and in my heart
contends a blind contrition, and a yearning, and an
enviousness, and yet a tender sort of amusement colours
all. Oh, God, there was never any other deity who
had such dear worshippers as You have had, and You
should be very proud of them.

"God of my grandmother, I cannot quite believe in
You, yet I am not as those who would come peering
at You reasonably. I, Jurgen, see You only through a
mist of tears. For You were loved by those whom I
loved greatly very long ago : and when I look at You
it is Your worshippers and the dear believers of old
that I remember. And it seems to me that dates and
manuscripts and the opinions of learned persons are
very trifling things besides what I remember, and what
I envy ! "

"Who could have expected such a monstrous clever
fellow ever to envy the illusions of old women ? " the
God of Jurgen's grandmother asked again : and yet His
countenance was not unfriendly.

"Why, but," said Jurgen, on a sudden, "why, but my
grandmother—in a way—was right about Heaven and
about You also. For certainly You seem to exist, and
to reign in just such estate as she described. And yet,
according to Your latest revelation, I too was right—
in a way—about these things being an old woman's
delusions. I wonder now——"

"Yes, Jurgen ? "

"Why, I wonder if everything is right, in a way ?   I

wonder if that is the large secret of everything? It would not be a bad solution, sir," said Jurgen, meditatively.

The God smiled. Then suddenly that part of Heaven was vacant, except for Jurgen, who stood there quite alone. And before him was the throne of the vanished God and the sceptre of the God, and Jurgen saw that the seven spots upon the great book were of red sealing-wax.

Jurgen was afraid : but he was particularly appalled by his consciousness that he was not going to falter. "What, you who have been duke and prince and king and emperor and pope! and do such dignities content a Jurgen? Why, not at all," says Jurgen.

So Jurgen ascended the throne of Heaven, and sat beneath that wondrous rainbow : and in his lap now was the book, and in his hand was the sceptre, of the God of Jurgen's grandmother.

Jurgen sat thus for a long while, regarding the bright vacant courts of Heaven. "And what will you do now?" says Jurgen, aloud. "Oh, fretful little Jurgen, you that have complained because you had not your desire, you are omnipotent over Earth and all the affairs of men. What now is your desire?" And sitting thus terribly enthroned, the heart of Jurgen was as lead within him, and he felt old and very tired. "For I do not know. Oh, nothing can help me, for I do not know what thing it is that I desire! And this book and this sceptre and this throne avail me nothing at all, and nothing can ever avail me : for I am Jurgen who seeks he knows not what."

So Jurgen shrugged, and climbed down from the throne of the God, and wandering at adventure, came presently to four archangels. They were seated upon a fleecy cloud, and they were eating milk and honey from gold porringers : and of these radiant beings Jurgen inquired the quickest way out of Heaven.

" For hereabouts are none of my illusions," said Jurgen,

" and I must now return to such illusions as are congenial. One must believe in something. And all that I have seen in Heaven I have admired and envied, but in none of these things could I believe, and with none of these things could I be satisfied. And while I think of it, I wonder now if any of you gentlemen can give me news of that Lisa who used to be my wife ? "

He described her; and they regarded him with compassion.

But these archangels, he found, had never heard of Lisa, and they assured him there was no such person in Heaven. For Steinvor had died when Jurgen was a boy, and so she had never seen Lisa; and in consequence, had not thought about Lisa one way or the other, when Steinvor outlined her notions to Koshchei who made things as they are.

Now Jurgen discovered, too, that, when his eyes first met the eyes of the God of Jurgen's grandmother, Jurgen had stayed motionless for thirty-seven days, forgetful of everything save that the God of his grandmother was love.

" Nobody else has willingly turned away so soon," Zachariel told him : " and we think that your insensibility is due to some evil virtue in the glittering garment which you are wearing, and of which the like was never seen in Heaven."

" I did but search for justice," Jurgen said : " and I could not find it in the eyes of your God, but only love and such forgiveness as troubled me."

" Because of that should you rejoice," the four archangels said; " and so should all that lives rejoice : and more particularly should we rejoice that dwell in Heaven, and hourly praise our Lord God's negligence of justice, whereby we are permitted to enter into this place."

CHAPTER XLII

TWELVE THAT ARE FRETTED HOURLY

SO it was upon Walburga's Eve, when almost anything is rather more than likely to happen, that Jurgen went hastily out of Heaven, without having gained or wasted any love there. St. Peter unbarred for him, not the main entrance, but a small private door, carved with innumerable fishes in bas-relief, because this exit opened directly upon any place you chose to imagine.

"For thus," St. Peter said, "you may return without loss of time to your own illusions."

"There was a cross," said Jurgen, "which I used to wear about my neck, through motives of sentiment, because it once belonged to my dead mother. For no woman has ever loved me save that Azra who was my mother——"

"I wonder if your mother told you that?" St. Peter asked him, smiling reminiscently. "Mine did, time and again. And sometimes I have wondered—— For, as you may remember, I was a married man, Jurgen: and my wife did not quite understand me," said St. Peter, with a sigh.

"Why, indeed," says Jurgen, "my case is not entirely dissimilar: and the more I marry, the less I find of comprehension. I should have had more sympathy with King Smoit, who was certainly my grandfather. Well, you conceive, St. Peter, these other women have trusted me, more or less, because they loved a phantom Jurgen.

271

But Azra trusted me not at all, because she loved me with clear eyes. She comprehended Jurgen, and yet loved him : though I for one, with all my cleverness, cannot do either of these things. None the less, in order to do the manly thing, in order to pleasure a woman,— and a married woman, too!—I flung away the little gold cross which was all that remained to me of my mother : and since then, St. Peter, the illusions of sentiment have given me a woefully wide berth. So I shall relinquish Heaven to seek a cross."

"That has been done before, Jurgen, and I doubt if much good came of it."

"Heyday, and did it not lead to the eternal glory of the first and greatest of the popes ? It seems to me, sir, that you have either very little memory or very little gratitude, and I am tempted to crow in your face."

"Why, now you talk like a cherub, Jurgen, and you ought to have better manners. Do you suppose that we Apostles enjoy hearing jokes made about the Church ? "

"Well, it is true, St. Peter, that you founded the Church——"

"Now, there you go again ! That is what those patronising seraphim and those impish cherubs are always telling us. You see, we Twelve sit together in Heaven, each on his white throne : and we behold everything that happens on Earth. Now from our station there has been no ignoring the growth and doings of what you might loosely call Christianity. And sometimes that which we see makes us very uncomfortable, Jurgen. Especially as just then some cherub is sure to flutter by, in a broad grin, and chuckle, ' But you started it.' And we did ; I cannot deny that in a way we did. Yet really we never anticipated anything of this sort, and it is not fair to tease us about it."

"Indeed, St. Peter, now I think of it, you ought to be held responsible for very little that has been said or done in the shadow of a steeple. For as I remember it, you Twelve attempted to convert a world to the teachings of Jesus : and good intentions ought to be respected, however drolly they may turn out."

It was apparent this sympathy was grateful to the old Saint, for he was moved to a more confidential tone. Meditatively he stroked his long white beard, then said with indignation : " If only they would not claim sib with us we could stand it : but as it is, for centuries we have felt like fools. It is particularly embarrassing for me, of course, being on the wicket ; for to cap it all, Jurgen, the little wretches die, and come to Heaven impudent as sparrows, and expect me to let them in ! From their thumbscrewings, and their auto-da-fés, and from their massacres, and patriotic sermons, and holy wars, and from every manner of abomination, they come to me, smirking. And millions upon millions of them, Jurgen ! There is no form of cruelty or folly that has not come to me for praise, and no sort of criminal idiot who has not claimed fellowship with me, who was an Apostle and a gentleman. Why, Jurgen, you may not believe it, but there was an eminent bishop came to me only last week in the expectation that I was going to admit him,—and I with the full record of his work for temperance, all fairly written out and in my hand ! "

Now Jurgen was surprised. " But temperance is surely a virtue, St. Peter."

" Ah, but his notion of temperance ! and his filthy ravings to my face, as though he were talking in some church or other ! Why, the slavering little blasphemer ! to my face he spoke against the first of my Master's miracles, and against the last injunction which was laid upon us Twelve, spluttering that the wine was unfermented ! To me he said this, look you, Jurgen ! to me, who drank of that noble wine at Cana and equally of that sustaining wine we had in the little upper room in Jerusalem when the hour of trial was near and our Master would have us at our best ! With me, who have since tasted of that unimaginable wine which the Master promised us in His kingdom, the busy wretch would be arguing! and would have convinced me, in the face of all my memories, that my Master, Who was a Man among men, was nourished by such thin swill as bred this niggling brawling wretch to plague me!"

"Well, but indeed, St. Peter, there is no denying that wine is often misused."

"So he informed me, Jurgen. And I told him by that argument he would prohibit the making of bishops, for reasons he would find in the mirror: and that, remembering what happened at the Crucifixion, he would clap every lumber dealer into jail. So they took him away still slavering," said St. Peter, wearily. "He was threatening to have somebody else elected in my place when I last heard him: but that was only old habit."

"I do not think, however, that I encountered any such bishop, sir, down yonder."

"In the Hell of your fathers? Oh, no: your fathers meant well, but their notions were limited. No, we have quite another eternal home for these blasphemers, in a region that was fitted out long ago, when the need grew pressing to provide a place for zealous Church-men."

"And who devised this place, St. Peter?"

"As a very special favour, we Twelve to whom is imputed the beginning and the patronising of such abominations were permitted to design and furnish this place. And, of course, we put it in charge of our former confrère, Judas. He seemed the appropriate person. Equally, of course, we put a very special roof upon it, the best imitation which we could contrive of the War Roof, so that none of those grinning cherubs could see what long reward it was we Twelve who founded Christianity had contrived for these blasphemers."

"Well, doubtless that was wise."

"Ah, and if we Twelve had our way there would be

just such another roof kept always over Earth. For
the slavering madman has left a many like him clamour-
ing and spewing about the churches that were named for
us Twelve, and in the pulpits of the churches that were
named for us : and we find it embarrassing. It is the
doctrine of Mahound they splutter, and not any doctrine
that we ever preached or even heard of : and they ought
to say so fairly, instead of libelling us who were Apostles
and gentlemen. But thus it is that the rascals make free
with our names : and the cherubs keep track of these
antics, and poke fun at us. So that it is not all pleasure,
this being a Holy Apostle in Heaven, Jurgen, though once
we Twelve were happy enough." And St. Peter sighed.

"One thing I did not understand, sir : and that was
when you spoke just now of the War Roof."

"It is a stone roof, made of the two tablets handed
down at Sinai, which God fits over Earth whenever men
go to war. For He is merciful : and many of us here
remember that once upon a time we were men and
women. So when men go to war God screens the sight
of what they do, because He wishes to be merciful to us."

"That must prevent, however, the ascent of all prayers
that are made in war-time."

"Why, but, of course, that is the roof's secondary
purpose," replied St. Peter. "What else would you
expect when the Master's teachings are being flouted?
Rumours get through, though, somehow, and horribly
preposterous rumours. For instance, I have actually
heard that in war-time prayers are put up to the Lord
God to back His favourites and take part in the murdering. Not," said the good Saint, in haste, " that I would
believe even a Christian bishop to be capable of such
blasphemy : I merely want to show you, Jurgen, what
wild stories get about. Still, I remember, back in
Cappadocia——" And then St. Peter slapped his
thigh. " But would you keep me gossiping here for ever,
Jurgen, with the Souls lining up at the main entrance

like ants that swarm to molasses? Come, out of Heaven
with you, Jurgen! and back to whatever place you
imagine will restore to you your own proper illusions!
and let me be returning to my duties."

"Well, then, St. Peter, I imagine Amneran Heath,
where I flung away my mother's last gift to me."

"And Amneran Heath it is," said St. Peter, as he
thrust Jurgen through the small private door that was
carved with fishes in bas-relief.

And Jurgen saw that the Saint spoke truthfully.

CHAPTER XLIII

POSTURES BEFORE A SHADOW

THUS Jurgen stood again upon Amneran Heath. And again it was Walburga's Eve, when almost anything is rather more than likely to happen: and the low moon was bright, so that the shadow of Jurgen was long and thin. And Jurgen searched for the gold cross that he had worn through motives of sentiment, but he could not find it, nor did he ever recover it: but barberry bushes and the thorns of barberry bushes he found in great plenty as he searched vainly. All the while that he searched, the shirt of Nessus glittered in the moonlight, and the shadow of Jurgen streamed long and thin, and every movement that was made by Jurgen the shadow parodied. And as always, it was the shadow of a lean woman, with her head wrapped in a towel.

Now Jurgen regarded this shadow, and to Jurgen it was abhorrent.

"Oh, Mother Sereda," says he, "for a whole year your shadow has dogged me. Many lands we have visited, and many sights we have seen: and at the end all that we have done is a tale that is told: and it is a tale that does not matter. So I stand where I stood at the beginning of my foiled journeying. The gift you gave me has availed me nothing: and I do not care whether I be young or old: and I have lost all that remained to me of my mother and of my mother's love, and I have betrayed my mother's pride in me, and I am weary."

Now a little whispering gathered upon the ground, as though dead leaves were moving there : and the whispering augmented (because this was upon Walburga's Eve, when almost anything is rather more than likely to happen), and the whispering became the ghost of a voice.

"You flattered me very cunningly, Jurgen, for you are a monstrous clever fellow." This it was that the voice said drily.

"A number of people might say that with tolerable justice," Jurgen declared : "and yet I guess who speaks. As for flattering you, godmother, I was only joking that day in Glathion : in fact, I was careful to explain as much, the moment I noticed your shadow seemed interested in my idle remarks and was writing them all down in a notebook. Oh, no, I can assure you I trafficked quite honestly, and have dealt fairly everywhere. For the rest, I really am very clever : it would be foolish of me to deny it."

"Vain fool!" said the voice of Mother Sereda.

Jurgen replied : "It may be that I am vain. But it is certain that I am clever. And even more certain is the fact that I am weary. For, look you, in the tinsel of my borrowed youth I have gone romancing through the world ; and into lands unvisited by other men have I ventured, playing at spillikins with women and gear and with the welfare of kingdoms ; and into Hell have I fallen, and into Heaven have I climbed, and into the place of the Lord God Himself have I crept stealthily : and nowhere have I found what I desired. Nor do I know what my desire is, even now. But I know that it is not possible for me to become young again, whatever I may appear to others."

"Indeed, Jurgen, youth has passed out of your heart, beyond the reach of Léshy : and the nearest you can come to regaining youth is to behave childishly."

Frank C. Pape

Every movement that was made by JURGEN the shadow parodied.

" O godmother, but do give rein to your better instincts and all that sort of thing, and speak with me more candidly ! Come now, dear lady, there should be no secrets between you and me. In Leukê you were reported to be Cybelê, the great Res Dea, the mistress of every tangible thing. In Cocaigne they spoke of you as Æsred. And at Cameliard Merlin called you Adères, dark Mother of the Little Gods. Well, but at your home in the forest, where I first had the honour of making your acquaintance, godmother, you told me you were Sereda, who takes the colour out of things, and controls all Wednesdays. Now these anagrams bewilder me, and I desire to know you frankly for what you are."

" It may be that I am all these. Meanwhile I bleach, and sooner or later I bleach everything. It may be that some day, Jurgen, I shall even take the colour out of a fool's conception of himself."

" Yes, yes ! but just between ourselves, godmother, is it not this shadow of you that prevents my entering, quite, into the appropriate emotion, the spirit of the occasion, as one might say, and robs my life of the zest which other persons apparently get out of living ? Come now, you know it is ! Well, and for my part, godmother, I love a jest as well as any man breathing, but I do prefer to have it intelligible."

" Now, let me tell you something plainly, Jurgen ! " Mother Sereda cleared her invisible throat, and began to speak rather indignantly.

* *

" Well, godmother, if you will pardon my frankness, I do not think it is quite nice to talk about such things, and certainly not with so much candour. However, dismissing these considerations of delicacy, let us revert to my original question. You have given me youth and all the appurtenances of youth : and therewith you have given, too, in your joking way—which nobody appreciates more heartily than I,—a shadow that renders all things not quite satisfactory, not wholly to be trusted, not to be met with frankness. Now—as you understand, I hope,—I concede the jest, I do not for a moment deny it is a master-stroke of humour. But, after all, just what exactly is the point of it? What does it mean?"

"It may be that there is no meaning anywhere. Could you face that interpretation, Jurgen?"

"No," said Jurgen: "I have faced god and devil, but that I will not face."

"No more would I, who have so many names, face that. You jested with me. So I jest with you. Probably Koshchei jests with all of us. And he, no doubt— even Koshchei who made things as they are,—is in turn the butt of some larger jest."

"He may be, certainly," said Jurgen: "yet, on the other hand——"

"About these matters I do not know. How should I? But I think that all of us take part in a moving and a shifting and a reasoned using of the things which are Koshchei's, a using such as we do not comprehend, and are not fit to comprehend."

"That is possible," said Jurgen: "but, none the less——!"

"It is as a chessboard whereon the pieces move diversely: the knights leaping sidewise, and the bishops darting obliquely, and the rooks charging straightforward, and the pawns laboriously hobbling from square to square, each at the player's will. There is no discernible order, all to the onlooker is manifestly in confusion: but to the player there is a meaning in the disposition of the pieces."

"I do not deny it: still, one must grant——"

"And I think it is as though each of the pieces, even the pawns, had a chessboard of his own which moves as he is moved, and whereupon he moves the pieces to suit his will, in the very moment wherein he is moved willy-nilly."

" You may be right : yet, even so——"

" And Koshchei who directs this infinite moving of puppets may well be the futile harried king in some yet larger game."

" Now, certainly I cannot contradict you : but, at the same time——! "

" So goes this criss-cross multitudinous moving as far as thought can reach : and beyond that the moving goes. All moves. All moves uncomprehendingly, and to the sound of laughter. For all moves in consonance with a higher power that understands the meaning of the movement. And each moves the pieces before him in consonance with his ability. So the game is endless and ruthless : and there is merriment overhead, but it is very far away."

" Nobody is more willing to concede that these are handsome fancies, Mother Sereda. But they make my head ache. Moreover, two people are needed to play chess, and your hypothesis does not provide anybody with an antagonist. Lastly, and above all, how do I know there is a word of truth in your high-sounding fancies ? "

" How can any of us know anything ? And what is Jurgen, that his knowing or his not knowing should matter to anybody ? "

Jurgen slapped his hands together. " Hah, Mother Sereda ! " says he, " but now I have you. It is that, precisely that damnable question, which your shadow has been whispering to me from the beginning of our companionship. And I am through with you. I will have no more of your gifts, which are purchased at the cost of hearing that whisper. I am resolved henceforward to be as other persons, and to believe implicitly in my own importance."

" But have you any reason to blame me ? I restored to you your youth. And when, just at the passing of that replevined Wednesday which I loaned, you rebuked the Countess Dorothy very edifyingly, I was pleased to find a man so chaste : and therefore I continued my grant of youth——"

" Ah, yes ! " said Jurgen : " then that was the way of it ! You were pleased, just in the nick of time, by my virtuous rebuke of the woman who tempted me. Yes, to be sure. Well, well ! come now, you know, that is very gratifying."

" None the less your chastity, however unusual, has proved a barren virtue. For what have you made of a year of youth ? Why, each thing that every man of forty-odd by ordinary regrets having done, you have done again, only more swiftly, compressing the follies of a quarter of a century into the space of one year. You have sought bodily pleasures. You have made jests. You have asked many idle questions. And you have doubted all things, including Jurgen. In the face of your memories, in the face of what you probably considered cordial repentance, you have made of your second youth just nothing. Each thing that every man of forty-odd regrets having done, you have done again."

" Yes : it is undeniable that I re-married," said Jurgen. " Indeed, now I think of it, there was Anaïtis and Chloris and Florimel, so that I have married thrice in one year. But I am largely the victim of heredity, you must remember, since it was without consulting me that Smoit of Glathion perpetuated his characteristics."

" Your marriages I do not criticise, for each was in accordance with the custom of the country : the law is always respectable ; and matrimony is an honourable estate, and has a steadying influence, in all climes. It is true my shadow reports several other affairs——"

" Oh, godmother, and what is this you are telling me ! "

" There was a Yolande and a Guenevere "—the voice of Mother Sereda appeared to read from a memorandum,—" and a Sylvia, who was your own step-grandmother, and a Stella, who was a yogini, whatever that may be; and a Phyllis and a Dolores, who were the queens of Hell and Philistia severally. Moreover, you visited the Queen of Pseudopolis in circumstances which could not but have been unfavourably viewed by her husband. Oh, yes, you have committed follies with divers women."

"Follies, it may be, but no crimes, not even a misdemeanour. Look you, Mother Sereda, does your shadow report in all this year one single instance of misconduct with a woman?" says Jurgen, sternly.

"No, dearie, as I joyfully concede. The very worst reported is that matters were sometimes assuming a more or less suspicious turn when you happened to put out the light. And, of course, shadows cannot exist in absolute darkness."

"See now," said Jurgen, "what a thing it is to be careful! Careful, I mean, in one's avoidance of even an appearance of evil. In what other young man of twenty-one may you look to find such continence? And yet you grumble!"

"I do not complain because you have lived chastely. That pleases me, and is the single reason you have been spared this long."

"Oh, godmother, and whatever are you telling me?"

"Yes, dearie, had you once sinned with a woman in the youth I gave, you would have been punished instantly and very terribly. For I was always a great believer in chastity, and in the old days I used to insure the chastity of all my priests in the only way that is infallible."

"In fact, I noticed something of the sort as you passed in Leukê."

"And over and over again I have been angered by my shadow's reports, and was about to punish you, my poor dearie, when I would remember that you held fast to the rarest of all virtues in a man, and that my shadow reported no irregularities with women. And that would please me, I acknowledge : so I would let matters run on a while longer. But it is a shiftless business, dearie, for you are making nothing of the youth I restored to you. And had you a thousand lives the result would be the same."

"Nevertheless, I am a monstrous clever fellow." Jurgen chuckled here.

"You are, instead, a palterer ; and your life, apart from that fine song you made about me, is sheer waste."

"Ah, if you come to that, there was a brown man in the Druid forest who showed me a very curious spectacle last June. And I am not apt to lose the memory of what he showed me, whatever you may say, and whatever I may have said to him."

"This and a many other curious spectacles you have seen and have made nothing of, in the false youth I gave you. And therefore my shadow was angry that in the revelation of so much futile trifling I did not take away the youth I gave—as I have half a mind to do, even now, I warn you, dearie, for there is really no putting up with you. But I spared you because of my shadow's grudging reports as to your continence, which is a virtue that we of the Léshy peculiarly revere."

Now Jurgen considered. "Eh ?—then it is within your ability to make me old again, or rather, an excellently preserved person of forty-odd, or say, thirty-nine, by the calendar, but not looking it by a long shot ? Such threats are easily voiced. But how can I know that you are speaking the truth ? "

"How can any of us know anything ? And what is Jurgen, that his knowing or his not knowing should matter to anybody ? "

"Ah, godmother, and must you still be mumbling that ! Come now, forget you are a woman, and be reasonable ! You exercise the fair and ancient privilege of kinship by calling me harsh names, but it is in the face of this plain fact : I got from you what never man has got before. I am a monstrous clever fellow, say what you will : for already I have cajoled you out of a year of youth, a year wherein I have neither builded nor robbed any churches, but have had upon the whole a very pleasant time. Ah, you may murmur platitudes and threats and axioms and anything else which happens to appeal to you : the fact remains that I got what I wanted. Yes, I cajoled you very neatly into giving me eternal youth. For, of course, poor dear, you are now powerless to take it back : and so I shall retain, in spite of you, the most desirable possession in life."

" I gave, in honour of your chastity, which is the one commendable trait that you possess——"

" My chastity, I grant you, is remarkable. Nevertheless, you really gave because I was the cleverer."

"—And what I give I can retract at will ! "

" Come, come, you know very well you can do nothing of the sort. I refer you to Sævius Nicanor. None of the Léshy can ever take back the priceless gift of youth. That is explicitly proved in the Appendix."

" Now, but I am becoming angry——"

" To the contrary, as I perceive with real regret, you are becoming ridiculous, since you dispute the authority of Sævius Nicanor."

"—And I will show you—oh, but I will show you, you jackanapes ! "

" Ah, but come now ! keep your temper in hand ! All fairly erudite persons know you cannot do the thing you threaten : and it is notorious that the weakest wheel of every cart creaks loudest. So do you cultivate a judicious taciturnity ! for really nobody is going to put up with petulance in an ugly and toothless woman of your age, as I tell you for your own good."

It always vexes people to be told anything for their own good. So what followed happened quickly. A fleece of cloud slipped over the moon. The night seemed bitterly cold, for the space of a heart-beat, and then matters were comfortable enough. The moon emerged in its full glory, and there in front of Jurgen was the proper shadow of Jurgen. He dazedly regarded his hands, and they were the hands of an elderly person. He felt the calves of his legs, and they were shrunken. He patted himself centrally, and underneath the shirt of Nessus the paunch of Jurgen was of impressive dimension. In other respects he had abated.

"Then, too, I have forgotten something very suddenly," reflected Jurgen. "It was something I wanted to forget. Ah, yes! but what was it that I wanted to forget? Why, there was a brown man—with something unusual about his feet.—He talked nonsense and behaved idiotically in a Druid forest.—He was probably insane. No, I do not remember what it was that I have forgotten: but I am sure it has gnawed away in the back of my mind, like a small ruinous maggot: and that, after all, it was of no importance."

Aloud he wailed, in his most moving tones: "Oh, Mother Sereda, I did not mean to anger you. It was not fair to snap me up on a thoughtless word! Have mercy upon me, Mother Sereda, for I would never have alluded to your being so old and plain-looking if I had known you were so vain!"

But Mother Sereda did not appear to be softened by this form of entreaty, for nothing happened.

"Well, then, thank goodness, that is over!" says Jurgen, to himself. "Of course, she may be listening still, and it is dangerous jesting with the Léshy: but really they do not seem to be very intelligent. Otherwise this irritable maunderer would have known that, everything else apart, I am heartily tired of the responsibilities of youth under any such constant surveillance. Now all is changed: there is no call to avoid a suspicion of wrongdoing by transacting all philosophical investigations in the dark: and I am no longer distrustful of lamps or candles, or even of sunlight. Old body, you are as grateful as old slippers, to a somewhat wearied man : and for the second time I have tricked Mother Sereda rather neatly. My knowledge of Lisa, however painfully acquired, is a decided advantage in dealing with anything that is feminine."

Then Jurgen regarded the black cave. " And that reminds me it still would be, I suppose, the manly thing to continue my quest for Lisa. The intimidating part is that if I go into this cave for the third time I shall almost certainly get her back. By every rule of tradition the third attempt is invariably successful. I wonder if I want Lisa back ? "

Jurgen meditated : and he shook a grizzled head. " I do not definitely know. She was an excellent cook. There were pies that I shall always remember with affection. And she meant well, poor dear ! But then if it was really her head that I sliced off last May—or if her temper is not any better.—Still, it is an interminable nuisance washing your own dishes : and I appear to have no aptitude whatever for sewing and darning things. But, to the other hand, Lisa nags so : and she does not understand me——"

Jurgen shrugged. " See-saw ! the argument for and against might run on indefinitely. Since I have no real preference, I will humour prejudice by doing the manly thing. For it seems only fair : and besides, it may fail after all."

Then he went into the cave for the third time.

CHAPTER XLIV

IN THE MANAGER'S OFFICE

THE tale tells that all was dark there, and Jurgen could see no one. But the cave stretched straight forward and downward, and at the far end was a glow of light. Jurgen went on and on, and so came to the place where Nessus had lain in wait for Jurgen. Again Jurgen stooped, and crawled through the opening in the cave's wall, and so came to where lamps were burning upon tall iron stands. Now, one by one, these lamps were going out, and there were now no women here : instead, Jurgen trod inch deep in fine white ashes, leaving the print of his feet upon them.

He went forward as the cave stretched. He came to a sharp turn in the cave, with the failing lamplight now behind him, so that his shadow confronted Jurgen, blurred but unarguable. It was the proper shadow of a commonplace and elderly pawnbroker, and Jurgen regarded it with approval.

Jurgen came then into a sort of underground chamber, from the roof of which was suspended a kettle of quivering red flames. Facing him was a throne, and back of this were rows of benches : but here, too, was nobody. Resting upright against the vacant throne was a triangular white shield : and when Jurgen looked more closely he could see there was writing upon it. Jurgen carried this shield as close as he could to the kettle of flames, for his eyesight was now not very good, and besides, the flames in the kettle were burning low : and

288

Jurgen deciphered the message that was written upon the shield, in black and red letters.

" Absent upon important affairs," it said. " Will be back in an hour."   And it was signed, " Thragnar R."

" I wonder now for whom King Thragnar left this notice ? " reflected Jurgen—" certainly not for me.   And I wonder, too, if he left it here a year ago or only this evening ?   And I wonder if it was Thragnar's head I removed in the black and silver pavilion ?   Ah, well, there are a number of things to wonder about in this incredible cave, wherein the lights are dying out, as I observe with some discomfort.   And I think the air grows chillier."

Then Jurgen looked to his right, at the stairway which he and Guenevere had ascended ; and he shook his head. " Glathion is no fit resort for a respectable pawnbroker. Chivalry is for young people, like the late Duke of Logreus.   But I must get out of this place, for certainly there is in the air a deathlike chill."

So Jurgen went on down the aisle between the rows of benches wherefrom Thragnar's warriors had glared at Jurgen when he was last in this part of the cave.   At the end of the aisle was a wooden door painted white. It was marked, in large black letters, " Office of the Manager—Keep Out."   So Jurgen opened this door.

He entered into a notable place illuminated by seven cresset lights.   These lights were the power of Assyria, and Nineveh, and Egypt, and Rome, and Athens, and Byzantium : six other cressets stood ready there, but fire had not yet been laid to these.   Back of all was a large blackboard with much figuring on it in red chalk. And here, too, was the black gentleman, who a year ago had given his blessing to Jurgen, for speaking civilly of the powers of darkness.   To-night the black gentleman wore a black dressing-gown that was embroidered with all the signs of the Zodiac.   He sat at a table, the top of which was curiously inlaid with thirty pieces of silver :

and he was copying entries from one big book into
another. He looked up from his writing pleasantly
enough, and very much as though he were expecting
Jurgen.

"You find me busy with the Stellar Accounts," says
he, "which appear to be in a fearful muddle. But what
more can I do for you, Jurgen,—for you, my friend,
who spoke a kind word for things as they are, and
furnished me with one or two really very acceptable
explanations as to why I had created evil?"

"I have been thinking, Prince——" begins the pawnbroker.

"And why do you call me a prince, Jurgen?"

"I do not know, sir. But I suspect that my quest is
ended, and that you are Koshchei the Deathless."

The black gentleman nodded. "Something of the
sort. Koshchei, or Ardnari, or Ptha, or Jaldalaoth, or
Abraxas,—it is all one what I may be called hereabouts.
My real name you never heard: no man has ever heard
my name. So that matter we need hardly go into."

"Precisely, Prince. Well, but it is a long way that I
have travelled roundabout, to win to you who made
things as they are. And it is eager I am to learn just
why you made things as they are."

Up went the black gentleman's eyebrows into regular
Gothic arches. "And do you really think, Jurgen, that
I am going to explain to you why I made things as they
are?"

"I fail to see, Prince, how my wanderings could have
any other equitable climax."

"But, friend, I have nothing to do with justice. To
the contrary, I am Koshchei who made things as they
are."

Jurgen saw the point. "Your reasoning, Prince, is
unanswerable. I bow to it. I should even have foreseen it. Do you tell me, then, what thing is this which
I desire, and cannot find in any realm that man has
known nor in any kingdom that man has imagined."

Koshchei was very patient. " I am not, I confess, anything like as well acquainted with what has been going on in this part of the universe as I ought to be. Of course, events are reported to me, in a general sort of way, and some of my people were put in charge of these stars, a while back : but they appear to have run the constellation rather shiftlessly. Still, I have recently been figuring on the matter, and I do not despair of putting the suns hereabouts to some profitable use, in one way or another, after all. Of course, it is not as if it were an important constellation. But I am an Economist, and I dislike waste——"

Then he was silent for an instant, not greatly worried by the problem, as Jurgen could see, but mildly vexed by his inability to divine the solution out of hand. Present Koshchei said :

" And in the meantime, Jurgen, I am afraid I cannot answer your question on the spur of the moment. You see, there appears to have been a great number of human beings, as you call them, evolved upon—oh, yes ! —upon Earth. I have the approximate figures over yonder, but they would hardly interest you. And the desires of each one of these human beings seem to have been multitudinous and inconstant. Yet, Jurgen, you might appeal to the local authorities, for I remember appointing some, at the request of a very charming old lady."

" In fine, you do not know what thing it is that I desire," said Jurgen, much surprised.

" Why, no, I have not the least notion," replied Koshchei. " Still, I suspect that if you got it you would protest it was a most unjust affliction. So why keep worrying about it ? "

Jurgen demanded, almost indignantly : " But have you not then, Prince, been guiding all my journeying during this last year ? "

" Now, really, Jurgen, I remember our little meeting very pleasantly. And I endeavoured forthwith to dispose of your most urgent annoyance. But I confess I have had one or two other matters upon my mind since then. You see, Jurgen, the universe is rather large, and the running of it is a considerable tax upon my time. I cannot manage to see anything like as much of my friends as I would be delighted to see of them. And so perhaps, what with one thing and another, I have not given you my undivided attention all through the year—not every moment of it, that is."

" Ah, Prince, I see that you are trying to spare my feelings, and it is kind of you. But the upshot is that you do not know what I have been doing, and you did not care what I was doing. Dear me! but this is a very sad come-down for my pride."

" Yes, but reflect how remarkable a possession is that pride of yours, and how I wonder at it, and how I envy it in vain,—I, who have nothing anywhere to contemplate save my own handiwork. Do you consider, Jurgen, what I would give if I could find, anywhere in this universe of mine, anything which would make me think myself one-half so important as you think Jurgen is ! " And Koshchei sighed.

But instead, Jurgen considered the humiliating fact that Koshchei had not been supervising Jurgen's travels. And of a sudden Jurgen perceived that this Koshchei the Deathless was not particularly intelligent. Then Jurgen wondered why he should ever have expected Koshchei to be intelligent. Koshchei was omnipotent, as men estimate omnipotence : but by what course of reasoning had people come to believe that Koshchei was clever, as men estimate cleverness ? The fact that, to the contrary, Koshchei seemed well-meaning, but rather slow of apprehension and a little needlessly fussy, went far toward explaining a host of matters which had long puzzled Jurgen. Cleverness was, of course, the most admirable of all traits : but cleverness was not at the top of things, and never had been.

" Very well, then ! " says Jurgen, with a shrug; " let us come to my third request and to the third thing that I have been seeking. Here, though, you ought to be more communicative. For I have been thinking, Prince, my wife's society is perhaps becoming to you a trifle burdensome."

" Eh, sirs, I am not unaccustomed to women. I may truthfully say that as I find them, so do I take them. And I was willing to oblige a fellow rebel."

" But I do not know, Prince, that I have ever rebelled. Far from it, I have everywhere conformed with custom."

" Your lips conformed, but all the while your mind made verses, Jurgen. And poetry is man's rebellion against being what he is."

" —And besides, you call me a fellow rebel. Now, how can it be possible that Koshchei, who made all things as they are, should be a rebel? unless, indeed, there is some power above even Koshchei. I would very much like to have that explained to me, sir."

" No doubt : but then why should I explain it to you, Jurgen ? " says the black gentleman.

" Well, be that as it may, Prince ! But—to return a little—I do not know that you have obliged me in carry-ing off my wife. I mean, of course, my first wife."

" Why, Jurgen," says the black gentleman, in high astonishment, " do you mean to tell me that you want the plague of your life back again ? "

" I do not know about that either, sir. She was certainly very hard to live with. On the other hand, I had become used to having her about. I rather miss her, now that I am again an elderly person. Indeed, I believe I have missed Lisa all along."

The black gentleman meditated. " Come, friend," he says, at last. " You were a poet of some merit. You displayed a promising talent which might have been cleverly developed, in any suitable environment. Now, I repeat, I am an Economist : I dislike waste : and you were never fitted to be anything save a poet. The trouble was "—and Koshchei lowered his voice to an impressive whisper,—" the trouble was your wife did not understand you. She hindered your art. Yes, that precisely sums it up: she interfered with your soul-development, and your instinctive need of self-expression, and all that sort of thing. You are very well rid of this woman, who converted a poet into a pawnbroker. To the other side, as is with point observed somewhere or other, it is not good for man to live alone. But, friend, I have just the wife for you."

"Well, Prince," said Jurgen, "I am willing to taste any drink once."

So Koshchei waved his hand: and there, quick as winking, was the loveliest lady that Jurgen had ever imagined.

CHAPTER XLV

THE FAITH OF GUENEVERE

ERY fair was this woman to look upon, with her shining grey eyes and small smiling lips, a fairer woman might no man boast of having seen. And she regarded Jurgen graciously, with her cheeks red and white, very lovely to observe. She was clothed in a robe of flame-coloured silk, and about her neck was a collar of red gold. And she told him, quite as though she spoke with a stranger, that she was Queen Guenevere.

"But Lancelot is turned monk, at Glastonbury: and Arthur is gone into Avalon," says she: "and I will be your wife if you will have me, Jurgen."

And Jurgen saw that Guenevere did not know him at all, and that even his name to her was meaningless. There were a many ways of accounting for this: but he put aside the unflattering explanation that she had simply forgotten all about Jurgen, in favour of the reflection that the Jurgen she had known was a scapegrace of twenty-one. Whereas he was now a staid and knowledgeable pawnbroker.

And it seemed to Jurgen that he had never really loved any woman save Guenevere, the daughter of Gogyrvan Gawr, and the pawnbroker was troubled.

"For again you make me think myself a god," says Jurgen. "Madame Guenevere, when man recognised himself to be Heaven's vicar upon earth, it was to serve and to glorify and to protect you and your radiant sisterhood that man consecrated his existence. You were beautiful, and you were frail; you were half goddess and half bric-à-brac. Ohimé, I recognise the call of chivalry, and my heart-strings resound : yet, for innumerable reasons, I hesitate to take you for my wife, and to concede myself your appointed protector, responsible as such to Heaven. For one matter, I am not altogether sure that I am Heaven's vicar here upon earth. Certainly the God of Heaven said nothing to me about it, and I cannot but suspect that Omniscience would have selected some more competent representative."

" It is so written, Messire Jurgen."

Jurgen shrugged. " I, too, in the intervals of business, have written much that is beautiful. Very often my verses were so beautiful that I would have given anything in the world in exchange for somewhat less sure information as to the author's veracity. Ah, no, madame, desire and knowledge are pressing me so sorely that, between them, I dare not love you, and still I cannot help it ! "

Then Jurgen gave a little wringing gesture with his hands. His smile was not merry ; and it seemed pitiful that Guenevere should not remember him.

" Madame and queen," says Jurgen, " once long and long ago there was a man who worshipped all women. To him they were one and all of sacred, sweet intimidating beauty. He shaped sonorous rhymes of this, in praise of the mystery and sanctity of women. Then a count's tow-headed daughter whom he loved, with such love as it puzzles me to think of now, was shown to him just as she was, as not even worthy of hatred. The goddess stood revealed, unveiled, and displaying in all things such mediocrity as he fretted to find in himself. That was unfortunate. For he began to suspect that women, also, are akin to their parents ; and are no wiser, and no more subtle, and no more immaculate, than the father who begot them. Madame and queen, it is not good for any man to suspect this."

" It is certainly not the conduct of a chivalrous person, nor of an authentic poet," says Queen Guenevere. " And yet your eyes are big with tears."

" Hah, madame," he replied, " but it amuses me to weep for a dead man with eyes that once were his.   For he was a dear lad before he went rampaging through the world, in the pride of his youth and in the armour of his hurt.   And songs he made for the pleasure of kings, and sword-play he made for the pleasure of men, and a whispering he made for the pleasure of women, in places where renown was, and where he trod boldly, giving pleasure to everybody in those fine days.   But for all his laughter, he could not understand his fellows, nor could he love them, nor could he detect anything in aught they said or did save their exceeding folly."

" Why, man's folly is indeed very great, Messire Jurgen, and the doings of this world are often inexplicable :   and so does it come about that man can be saved by faith alone."

" Ah, but this boy had lost his fellows' cordial common faith in the importance of what use they made of half-hours and months and years ;   and because a jill-flirt had opened his eyes so that they saw too much, he had lost faith in the importance of his own actions, too.   There was a little time of which the passing might be made not unendurable ;   beyond gaped unpredictable darkness ;   and that was all there was of certainty anywhere.   Meanwhile, he had the loan of a brain which played with ideas, and a body that went delicately down pleasant ways. And so he was never the mate for you, dear Guenevere, because he had not sufficient faith in anything at all, not even in his own deductions."

Now said Queen Guenevere :   " Farewell to you, then, Jurgen, for it is I that am leaving you for ever.   I was to them that served me the lovely and excellent master-work of God : in Caerleon and Northgalis and at Joyeuse Garde might men behold me with delight, because, men said, to view me was to comprehend the power and kindliness of their Creator. Very beautiful was Iseult, and the face of Luned sparkled like a moving gem; Morgaine and Enid and Viviane and shrewd Nimuë were lovely, too; and the comeliness of Ettarde exalted the beholder like a proud music : these, going statelily about Arthur's hall, seemed Heaven's finest craftsmanship until the Queen came to her daïs, as the moon among glowing stars : men then affirmed that God in making Guenevere had used both hands. And it is I that am leaving you for ever. My beauty was no human white and red, said they, but an explicit sign of Heaven's might. In approaching me men thought of God, because in me, they said, His splendour was incarnate. That which I willed was neither right nor wrong : it was divine. This thing it was that the knights saw in me; this surety, as to the power and kindliness of their great Father, it was of which the chevaliers of yesterday were conscious in beholding me, and of men's need to be worthy of such parentage; and it is I that am leaving you for ever."

Said Jurgen : " I could not see all this in you, not quite all this, because of a shadow that followed me. Now it is too late, and this is a sorrowful thing which is happening. I am become as a rudderless boat that goes from wave to wave : I am turned to unfertile dust which a whirlwind makes coherent, and presently lets fall. And so, farewell to you, Queen Guenevere, for it is a sorrowful thing and a very unfair thing that is happening."

Thus he cried farewell to the daughter of Gogyrvan blawr. And instantly she vanished like the flame of a Gown out altar-candle.

CHAPTER XLVI

THE DESIRE OF ANAÏTIS

ND again Koshchei waved his hand. Then came to Jurgen a woman who was strangely gifted and perverse. Her dark eyes glittered : upon her head was a network of red coral, with branches radiating downward, and her tunic was of two colours, being shot with black and crimson curiously mingled.

And Anaïtis also had forgotten Jurgen, or else she did not recognise him in this man of forty-and-something : and again belief awoke in Jurgen's heart that this was the only woman whom Jurgen had really loved, as he listened to Anaïtis and to her talk of marvellous things.

Of the lore of Thaïs she spoke, and of the schooling of Sappho, and of the secrets of Rhodopê, and of the mourning for Adonis : and the refrain of all her talking was not changed. " For we have but a little while to live, and none knows his fate thereafter. So that a man possesses nothing certainly save a brief loan of his own body : and yet the body of man is capable of much curious pleasure. As thus and thus," says she. And the bright-coloured pensive woman spoke with antique directness of matters that Jurgen, being no longer a scapegrace of twenty-one, found rather embarrassing.

" Come, come ! " thinks he, " but it will never do to seem provincial. I believe that I am actually blushing."

Aloud he said : " Sweetheart, there was—why, not a half-hour since !—a youth who sought quite zealously for the over-mastering frenzies you prattle about. But, candidly, he could not find the flesh whose touch would rouse insanity. The lad had opportunities, too, let me tell you! Hah, I recall with tenderness the glitter of eyes and hair, and the gay garments, and the soft voices of those fond foolish women, even now. But he went from one pair of lips to another, with an ardour that was always half-feigned, and with protestations which were conscious echoes of some romance or other. Such escapades were pleasant enough : but they were not very serious, after all. For these things concerned his body alone : and I am more than an edifice of viands reared by my teeth. To pretend that what my body does or endures is of importance seems rather silly nowadays. I prefer to regard it as a necessary beast of burden, which I maintain at considerable expense and trouble. So I shall make no more pother about it."

But then again Queen Anaïtis spoke of marvellous things ; and he listened, fair-mindedly ; for the Queen spoke now of that which was hers to share with him.

"Well, I have heard," says Jurgen, "that you have a notable residence in Cocaigne."

"But that is only a little country place, to which I sometimes repair in summer, in order to live rustically. No, Jurgen, you must see my palaces. In Babylon I have a palace where many abide with cords about them and burn bran for perfume, while they await that thing which is to befall them. In Armenia I have a palace surrounded by vast gardens, where only strangers have the right to enter : they there receive a hospitality that is more than gallant. In Paphos I have a palace wherein is a little pyramid of white stone, very curious to see : but still more curious is the statue in my palace at Amathus, of a bearded woman, which displays other features that women do not possess. And in Alexandria I have a palace that is tended by thirty-six exceedingly wise and sacred persons, and wherein it is always night :

and there folk seek for monstrous pleasures, even at the price of instant death, and win to both of these swiftly. Everywhere my palaces stand upon high places near the sea : so they are beheld from afar by those whom I hold dearest, my beautiful broad-chested mariners, who do not fear even me, but know that in my palaces they will find notable employment. For I must tell you of what is to be encountered within these places that are mine, and of how pleasantly we pass our time there." Then she told him.

Now he listened more attentively than ever, and his eyes were narrowed, and his lips were lax and motionless and foolish-looking, and he was deeply interested. For Anaïtis had thought of some new diversions since their last meeting : and to Jurgen, even at forty-and-something, this queen's voice was all a horrible and strange and lovely magic. " She really tempts very nicely, too," he reflected, with a sort of pride in her.

Then Jurgen growled and shook himself, half angrily : and he tweaked the ear of Queen Anaïtis.

" Sweetheart," says he, " you paint a glowing picture : but you are shrewd enough to borrow your pigments from the day-dreams of inexperience. What you prattle about is not at all as you describe it. You forget you are talking to a widely married man of varied experience. Moreover, I shudder to think of what might happen if Lisa were to walk in unexpectedly. And for the rest, all this to-do over nameless delights and unspeakable caresses and other anonymous antics seems rather naïve. My ears are beset by eloquent grey hairs which plead at closer quarters than does that fibbing little tongue of yours. And so be off with you ! "

With that Queen Anaïtis smiled very cruelly, and she said : " Farewell to you, then, Jurgen, for it is I that am leaving you for ever. Henceforward you must fret away much sunlight by interminably shunning discomfort and by indulging tepid preferences. For I, and none but I,

can waken that desire which uses all of a man, and so
wastes nothing, even though it leave that favoured man
for ever after like wan ashes in the sunlight.   And with
you I have no more concern, for it is I that am leaving
you for ever.   Join with your greying fellows, then ! and
help them to affront the clean sane sunlight, by making
guilds and laws and solemn phrases wherewith to rid the
world of me.   I, Anaïtis, laugh, and my heart is a wave
in the sunlight.   For there is no power like my power,
and no living thing which can withstand my power;
and those who deride me, as I well know, are but the
dead dry husks that a wind moves, with hissing noises,
while I harvest in open sunlight.   For I am the desire
that uses all of a man : and it is I that am leaving you
for ever."

Said Jurgen : " I could not see all this in you, not
quite all this, because of a shadow that followed me.
Now it is too late, and this is a sorrowful thing which
is happening.   I am become as a puzzled ghost who
furtively observes the doings of loud-voiced ruddy
persons : and I am compact of weariness and apprehension, for I no longer discern what thing is I, nor what
is my desire, and I fear that I am already dead.   So
farewell to you, Queen Anaïtis, for this, too, is a sorrowful thing and a very unfair thing that is happening."

Thus he cried farewell to the Sun's daughter.   And
all the colours of her loveliness flickered and merged into
the likeness of a tall thin flame that aspired ; and then
this flame was extinguished.

CHAPTER XLVII

THE VISION OF HELEN

AND for the third time Koshchei waved his hand. Now came to Jurgen a gold-haired woman, clothed all in white. She was tall, and lovely and tender to regard: and hers was not the red and white comeliness of many ladies that were famed for beauty, but rather it had the even glow of ivory. Her nose was large and high in the bridge, her flexible mouth was not of the smallest; and yet, whatever other persons might have said, to Jurgen this woman's countenance was in all things perfect. And, beholding her, Jurgen kneeled.

He hid his face in her white robe: and he stayed thus, without speaking, for a long while.

"Lady of my vision," he said, and his voice broke—"there is that in you which wakes old memories. For now assuredly I believe your father was not Dom Manuel but that ardent bird which nestled very long ago in Leda's bosom. And now Troy's sons are all in Adês' keeping, in the world below; fire has consumed the walls of Troy, and the years have forgotten her tall conquerors; but still you are bringing woe on woe to hapless sufferers."

And again his voice broke. For the world seemed cheerless, and like a house that none has lived in for a great while.

Queen Helen, the delight of gods and men, replied nothing at all, because there was no need, inasmuch as the man who has once glimpsed her loveliness is beyond saving, and beyond the desire of being saved.

"To-night," says Jurgen, "as once through the grey art of Phobetor, now through the will of Koshchei, it appears that you stand within arm's reach. Hah, lady, were that possible—and I know very well it is not possible, whatever my senses may report,—I am not fit to mate with your perfection. At the bottom of my heart, I no longer desire perfection. For we who are tax-payers as well as immortal souls must live by politic evasions and formulæ and catchwords that fret away our lives as moths waste a garment; we fall insensibly to common sense as to a drug; and it dulls and kills whatever in us is rebellious and fine and unreasonable; and so you will find no man of my years with whom living is not a mechanism which gnaws away time unprompted. For within this hour I have become again a creature of use and wont; I am the lackey of prudence and half-measures; and I have put my dreams upon an allowance. Yet even now I love you more than I love books and indolence and flattery and the charitable wine which cheats me into a favourable opinion of myself. What more can an old poet say? For that reason, lady, I pray you begone, because your loveliness is a taunt which I find unendurable."

But his voice yearned, because this was Queen Helen, the delight of gods and men, who regarded him with grave, kind eyes. She seemed to view, as one appraises the pattern of an unrolled carpet, every action of Jurgen's life: and she seemed, too, to wonder, without reproach or trouble, how men could be so foolish, and of their own accord become so miry.

"Oh, I have failed my vision!" cries Jurgen. "I have failed, and I know very well that every man must fail: and yet my shame is no less bitter. For I am transmuted by time's handling! I shudder at the

And so farewell to you, Queen Helen!

thought of living day-in and day-out with my vision!
And so I will have none of you for my wife."

Then, trembling, Jurgen raised toward his lips the
hand of her who was the world's darling.

"And so farewell to you, Queen Helen! Oh, very
long ago I found your beauty mirrored in a wanton's
face! and often in a woman's face I have found one
or another feature wherein she resembled you, and for
the sake of it have lied to that woman glibly. And all
my verses, as I know now, were vain enchantments
striving to evoke that hidden loveliness of which I knew
by dim report alone. Oh, all my life was a foiled quest
of you, Queen Helen, and an unsatiated hungering.
And for a while I served my vision, honouring you with
clean-handed deeds. Yes, certainly it should be graved
upon my tomb, 'Queen Helen ruled this earth while it
stayed worthy.' But that was very long ago.

"And so farewell to you, Queen Helen! Your beauty
has been to me as a robber that stripped my life of
joy and sorrow, and I desire not ever to dream of your
beauty any more. For I have been able to love nobody.
And I know that it is you who have prevented this,
Queen Helen, at every moment of my life since the
disastrous moment when I first seemed to find your
loveliness in the face of Madame Dorothy. It is the
memory of your beauty, as I then saw it mirrored in
the face of a jill-flirt, which has enfeebled me for such
honest love as other men give women; and I envy these
other men. For Jurgen has loved nothing—not even
you, not even Jurgen!—quite whole-heartedly.

"And so farewell to you, Queen Helen! Hereafter
I rove no more a-questing anything; instead, I potter
after hearthside comforts, and play the physician with
myself, and strive painstakingly to make old bones. And
no man's notion anywhere seems worth a cup of mulled
wine; and for the sake of no notion would I endanger
the routine which so hideously bores me. For I am

transmuted by time's handling; I have become the lackey of prudence and half-measures; and it does not seem fair, but there is no help for it. So it is necessary that I now cry farewell to you, Queen Helen: for I have failed in the service of my vision, and I deny you utterly!"

Thus he cried farewell to the Swan's daughter: and Queen Helen vanished as a bright mist passes, not departing swiftly, as had departed Queen Guenevere and Queen Anaïtis; and Jurgen was alone with the black gentleman. And to Jurgen the world seemed cheerless and like a house that none has lived in for a great while.

CHAPTER XLVIII

CANDID OPINIONS OF DAME LISA

"EH, sirs!" observes Koshchei the Death-less, "but some of us are certainly hard to please."

And now Jurgen was already intent to shrug off his display of emotion. " In selecting a wife, sir," submitted Jurgen, " there are all sorts of matters to be considered——"

Then bewilderment smote him. For it occurred to Jurgen that his previous commerce with these three women was patently unknown to Koshchei. Why, Koshchei, who made all things as they are—Koshchei, no less—was now doing for Jurgen Koshchei's utmost : and that utmost amounted to getting for Jurgen what Jurgen had once, with the aid of youth and impudence, got for himself. Not even Koshchei, then, could do more for Jurgen than might be accomplished by that youth and impudence and tendency to pry into things generally which Jurgen had just relinquished as over-restless nuisances. Jurgen drew the inference, and shrugged; decidedly, cleverness was not at the top. However, there was no pressing need to enlighten Koshchei, and no wisdom in attempting it.

"—For you must understand, sir," continued Jurgen, smoothly, " that, whatever the first impulse of the moment, it was apparent to any reflective person that in the past of each of these ladies there was much to suggest inborn inaptitude for domestic life. And I am a peace-loving fellow, sir; nor do I hold with moral

laxity, now that I am forty-odd, except, of course, in
talk when it promotes sociability, and in verse-making
wherein it is esteemed as a conventional ornament.
Still, Prince, the chance I lost! I do not refer to
matrimony, you conceive. But in the presence of these
famous fair ones now departed from me for ever, with
what glowing words I ought to have spoken! upon a
wondrous ladder of tropes, metaphors and recondite
allusions, to what stylistic heights of Asiatic prose I
ought to have ascended! and instead, I twaddled like
a schoolmaster. Decidedly, Lisa is right, and I am
good-for-nothing. However," Jurgen added, hopefully,
" it appeared to me that when I last saw her, a year ago
this evening, Lisa was somewhat less outspoken than
usual."

" Eh, sirs, but she was under a very potent spell. I
found that necessary in the interest of law and order hereabouts. I, who made things as they are, am not accustomed to the excesses of practical persons who are
ruthlessly bent upon reforming their associates. Indeed,
it is one of the advantages of my situation that such
folk do not consider things as they are, and in consequence very rarely bother me." And the black gentleman in turn shrugged. " You will pardon me, but I
notice in my accounts that I am positively committed to
colour this year's anemones to-night, and there is a rather
large planetary system to be discontinued at half-past
ten. So time presses."

" And time is inexorable. Prince, with all due respect,
I fancy it is precisely this truism which you have overlooked. You produce the most charming of women, in
a determined onslaught upon my fancy; but you forget
you are displaying them to a man of forty-and-something."

" And does that make so great a difference ? "

" Oh, a sad difference, Prince ! For as a man gets on
in life he changes in many ways. He handles sword and

lance less creditably, and does not carry as heavy a staff
as he once flourished. He takes less interest in conversation, and his flow of humour diminishes. He is not the
tireless mathematician that he was, if only because his
faith in his personal endowments slackens. He recognises his limitations, and in consequence the unimportance of his opinions, and indeed he recognises the
probable unimportance of all fleshly matters. So he
relinquishes trying to figure out things, and sceptres
and candles appear to him about equivalent; and he
is inclined to give up philosophical experiments, and to
let things pass unplumbed. Oh, yes, it makes a difference." And Jurgen sighed. " And yet, for all that, it
is a relief, sir, in a way."

" Nevertheless," said Koshchei, " now that you have
inspected the flower of womanhood, I cannot soberly
believe you prefer your termagant of a wife."

" Frankly, Prince, I also am, as usual, undecided.
You may be right in all you have urged; and certainly
I cannot go so far as to say you are wrong; but still, at
the same time——! Come now, could you not let me
see my first wife for just a moment ? "

This was no sooner asked than granted; for there,
sure enough, was Dame Lisa. She was no longer re-
stricted to quiet speech by any stupendous necromancy :
and uncommonly plain she looked, after the passing of
those lovely ladies.

" Aha, you rascal ! " begins Dame Lisa, addressing
Jurgen; " and so you thought to be rid of me ! Oh, a
precious lot you are ! and a deal of thanks I get for my
scrimping and slaving ! " And she began scolding away.

But she began, somewhat to Jurgen's astonishment,
by stating that he was even worse than the Countess
Dorothy. Then he recollected that, by not the most
disastrous piece of luck conceivable, Dame Lisa's latest
news from the outside world had been rendered by her
sister, the notary's wife, a twelvemonth back.

And rather unaccountably Jurgen fell to thinking of how unsubstantial seemed these curious months devoted to other women, as set against the commonplace years which he and Lisa had fretted through together; of the fine and merry girl that Lisa had been before she married him; of how well she knew his tastes in cookery and all his little preferences, and of how cleverly she humoured them on those rare days when nothing had occurred to vex her; of all the buttons she had replaced, and all the socks she had darned, and of what tempests had been loosed when anyone else had had the audacity to criticise Jurgen; and of how much more unpleasant—everything considered—life was without her than with her. She was so unattractive looking, too, poor dear, that you could not but be sorry for her. And Jurgen's mood was half yearning and half penitence.

" I think I will take her back, Prince," says Jurgen, very subdued,—" now that I am forty-and-something. For I do not know but it is as hard on her as on me."

" My friend, do you forget the poet that you might be, even yet? No rational person would dispute that the society and amiable chat of Dame Lisa must naturally be a desideratum——"

But Dame Lisa was always resentful of long words. " Be silent, you black scoffer, and do not allude to such disgraceful things in the presence of respectable people! For I am a decent Christian woman, I would have you understand. But everybody knows your reputation! and a very fit companion you are for that scamp yonder! and volumes could not say more! "

Thus casually, and with comparative lenience, did Dame Lisa dispose of Koshchei, who made things as they are, for she believed him to be merely Satan. And to her husband Dame Lisa now addressed herself more particularly.

" Jurgen, I always told you you would come to this, and now I hope you are satisfied. Jurgen, do not stand there with your mouth open, like a scared fish, when I ask you a civil question! but answer when you are spoken to! Yes, and you need not try to look so idiotically innocent, Jurgen, because I am disgusted with you. For, Jurgen, you heard perfectly well what your very suitable friend just said about me, with my own husband standing by. No—now I beg of you!—do not ask me what he said, Jurgen! I leave that to your conscience, and I prefer to talk no more about it. You know that when I am once disappointed in a person I am through with that person. So, very luckily, there is no need at all for you to pile hypocrisy on cowardice, because if my own husband has not the feelings of a man, and cannot protect me from insults and low company, I had best be going home and getting supper ready. I dare say the house is like a pig-sty : and I can see by looking at you that you have been ruining your eyes by reading in bed again. And to think of your going about in public, even among such associates, with a button off your shirt ! "

She was silent for one terrible moment; then Lisa spoke in frozen despair.

" And now I look at that shirt, I ask you fairly, Jurgen, do you consider that a man of your age has any right to be going about in a shirt that nobody—in a shirt which —in a shirt that I can only——? Ah, but I never saw such a shirt ! and neither did anybody else ! You simply cannot imagine what a figure you cut in it, Jurgen. Jurgen, I have been patient with you ; I have put up with a great deal, saying nothing where many women would have lost their temper; but I simply cannot permit you to select your own clothes, and so ruin the business and take the bread out of our mouths. In short, you are enough to drive a person mad ; and I warn you that I am done with you for ever."

Dame Lisa went with dignity to the door of Koshchei's office.

" So you can come with me or not, precisely as you

elect. It is all one to me, I can assure you, after the cruel things you have said, and the way you have stormed at me, and have encouraged that notorious blackamoor to insult me in terms which I, for one, would not soil my lips by repeating. I do not doubt you consider it is all very clever and amusing, but you know now what I think about it. And upon the whole, if you do not feel the exertion will kill you, you had better come home the long way, and stop by Sister's and ask her to let you have a half-pound of butter; for I know you too well to suppose you have been attending to the churning."

Dame Lisa here evinced a stately sort of mirth such as is unimaginable by bachelors.

" You churning while I was away !—oh, no, not you ! There is probably not so much as an egg in the house. For my lord and gentleman has had other fish to fry, in his fine new courting clothes. And that—and on a man of your age, with a paunch to you like a beer-barrel and with legs like pipe-stems !—yes, that infamous shirt of yours is the reason you had better, for your own comfort, come home the long way. For I warn you, Jurgen, that the style in which I have caught you rigged out has quite decided me, before I go home or anywhere else, to stop by for a word or so with your high and mighty Madame Dorothy. So you had just as well not be along with me, for there is no pulling wool over my eyes any longer, and you two need never think to hoodwink me again about your goings-on. No, Jurgen, you cannot fool me; for I can read you like a book. And such behaviour, at your time of life, does not surprise me at all, because it is precisely what I would have expected of you."

With that Dame Lisa passed through the door and went away, still talking. It was of Heitman Michael's wife that the wife of Jurgen spoke, discoursing of the personal traits, and of the past doings, and (with augmented fervour) of the figure and visage of Madame

Dorothy, as all these abominations appeared to the eye of discernment, and must be revealed by the tongue of candour, as a matter of public duty.

So passed Dame Lisa, neither as flame nor mist, but as the voice of judgment.

CHAPTER XLIX

OF THE COMPROMISE WITH KOSHCHEI

"HEW!" said Koshchei, in the ensuing silence: "you had better stay overnight, in any event. I really think, friend, you will be more comfortable, just now at least, in this quiet cave."

But Jurgen had taken up his hat. "No! I dare say I, too, had better be going," says Jurgen. "I thank you very heartily for your intended kindness, sir, still I do not know but it is better as it is. And is there anything"—Jurgen coughed delicately—"and is there anything to pay, sir?"

"Oh, just a trifle, first of all, for a year's maintenance of Dame Lisa. You see, Jurgen, that is an almighty fine shirt you are wearing: it rather appeals to me; and I fancy, from something your wife let drop just now, it did not impress her as being quite suited to you. So, in the interest of domesticity, suppose you ransom Dame Lisa with that fine shirt of yours?"

"Why, willingly," said Jurgen, and he took off the shirt of Nessus.

"You have worn this for some time, I understand," said Koshchei, meditatively: "and did you ever notice any inconvenience in wearing this garment?"

"Not that I could detect, Prince; it fitted me, and seemed to impress everybody most favourably."

"There!" said Koshchei; "that is what I have always contended. To the strong man, and to wholesome matter-of-fact people generally, it is a fatal irritant;

but persons like you can wear the shirt of Nessus very comfortably for a long, long while, and be generally admired; and you end by exchanging it for your wife's society. But now, Jurgen, about yourself. You probably noticed that my door was marked Keep Out. One must have rules, you know. Often it is a nuisance, but still rules are rules; and so I must tell you, Jurgen, it is not permitted any person to leave my presence unmaimed, if not actually annihilated. One really must have rules, you know."

"You would chop off an arm? or a hand? or a whole finger? Come now, Prince, you must be joking!"

Koshchei the Deathless was very grave as he sat there, in meditation, drumming with his long jet-black fingers upon the table-top that was curiously inlaid with thirty pieces of silver. In the lamplight his sharp nails glittered like flame-points, and the colour suddenly withdrew from his eyes, so that they showed like small white eggs.

"But, man, how strange you are!" said Koshchei, presently; and life flowed back into his eyes, and Jurgen ventured the liberty of breathing. "Inside, I mean. Why, there is hardly anything left. Now rules are rules, of course; but you, who are the remnant of a poet, may depart unhindered whenever you will, and I shall take nothing from you. For really it is necessary to draw the line somewhere."

Jurgen meditated this clemency; and with a sick heart he seemed to understand. "Yes; that is probably the truth; for I have not retained the faith, nor the desire, nor the vision. Yes, that is probably the truth. Well, at all events, Prince, I very unfeignedly admired each of the ladies to whom you were friendly enough to present me, and I was greatly flattered by their offers. More than generous I thought them. But it really would not do for me to take up with any one of them now. For Lisa is my wife, you see. A great deal has passed between us, sir, in the last ten years. And I have been a sore disappointment to her, in many ways. And I am used to her——"

Then Jurgen considered, and regarded the black gentleman with mingled envy and commiseration. "Why, no, you probably would not understand, sir, on account of your not being, I suppose, a married person. But I can assure you it is always pretty much like that."

"I lack grounds to dispute your aphorism," observed Koshchei, "inasmuch as matrimony was certainly not included in my doom. None the less, to a by-stander, the conduct of you both appears remarkable. I could not understand, for example, just how your wife proposed to have you keep out of her sight for ever and still have supper with her to-night; nor why she should desire to sup with such a reprobate as she described with unbridled pungency and disapproval."

"Ah, but again, it is always pretty much like that, sir. And the truth of it, Prince, is a great symbol. The truth of it is, we have lived together so long that my wife has become rather foolishly fond of me. So she is not, as one might say, quite reasonable about me. No, sir; it is the fashion of women to discard civility toward those for whom they suffer most willingly; and whom a woman loveth she chasteneth, after a good precedent."

"But her talking, Jurgen, has nowhere any precedent. Why, it deafens, it appals, it submerges you in an up-roarious sea of fault-finding; and in a word, you might as profitably oppose a hurricane. Yet you want her back! Now assuredly, Jurgen, I do not think very highly of your wisdom, but by your bravery I am astounded."

"Ah, Prince, it is because I can perceive that all women are poets, though the medium they work in is not always ink. So the moment Lisa is set free from what, in a manner of speaking, sir, inconsiderate persons might, in their unthinking way, refer to as the terrors of an underground establishment that I do not for an instant doubt to be conducted after a system which furthers the true interests of everybody, and so reflects vast credit upon its officials, if you will pardon my frankness "—and Jurgen smiled ingratiatingly,—" why, at that moment Lisa's thoughts take form in very much the high denunciatory style of Jeremiah and Amos, who were remarkably fine poets. Her concluding observations as to the Countess, in particular, I consider to have been an example of sustained invective such as one rarely encounters in this degenerate age. Well, her next essay in creative composition is my supper, which will be an equally spirited impromptu. To-morrow she will darn and sew me an epic; and her desserts will continue to be in the richest lyric vein. Such, sir, are the poems of Lisa, all addressed to me, who came so near to gallivanting with mere queens ! "

" What, can it be that you are remorseful? " said Koshchei.

" Oh, Prince, when I consider steadfastly the depth and the intensity of that devotion which, for so many years, has tended me, and has endured the society of that person whom I peculiarly know to be the most tedious and irritating of companions, I stand aghast, before a miracle. And I cry, Oh, certainly a goddess ! and I can think of no queen who is fairly mentionable in the same breath. Hah, all we poets write a deal about love : but none of us may grasp the word's full meaning until he reflects that this is a passion mighty enough to induce a woman to put up with him."

" Even so, it does not seem to induce quite thorough confidence. Jurgen, I was grieved to see that Dame Lisa evidently suspects you of running after some other woman in your wife's absence."

" Think upon that now ! And you saw for yourself how little the handsomest of women could tempt me. Yet even Lisa's absurd notion I can comprehend and

pardon. And again, you probably would not understand
my overlooking such a thing, sir, on account of your not
being a married person. Nevertheless, my forgiveness
also is a great symbol."

Then Jurgen sighed and he shook hands, very cir-
cumspectly, with Koshchei, who made things as they
are; and Jurgen started out of the office.

"But I will bear you company a part of the way,"
says Koshchei.

So Koshchei removed his dressing-gown, and he put
on the fine laced coat which was hung over the back
of a strange-looking chair with three legs, each of a
different metal; the shirt of Nessus Koshchei folded
and put aside, saying that some day he might be able
to use it somehow. And Koshchei paused before the
blackboard and he scratched his head reflectively. Jurgen
saw that this board was nearly covered with figures which
had not yet been added up; and this blackboard seemed
to him the most frightful thing he had faced anywhere.

Then Koshchei came out of the cave with Jurgen, and
Koshchei walked with Jurgen across Amneran Heath,
and through Morven, in the late evening. And Koshchei
talked as they went; and a queer thing Jurgen noticed,
and it was that the moon was sinking in the east, as
though the time were getting earlier and earlier. But
Jurgen did not presume to criticise this, in the presence
of Koshchei, who made things as they are.

"And I manage affairs as best I can, Jurgen. But
they get in a fearful muddle sometimes. Eh, sirs, I
have no competent assistants. I have to look out for
everything, absolutely everything! And of course,
while in a sort of way I am infallible, mistakes will occur
every now and then in the actual working out of plans
that in the abstract are right enough. So it really does
please me to hear anybody putting in a kind word for
things as they are, because, between ourselves, there is
a deal of dissatisfaction about. And I was honestly

delighted, just now, to hear you speaking up for evil in the fact of that rapscallion monk. So I give you thanks and many thanks, Jurgen, for your kind word."

"'Just now!'" thinks Jurgen. He perceived that they had passed the Cistercian Abbey, and were approaching Bellegarde. And it was as in a dream that Jurgen was speaking. "*Who are you, and why do you thank me?*" asks Jurgen.

"*My name is no great matter. But you have a kind heart, Jurgen. May your life be free from care.*"

"*Save us from hurt and harm, friend, but I am already married——*" Then resolutely Jurgen put aside the spell that was befogging him. "See here, Prince, are you beginning all over again? For I really cannot stand any more of your benevolences."

Koshchei smiled. "No, Jurgen, I am not beginning all over again. For now I have never begun, and now there is no word of truth in anything which you remember of the year just past. Now none of these things has ever happened."

"But how can that be, Prince?"

"Why should I tell you, Jurgen? Let it suffice that what I will, not only happens, but has already happened, beyond the ancientest memory of man and his mother. How otherwise could I be Koshchei? And so farewell to you, poor Jurgen, to whom nothing in particular has happened now. It is not justice I am giving you, but something infinitely more acceptable to you and all your kind."

"But, to be sure!" says Jurgen. "I fancy that nobody anywhere cares much for justice. So farewell to you, Prince. And at our parting I ask no more questions of you, for I perceive it is scant comfort a man gets from questioning Koshchei, who made things as they are. But I am wondering what pleasure you get out of it all?"

"Eh, sirs," says Koshchei, with not the most candid

of smiles, " I contemplate the spectacle with appropriate emotions."

And so speaking, Koshchei quitted Jurgen for ever.

" Yet how may I be sure," thought Jurgen, instantly, " that this black gentleman was really Koshchei? He said he was. Why, yes; and Horvendile to all intents told me that Horvendile was Koshchei. Aha, and what else did Horvendile say!—' This is one of the romancer's most venerable devices that is being practised.' Why, but there was Smoit of Glathion, also, so that this is the third time I have been fobbed off with the explanation I was dreaming! and left with no proof, one way or the other."

Thus Jurgen, indignantly, and then he laughed. " Why, but, of course! I may have talked face to face with Koshchei, who made all things as they are; and again, I may not have. That is the whole point of it —the cream, as one might say, of the jest—that I cannot ever be sure. Well!"—and Jurgen shrugged here— " well, and what could I be expected to do about it?"

CHAPTER L

THE MOMENT THAT DID NOT COUNT

AND that is really all the story save for the moment Jurgen paused on his way home. For Koshchei (if it, indeed, was Koshchei) had quitted Jurgen just as they approached Bellegarde: and as the pawnbroker walked on alone in the pleasant April evening one called to him from the terrace. Even in the dusk he knew this was the Countess Dorothy.

"May I speak with you a moment?" says she.

"Very willingly, madame." And Jurgen ascended from the highway to the terrace.

"I thought it would be near your supper hour. So I was waiting here until you passed. You conceive, it is not quite convenient for me to seek you out at the shop."

"Why, no, madame. There is a prejudice," said Jurgen, soberly. And he waited.

He saw that Madame Dorothy was perfectly composed, yet anxious to speed the affair. "You must know," said she, " that my husband's birthday approaches, and I wish to surprise him with a gift. It is therefore necessary that I raise some money without troubling him. How much—abominable usurer!—could you advance me upon this necklace?"

Jurgen turned it in his hand. It was a handsome piece of jewelry, familiar to him as formerly the property of Heitman Michael's mother. Jurgen named a sum.

"But that," the Countess says, "is not a fraction of its worth!"

"Times are very hard, madame. Of course, if you cared to sell outright I could deal more generously."

"Old monster, I could not do that. It would not be convenient." She hesitated here. "It would not be explicable."

"As to that, madame, I could make you an imitation in paste which nobody could distinguish from the original. I can amply understand that you desire to veil from your husband any sacrifices that are entailed by your affection."

"It is my affection for him," said the Countess quickly.

"I alluded to your affection for him," said Jurgen— "naturally."

Then Countess Dorothy named a price for the necklace. "For it is necessary I have that much, and not a penny less." And Jurgen shook his head dubiously, and vowed that ladies were unconscionable bargainers: but Jurgen agreed to what she asked, because the necklace was worth almost as much again. Then Jurgen suggested that the business could be most conveniently concluded through an emissary.

"If Messire de Nérac, for example, could have matters explained to him, and could manage to visit me to-morrow, I am sure we could carry through this amiable imposture without any annoyance whatever to Heitman Michael," says Jurgen, smoothly.

"Nérac will come then," says the Countess. "And you may give him the money, precisely as though it were for him."

"But certainly, madame. A very estimable young nobleman, that! and it is a pity his debts are so large. I heard that he had lost heavily at cards within the last month; and I grieved, madame."

"He has promised me when these debts are settled

to play no more.—But again what am I saying? I mean, Master Inquisitive, that I take considerable interest in the welfare of Messire de Nérac: and so I have sometimes chided him on his wild courses. And that is all I mean."

"Precisely, madame. And so Messire de Nérac will come to me to-morrow for the money: and there is no more to say."

Jurgen paused. The moon was risen now. These two sat together upon a bench of carved stone near the balustrade: and before them, upon the other side of the highway, were luminous valleys and tree-tops. Fleetingly Jurgen recollected the boy and girl who had once sat in this place, and had talked of all the splendid things which Jurgen was to do, and of the happy life that was to be theirs together. Then he regarded the composed and handsome woman beside him, and he considered that the money to pay her latest lover's debts had been assured with a suitable respect for appearances.

"Come, but this is a gallant lady, who would defy the almanac," reflected Jurgen. "Even so, thirty-eight is an undeniable and somewhat autumnal figure, and I suspect young Nérac is bleeding his elderly mistress. Well, but at his age nobody has a conscience. Yes, and Madame Dorothy is handsome still; and still my pulse is playing me queer tricks, because she is near me, and my voice has not the intonation I intend, because she is near me; and still I am three-quarters in love with her. Yes, in the light of such cursed folly as even now possesses me, I have good reason to give thanks for the regained infirmities of age. Yet living seems to me a wasteful and inequitable process, for this is a poor outcome for the boy and girl that I remember. And weighing this outcome, I am tempted to weep and to talk romantically, even now."

But he did not. For really weeping was not requisite. Jurgen was making his fair profit out of the Countess's folly, and it was merely his duty to see that this little business transaction was managed without any scandal.

"So there is nothing more to say," observed Jurgen, as he rose in the moonlight, "save that I shall always be delighted to serve you, madame, and I may reasonably boast that I have earned a reputation for fair dealing."

And he thought: "In effect, since certainly as she grows older she will need yet more money for her lovers, I am offering to pimp for her." Then Jurgen shrugged. "That is one side of the affair. The other is that I transact my legitimate business,—I, who am that which the years have made of me."

Thus it was that Jurgen quitted the Countess Dorothy, whom, as you have heard, this pawnbroker had loved in his first youth under the name of Heart's Desire; and whom in the youth that was loaned him by Mother Sereda he had loved as Queen Helen, the delight of gods and men. For Jurgen was quitting Madame Dorothy after the simplest of business transactions, which consumed only a moment, and did not actually count one way or the other.

And after this moment which did not count, the pawnbroker resumed his journey, and so came presently to his home. He peeped through the window. And there in a snug room, with supper laid, sat Dame Lisa about some sewing, and evidently in a quite amiable frame of mind.

Then terror smote the Jurgen who had faced sorcerers and gods and devils intrepidly. "For I forgot about the butter!"

But immediately afterward he recollected that, now, not even what Lisa had said to him in the cave was real. Neither he nor Lisa, now, had ever been in the cave, and probably there was no longer any such place, and now there never had been any such place. It was rather confusing.

" Ah, but I must remember carefully," said Jurgen,
" that I have not seen Lisa since breakfast this morning.
Nothing whatever has happened. There has been no
requirement laid upon me, after all, to do the manly
thing. So I retain my wife, such as she is, poor dear !
I retain my home. I retain my shop and a fair line of
business. Yes, Koshchei—if it was really Koshchei—
has dealt with me very justly. And probably his methods
are everything they should be ; certainly I cannot go so
far as to say that they are wrong : but still, at the same
time—— ! "

Then Jurgen sighed, and entered his snug home.
Thus it was in the old days.

A CATALOGUE OF SELECTED DOVER BOOKS
IN ALL FIELDS OF INTEREST

A CATALOGUE OF SELECTED DOVER BOOKS
IN ALL FIELDS OF INTEREST

THE DEVIL'S DICTIONARY, Ambrose Bierce. Barbed, bitter, brilliant witticisms in the form of a dictionary. Best, most ferocious satire America has produced. 145pp. 20487-1 Pa. $1.50

ABSOLUTELY MAD INVENTIONS, A.E. Brown, H.A. Jeffcott. Hilarious, useless, or merely absurd inventions all granted patents by the U.S. Patent Office. Edible tie pin, mechanical hat tipper, etc. 57 illustrations. 125pp. 22596-8 Pa. $1.50

AMERICAN WILD FLOWERS COLORING BOOK, Paul Kennedy. Planned coverage of 48 most important wildflowers, from Rickett's collection; instructive as well as entertaining. Color versions on covers. 48pp. 8¼ x 11. 20095-7 Pa. $1.35

BIRDS OF AMERICA COLORING BOOK, John James Audubon. Rendered for coloring by Paul Kennedy. 46 of Audubon's noted illustrations: red-winged blackbird, cardinal, purple finch, towhee, etc. Original plates reproduced in full color on the covers. 48pp. 8¼ x 11. 23049-X Pa. $1.35

NORTH AMERICAN INDIAN DESIGN COLORING BOOK, Paul Kennedy. The finest examples from Indian masks, beadwork, pottery, etc. — selected and redrawn for coloring (with identifications) by well-known illustrator Paul Kennedy. 48pp. 8¼ x 11. 21125-8 Pa. $1.35

UNIFORMS OF THE AMERICAN REVOLUTION COLORING BOOK, Peter Copeland. 31 lively drawings reproduce whole panorama of military attire; each uniform has complete instructions for accurate coloring. (Not in the Pictorial Archives Series). 64pp. 8¼ x 11. 21850-3 Pa. $1.50

THE WONDERFUL WIZARD OF OZ COLORING BOOK, L. Frank Baum. Color the Yellow Brick Road and much more in 61 drawings adapted from W.W. Denslow's originals, accompanied by abridged version of text. Dorothy, Toto, Oz and the Emerald City. 61 illustrations. 64pp. 8¼ x 11. 20452-9 Pa. $1.50

CUT AND COLOR PAPER MASKS, Michael Grater. Clowns, animals, funny faces... simply color them in, cut them out, and put them together and you have 9 paper masks to play with and enjoy. Complete instructions. Assembled masks shown in full color on the covers. 32pp. 8¼ x 11. 23171-2 Pa. $1.50

STAINED GLASS CHRISTMAS ORNAMENT COLORING BOOK, Carol Belanger Grafton. Brighten your Christmas season with over 100 Christmas ornaments done in a stained glass effect on translucent paper. Color them in and then hang at windows, from lights, anywhere. 32pp. 8¼ x 11. 20707-2 Pa. $1.75

MOTHER GOOSE'S MELODIES. Facsimile of fabulously rare Munroe and Francis "copyright 1833" Boston edition. Familiar and unusual rhymes, wonderful old woodcut illustrations. Edited by E.F. Bleiler. 128pp. 4½ x 6⅜. 22577-1 Pa. $1.00

MOTHER GOOSE IN HIEROGLYPHICS. Favorite nursery rhymes presented in rebus form for children. Fascinating 1849 edition reproduced in toto, with key. Introduction by E.F. Bleiler. About 400 woodcuts. 64pp. 6⅞ x 5¼. 20745-5 Pa. $1.00

PETER PIPER'S PRACTICAL PRINCIPLES OF PLAIN & PERFECT PRONUNCIATION. Alliterative jingles and tongue-twisters. Reproduction in full of 1830 first American edition. 25 spirited woodcuts. 32pp. 4½ x 6⅜. 22560-7 Pa. $1.00

MARMADUKE MULTIPLY'S MERRY METHOD OF MAKING MINOR MATHEMATICIANS. Fellow to Peter Piper, it teaches multiplication table by catchy rhymes and woodcuts. 1841 Munroe & Francis edition. Edited by E.F. Bleiler. 103pp. 4⅝ x 6.
22773-1 Pa. $1.25
20171-6 Clothbd. $3.00

THE NIGHT BEFORE CHRISTMAS, Clement Moore. Full text, and woodcuts from original 1848 book. Also critical, historical material. 19 illustrations. 40pp. 4⅝ x 6. 22797-9 Pa. $1.00

THE KING OF THE GOLDEN RIVER, John Ruskin. Victorian children's classic of three brothers, their attempts to reach the Golden River, what becomes of them. Facsimile of original 1889 edition. 22 illustrations. 56pp. 4⅝ x 6⅜.
20066-3 Pa. $1.25

DREAMS OF THE RAREBIT FIEND, Winsor McCay. Pioneer cartoon strip, unexcelled for beauty, imagination, in 60 full sequences. Incredible technical virtuosity, wonderful visual wit. Historical introduction. 62pp. 8⅜ x 11¼. 21347-1 Pa. $2.00

THE KATZENJAMMER KIDS, Rudolf Dirks. In full color, 14 strips from 1906-7; full of imagination, characteristic humor. Classic of great historical importance. Introduction by August Derleth. 32pp. 9¼ x 12¼. 23005-8 Pa. $2.00

LITTLE ORPHAN ANNIE AND LITTLE ORPHAN ANNIE IN COSMIC CITY, Harold Gray. Two great sequences from the early strips: our curly-haired heroine defends the Warbucks' financial empire and, then, takes on meanie Phineas P. Pinchpenny. Leapin' lizards! 178pp. 6⅛ x 8⅜. 23107-0 Pa. $2.00

WHEN A FELLER NEEDS A FRIEND, Clare Briggs. 122 cartoons by one of the greatest newspaper cartoonists of the early 20th century — about growing up, making a living, family life, daily frustrations and occasional triumphs. 121pp. 8½ x 9½.
23148-8 Pa. $2.50

THE BEST OF GLUYAS WILLIAMS. 100 drawings by one of America's finest cartoonists: The Day a Cake of Ivory Soap Sank at Proctor & Gamble's, At the Life Insurance Agents' Banquet, and many other gems from the 20's and 30's. 118pp. 8⅜ x 11¼. 22737-5 Pa. $2.50

150 MASTERPIECES OF DRAWING, edited by Anthony Toney. 150 plates, early 15th century to end of 18th century; Rembrandt, Michelangelo, Dürer, Fragonard, Watteau, Wouwerman, many others. 150pp. 8⅜ x 11¼.   21032-4 Pa. $3.50

THE GOLDEN AGE OF THE POSTER, Hayward and Blanche Cirker. 70 extraordinary posters in full colors, from Maîtres de l'Affiche, Mucha, Lautrec, Bradley, Cheret, Beardsley, many others. 9⅜ x 12¼.   22753-7 Pa. $4.95
21718-3 Clothbd. $7.95

SIMPLICISSIMUS, selection, translations and text by Stanley Appelbaum. 180 satirical drawings, 16 in full color, from the famous German weekly magazine in the years 1896 to 1926. 24 artists included: Grosz, Kley, Pascin, Kubin, Kollwitz, plus Heine, Thöny, Bruno Paul, others. 172pp. 8½ x 12¼.   23098-8 Pa. $5.00
23099-6 Clothbd. $10.00

THE EARLY WORK OF AUBREY BEARDSLEY, Aubrey Beardsley. 157 plates, 2 in color: Manon Lescaut, Madame Bovary, Morte d'Arthur, Salome, other. Introduction by H. Marillier. 175pp. 8½ x 11.   21816-3 Pa. $3.50

THE LATER WORK OF AUBREY BEARDSLEY, Aubrey Beardsley. Exotic masterpieces of full maturity: Venus and Tannhäuser, Lysistrata, Rape of the Lock, Volpone, Savoy material, etc. 174 plates, 2 in color. 176pp. 8½ x 11.   21817-1 Pa. $3.75

DRAWINGS OF WILLIAM BLAKE, William Blake. 92 plates from Book of Job, Divine Comedy, Paradise Lost, visionary heads, mythological figures, Laocoön, etc. Selection, introduction, commentary by Sir Geoffrey Keynes. 178pp. 8½ x 11.
22303-5 Pa. $3.50

LONDON: A PILGRIMAGE, Gustave Doré, Blanchard Jerrold. Squalor, riches, misery, beauty of mid-Victorian metropolis; 55 wonderful plates, 125 other illustrations, full social, cultural text by Jerrold. 191pp. of text. 8⅛ x 11.
22306-X Pa. $5.00

THE COMPLETE WOODCUTS OF ALBRECHT DÜRER, edited by Dr. W. Kurth. 346 in all: Old Testament, St. Jerome, Passion, Life of Virgin, Apocalypse, many others. Introduction by Campbell Dodgson. 285pp. 8½ x 12¼.   21097-9 Pa. $6.00

THE DISASTERS OF WAR, Francisco Goya. 83 etchings record horrors of Napoleonic wars in Spain and war in general. Reprint of 1st edition, plus 3 additional plates. Introduction by Philip Hofer. 97pp. 9⅜ x 8¼.   21872-4 Pa. $2.50

ENGRAVINGS OF HOGARTH, William Hogarth. 101 of Hogarth's greatest works: Rake's Progress, Harlot's Progress, Illustrations for Hudibras, Midnight Modern Conversation, Before and After, Beer Street and Gin Lane, many more. Full commentary. 256pp. 11 x 14.   22479-1 Pa. $6.00
23023-6 Clothbd. $13.50

PRIMITIVE ART, Franz Boas. Great anthropologist on ceramics, textiles, wood, stone, metal, etc.; patterns, technology, symbols, styles. All areas, but fullest on Northwest Coast Indians. 350 illustrations. 378pp.   20025-6 Pa. $3.50

HOUDINI ON MAGIC, Harold Houdini. Edited by Walter Gibson, Morris N. Young. How he escaped; exposés of fake spiritualists; instructions for eye-catching tricks; other fascinating material by and about greatest magician. 155 illustrations. 280pp. 20384-0 Pa. $2.50

HANDBOOK OF THE NUTRITIONAL CONTENTS OF FOOD, U.S. Dept. of Agriculture. Largest, most detailed source of food nutrition information ever prepared. Two mammoth tables: one measuring nutrients in 100 grams of edible portion; the other, in edible portion of 1 pound as purchased. Originally titled Composition of Foods. 190pp. 9 x 12. 21342-0 Pa. $4.00

COMPLETE GUIDE TO HOME CANNING, PRESERVING AND FREEZING, U.S. Dept. of Agriculture. Seven basic manuals with full instructions for jams and jellies; pickles and relishes; canning fruits, vegetables, meat; freezing anything. Really good recipes, exact instructions for optimal results. Save a fortune in food. 156 illustrations. 214pp. 6⅛ x 9¼. 22911-4 Pa. $2.50

THE BREAD TRAY, Louis P. De Gouy. Nearly every bread the cook could buy or make: bread sticks of Italy, fruit breads of Greece, glazed rolls of Vienna, everything from corn pone to croissants. Over 500 recipes altogether. including buns, rolls, muffins, scones, and more. 463pp. 23000-7 Pa. $3.50

CREATIVE HAMBURGER COOKERY, Louis P. De Gouy. 182 unusual recipes for casseroles, meat loaves and hamburgers that turn inexpensive ground meat into memorable main dishes: Arizona chili burgers, burger tamale pie, burger stew, burger corn loaf, burger wine loaf, and more. 120pp. 23001-5 Pa. $1.75

LONG ISLAND SEAFOOD COOKBOOK, J. George Frederick and Jean Joyce. Probably the best American seafood cookbook. Hundreds of recipes. 40 gourmet sauces, 123 recipes using oysters alone! All varieties of fish and seafood amply represented. 324pp. 22677-8 Pa. $3.00

THE EPICUREAN: A COMPLETE TREATISE OF ANALYTICAL AND PRACTICAL STUDIES IN THE CULINARY ART, Charles Ranhofer. Great modern classic. 3,500 recipes from master chef of Delmonico's, turn-of-the-century America's best restaurant. Also explained, many techniques known only to professional chefs. 775 illustrations. 1183pp. 6⅝ x 10. 22680-8 Clothbd. $17.50

THE AMERICAN WINE COOK BOOK, Ted Hatch. Over 700 recipes: old favorites livened up with wine plus many more: Czech fish soup, quince soup, sauce Perigueux, shrimp shortcake, filets Stroganoff, cordon bleu goulash, jambonneau, wine fruit cake, more. 314pp. 22796-0 Pa. $2.50

DELICIOUS VEGETARIAN COOKING, Ivan Baker. Close to 500 delicious and varied recipes: soups, main course dishes (pea, bean, lentil, cheese, vegetable, pasta, and egg dishes), savories, stews, whole-wheat breads and cakes, more. 168pp. USO 22834-7 Pa. $1.75

DRIED FLOWERS, Sarah Whitlock and Martha Rankin. Concise, clear, practical guide to dehydration, glycerinizing, pressing plant material, and more. Covers use of silica gel. 12 drawings. Originally titled "New Techniques with Dried Flowers." 32pp. 21802-3 Pa. $1.00

ABC OF POULTRY RAISING, J.H. Florea. Poultry expert, editor tells how to raise chickens on home or small business basis. Breeds, feeding, housing, laying, etc. Very concrete, practical. 50 illustrations. 256pp. 23201-8 Pa. $3.00

HOW INDIANS USE WILD PLANTS FOR FOOD, MEDICINE & CRAFTS, Frances Densmore. Smithsonian, Bureau of American Ethnology report presents wealth of material on nearly 200 plants used by Chippewas of Minnesota and Wisconsin. 33 plates plus 122pp. of text. 6⅛ x 9¼. 23019-8 Pa. $2.50

THE HERBAL OR GENERAL HISTORY OF PLANTS, John Gerard. The 1633 edition revised and enlarged by Thomas Johnson. Containing almost 2850 plant descriptions and 2705 superb illustrations, Gerard's Herbal is a monumental work, the book all modern English herbals are derived from, and the one herbal every serious enthusiast should have in its entirety. Original editions are worth perhaps $750. 1678pp. 8½ x 12¼. 23147-X Clothbd. $50.00

A MODERN HERBAL, Margaret Grieve. Much the fullest, most exact, most useful compilation of herbal material. Gigantic alphabetical encyclopedia, from aconite to zedoary, gives botanical information, medical properties, folklore, economic uses, and much else. Indispensable to serious reader. 161 illustrations. 888pp. 6½ x 9¼. USO 22798-7, 22799-5 Pa., Two vol. set $10.00

HOW TO KNOW THE FERNS, Frances T. Parsons. Delightful classic. Identification, fern lore, for Eastern and Central U.S.A. Has introduced thousands to interesting life form. 99 illustrations. 215pp. 20740-4 Pa. $2.50

THE MUSHROOM HANDBOOK, Louis C.C. Krieger. Still the best popular handbook. Full descriptions of 259 species, extremely thorough text, habitats, luminescence, poisons, folklore, etc. 32 color plates; 126 other illustrations. 560pp. 21861-9 Pa. $4.50

HOW TO KNOW THE WILD FRUITS, Maude G. Peterson. Classic guide covers nearly 200 trees, shrubs, smaller plants of the U.S. arranged by color of fruit and then by family. Full text provides names, descriptions, edibility, uses. 80 illustrations. 400pp. 22943-2 Pa. $3.00

COMMON WEEDS OF THE UNITED STATES, U.S. Department of Agriculture. Covers 220 important weeds with illustration, maps, botanical information, plant lore for each. Over 225 illustrations. 463pp. 6⅛ x 9¼. 20504-5 Pa. $4.50

HOW TO KNOW THE WILD FLOWERS, Mrs. William S. Dana. Still best popular book for East and Central USA. Over 500 plants easily identified, with plant lore; arranged according to color and flowering time. 174 plates. 459pp. 20332-8 Pa. $3.50

CONSTRUCTION OF AMERICAN FURNITURE TREASURES, Lester Margon. 344 detail drawings, complete text on constructing exact reproductions of 38 early American masterpieces: Hepplewhite sideboard, Duncan Phyfe drop-leaf table, mantel clock, gate-leg dining table, Pa. German cupboard, more. 38 plates. 54 photographs. 168pp. 8⅜ x 11¼. 23056-2 Pa. $4.00

JEWELRY MAKING AND DESIGN, Augustus F. Rose, Antonio Cirino. Professional secrets revealed in thorough, practical guide: tools, materials, processes; rings, brooches, chains, cast pieces, enamelling, setting stones, etc. Do not confuse with skimpy introductions: beginner can use, professional can learn from it. Over 200 illustrations. 306pp. 21750-7 Pa. $3.00

METALWORK AND ENAMELLING, Herbert Maryon. Generally coneeded best all-around book. Countless trade secrets: materials, tools, soldering, filigree, setting, inlay, niello, repoussé, casting, polishing, etc. For beginner or expert. Author was foremost British expert. 330 illustrations. 335pp. 22702-2 Pa. $3.50

WEAVING WITH FOOT-POWER LOOMS, Edward F. Worst. Setting up a loom, beginning to weave, constructing equipment, using dyes, more, plus over 285 drafts of traditional patterns including Colonial and Swedish weaves. More than 200 other figures. For beginning and advanced. 275pp. 8¾ x 6⅜. 23064-3 Pa. $4.00

WEAVING A NAVAJO BLANKET, Gladys A. Reichard. Foremost anthropologist studied under Navajo women, reveals every step in process from wool, dyeing, spinning, setting up loom, designing, weaving. Much history, symbolism. With this book you could make one yourself. 97 illustrations. 222pp. 22992-0 Pa. $3.00

NATURAL DYES AND HOME DYEING, Rita J. Adrosko. Use natural ingredients: bark, flowers, leaves, lichens, insects etc. Over 135 specific recipes from historical sources for cotton, wool, other fabrics. Genuine premodern handicrafts. 12 illustrations. 160pp. 22688-3 Pa. $2.00

THE HAND DECORATION OF FABRICS, Francis J. Kafka. Outstanding, profusely illustrated guide to stenciling, batik, block printing, tie dyeing, freehand painting, silk screen printing, and novelty decoration. 356 illustrations. 198pp. 6 x 9. 21401-X Pa. $3.00

THOMAS NAST: CARTOONS AND ILLUSTRATIONS, with text by Thomas Nast St. Hill. Father of American political cartooning. Cartoons that destroyed Tweed Ring; inflation, free love, church and state; original Republican elephant and Democratic donkey; Santa Claus; more. 117 illustrations. 146pp. 9 x 12.
22983-1 Pa. $4.00
23067-8 Clothbd. $8.50

FREDERIC REMINGTON: 173 DRAWINGS AND ILLUSTRATIONS. Most famous of the Western artists, most responsible for our myths about the American West in its untamed days. Complete reprinting of *Drawings of Frederic Remington* (1897), plus other selections. 4 additional drawings in color on covers. 140pp. 9 x 12.
20714-5 Pa. $3.95

THE MAGIC MOVING PICTURE BOOK, Bliss, Sands & Co. The pictures in this book move! Volcanoes erupt, a house burns, a serpentine dancer wiggles her way through a number. By using a specially ruled acetate screen provided, you can obtain these and 15 other startling effects. Originally "The Motograph Moving Picture Book." 32pp. 8¼ x 11. 23224-7 Pa. $1.75

STRING FIGURES AND HOW TO MAKE THEM, Caroline F. Jayne. Fullest, clearest instructions on string figures from around world: Eskimo, Navajo, Lapp, Europe, more. Cats cradle, moving spear, lightning, stars. Introduction by A.C. Haddon. 950 illustrations. 407pp. 20152-X Pa. $3.00

PAPER FOLDING FOR BEGINNERS, William D. Murray and Francis J. Rigney. Clearest book on market for making origami sail boats, roosters, frogs that move legs, cups, bonbon boxes. 40 projects. More than 275 illustrations. Photographs. 94pp. 20713-7 Pa. $1.25

INDIAN SIGN LANGUAGE, William Tomkins. Over 525 signs developed by Sioux, Blackfoot, Cheyenne, Arapahoe and other tribes. Written instructions and diagrams: how to make words, construct sentences. Also 290 pictographs of Sioux and Ojibway tribes. 111pp. 6⅛ x 9¼. 22029-X Pa. $1.50

BOOMERANGS: HOW TO MAKE AND THROW THEM, Bernard S. Mason. Easy to make and throw, dozens of designs: cross-stick, pinwheel, boomabird, tumblestick, Australian curved stick boomerang. Complete throwing instructions. All safe. 99pp. 23028-7 Pa. $1.50

25 KITES THAT FLY, Leslie Hunt. Full, easy to follow instructions for kites made from inexpensive materials. Many novelties. Reeling, raising, designing your own. 70 illustrations. 110pp. 22550-X Pa. $1.25

TRICKS AND GAMES ON THE POOL TABLE, Fred Herrmann. 79 tricks and games, some solitaires, some for 2 or more players, some competitive; mystifying shots and throws, unusual carom, tricks involving cork, coins, a hat, more. 77 figures. 95pp. 21814-7 Pa. $1.25

WOODCRAFT AND CAMPING, Bernard S. Mason. How to make a quick emergency shelter, select woods that will burn immediately, make do with limited supplies, etc. Also making many things out of wood, rawhide, bark, at camp. Formerly titled Woodcraft. 295 illustrations. 580pp. 21951-8 Pa. $4.00

AN INTRODUCTION TO CHESS MOVES AND TACTICS SIMPLY EXPLAINED, Leonard Barden. Informal intermediate introduction: reasons for moves, tactics, openings, traps, positional play, endgame. Isolates patterns. 102pp. USO 21210-6 Pa. $1.35

LASKER'S MANUAL OF CHESS, Dr. Emanuel Lasker. Great world champion offers very thorough coverage of all aspects of chess. Combinations, position play, openings, endgame, aesthetics of chess, philosophy of struggle, much more. Filled with analyzed games. 390pp. 20640-8 Pa. $3.50

INCIDENTS OF TRAVEL IN YUCATAN, John L. Stephens. Classic (1843) exploration of jungles of Yucatan, looking for evidences of Maya civilization. Travel adventures, Mexican and Indian culture, etc. Total of 669pp.
20926-1, 20927-X Pa., Two vol. set $5.50

LIVING MY LIFE, Emma Goldman. Candid, no holds barred account by foremost American anarchist: her own life, anarchist movement, famous contemporaries, ideas and their impact. Struggles and confrontations in America, plus deportation to U.S.S.R. Shocking inside account of persecution of anarchists under Lenin. 13 plates. Total of 944pp.
22543-7, 22544-5 Pa., Two vol. set $9.00

AMERICAN INDIANS, George Catlin. Classic account of life among Plains Indians: ceremonies, hunt, warfare, etc. Dover edition reproduces for first time all original paintings. 312 plates. 572pp. of text. 6⅛ x 9¼.
22118-0, 22119-9 Pa., Two vol. set $8.00
22140-7, 22144-X Clothbd., Two vol. set $16.00

THE INDIANS' BOOK, Natalie Curtis. Lore, music, narratives, drawings by Indians, collected from cultures of U.S.A. 149 songs in full notation. 45 illustrations. 583pp. 6⅝ x 9⅜.
21939-9 Pa. $5.00

INDIAN BLANKETS AND THEIR MAKERS, George Wharton James. History, old style wool blankets, changes brought about by traders, symbolism of design and color, a Navajo weaver at work, outline blanket, Kachina blankets, more. Emphasis on Navajo. 130 illustrations, 32 in color. 230pp. 6⅛ x 9¼.
22996-3 Pa. $5.00
23068-6 Clothbd. $10.00

AN INTRODUCTION TO THE STUDY OF THE MAYA HIEROGLYPHS, Sylvanus Griswold Morley. Classic study by one of the truly great figures in hieroglyph research. Still the best introduction for the student for reading Maya hieroglyphs. New introduction by J. Eric S. Thompson. 117 illustrations. 284pp.
23108-9 Pa. $4.00

THE ANALECTS OF CONFUCIUS, THE GREAT LEARNING, DOCTRINE OF THE MEAN, Confucius. Edited by James Legge. Full Chinese text, standard English translation on same page, Chinese commentators, editor's annotations; dictionary of characters at rear, plus grammatical comment. Finest edition anywhere of one of world's greatest thinkers. 503pp.
22746-4 Pa. $4.50

THE I CHING (THE BOOK OF CHANGES), translated by James Legge. Complete translation of basic text plus appendices by Confucius, and Chinese commentary of most penetrating divination manual ever prepared. Indispensable to study of early Oriental civilizations, to modern inquiring reader. 448pp.
21062-6 Pa. $3.50

THE EGYPTIAN BOOK OF THE DEAD, E.A. Wallis Budge. Complete reproduction of Ani's papyrus, finest ever found. Full hieroglyphic text, interlinear transliteration, word for word translation, smooth translation. Basic work, for Egyptology, for modern study of psychic matters. Total of 533pp. 6½ x 9¼.
EBE 21866-X Pa. $4.95

MODERN CHESS STRATEGY, Ludek Pachman. The use of the queen, the active king, exchanges, pawn play, the center, weak squares, etc. Section on rook alone worth price of the book. Stress on the moderns. Often considered the most important book on strategy. 314pp. 20290-9 Pa. $3.00

CHESS STRATEGY, Edward Lasker. One of half-dozen great theoretical works in chess, shows principles of action above and beyond moves. Acclaimed by Capablanca, Keres, etc. 282pp. USO 20528-2 Pa. $2.50

CHESS PRAXIS, THE PRAXIS OF MY SYSTEM, Aron Nimzovich. Founder of hypermodern chess explains his profound, influential theories that have dominated much of 20th century chess. 109 illustrative games. 369pp. 20296-8 Pa. $3.50

HOW TO PLAY THE CHESS OPENINGS, Eugene Znosko-Borovsky. Clear, profound examinations of just what each opening is intended to do and how opponent can counter. Many sample games, questions and answers. 147pp. 22795-2 Pa. $2.00

THE ART OF CHESS COMBINATION, Eugene Znosko-Borovsky. Modern explanation of principles, varieties, techniques and ideas behind them, illustrated with many examples from great players. 212pp. 20583-5 Pa. $2.00

COMBINATIONS: THE HEART OF CHESS, Irving Chernev. Step-by-step explanation of intricacies of combinative play. 356 combinations by Tarrasch, Botvinnik, Keres, Steinitz, Anderssen, Morphy, Marshall, Capablanca, others, all annotated. 245 pp. 21744-2 Pa. $2.50

HOW TO PLAY CHESS ENDINGS, Eugene Znosko-Borovsky. Thorough instruction manual by fine teacher analyzes each piece individually; many common endgame situations. Examines games by Steinitz, Alekhine, Lasker, others. Emphasis on understanding. 288pp. 21170-3 Pa. $2.75

MORPHY'S GAMES OF CHESS, Philip W. Sergeant. Romantic history, 54 games of greatest player of all time against Anderssen, Bird, Paulsen, Harrwitz; 52 games at odds; 52 blindfold; 100 consultation, informal, other games. Analyses by Anderssen, Steinitz, Morphy himself. 352pp. 20386-7 Pa. $2.75

500 MASTER GAMES OF CHESS, S. Tartakower, J. du Mont. Vast collection of great chess games from 1798-1938, with much material nowhere else readily available. Fully annotated, arranged by opening for easier study. 665pp. 23208-5 Pa. $6.00

THE SOVIET SCHOOL OF CHESS, Alexander Kotov and M. Yudovich. Authoritative work on modern Russian chess. History, conceptual background. 128 fully annotated games (most unavailable elsewhere) by Botvinnik, Keres, Smyslov, Tal, Petrosian, Spassky, more. 390pp. 20026-4 Pa. $3.95

WONDERS AND CURIOSITIES OF CHESS, Irving Chernev. A lifetime's accumulation of such wonders and curiosities as the longest won game, shortest game, chess problem with mate in 1220 moves, and much more unusual material — 356 items in all, over 160 complete games. 146 diagrams. 203pp. 23007-4 Pa. $3.50

CATALOGUE OF DOVER BOOKS

THE ART DECO STYLE, ed. by Theodore Menten. Furniture, jewelry, metalwork, ceramics, fabrics, lighting fixtures, interior decors, exteriors, graphics from pure French sources. Best sampling around. Over 400 photographs. 183pp. 8⅜ x 11¼.
22824-X Pa. $4.00

THE GENTLEMAN AND CABINET MAKER'S DIRECTOR, Thomas Chippendale. Full reprint, 1762 style book, most influential of all time; chairs, tables, sofas, mirrors, cabinets, etc. 200 plates, plus 24 photographs of surviving pieces. 249pp. 9⅞ x 12¾.
21601-2 Pa. $5.00

PINE FURNITURE OF EARLY NEW ENGLAND, Russell H. Kettell. Basic book. Thorough historical text, plus 200 illustrations of boxes, highboys, candlesticks, desks, etc. 477pp. 7⅞ x 10¾.
20145-7 Clothbd. $12.50

ORIENTAL RUGS, ANTIQUE AND MODERN, Walter A. Hawley. Persia, Turkey, Caucasus, Central Asia, China, other traditions. Best general survey of all aspects: styles and periods, manufacture, uses, symbols and their interpretation, and identification. 96 illustrations, 11 in color. 320pp. 6⅛ x 9¼.
22366-3 Pa. $5.00

DECORATIVE ANTIQUE IRONWORK, Henry R. d'Allemagne. Photographs of 4500 iron artifacts from world's finest collection, Rouen. Hinges, locks, candelabra, weapons, lighting devices, clocks, tools, from Roman times to mid-19th century. Nothing else comparable to it. 420pp. 9 x 12.
22082-6 Pa. $8.50

THE COMPLETE BOOK OF DOLL MAKING AND COLLECTING, Catherine Christopher. Instructions, patterns for dozens of dolls, from rag doll on up to elaborate, historically accurate figures. Mould faces, sew clothing, make doll houses, etc. Also collecting information. Many illustrations. 288pp. 6 x 9. 22066-4 Pa. $3.00

ANTIQUE PAPER DOLLS: 1915-1920, edited by Arnold Arnold. 7 antique cut-out dolls and 24 costumes from 1915-1920, selected by Arnold Arnold from his collection of rare children's books and entertainments, all in full color. 32pp. 9¼ x 12¼.
23176-3 Pa. $2.00

ANTIQUE PAPER DOLLS: THE EDWARDIAN ERA, Epinal. Full-color reproductions of two historic series of paper dolls that show clothing styles in 1908 and at the beginning of the First World War. 8 two-sided, stand-up dolls and 32 complete, two-sided costumes. Full instructions for assembling included. 32pp. 9¼ x 12¼.
23175-5 Pa. $2.00

A HISTORY OF COSTUME, Carl Köhler, Emma von Sichardt. Egypt, Babylon, Greece up through 19th century Europe; based on surviving pieces, art works, etc. Full text and 595 illustrations, including many clear, measured patterns for reproducing historic costume. Practical. 464pp. 21030-8 Pa. $4.00

EARLY AMERICAN LOCOMOTIVES, John H. White, Jr. Finest locomotive engravings from late 19th century: historical (1804-1874), main-line (after 1870), special, foreign, etc. 147 plates. 200pp. 11⅜ x 8¼. 22772-3 Pa. $3.50

SLEEPING BEAUTY, illustrated by Arthur Rackham. Perhaps the fullest, most delightful version ever, told by C.S. Evans. Rackham's best work. 49 illustrations. 110pp. 7⅞ x 10¾. —————— 22756-1 Pa. $2.00

THE WONDERFUL WIZARD OF OZ, L. Frank Baum. Facsimile in full color of America's finest children's classic. Introduction by Martin Gardner. 143 illustrations by W.W. Denslow. 267pp. 20691-2 Pa. $2.50

GOOPS AND HOW TO BE THEM, Gelett Burgess. Classic tongue-in-cheek masquerading as etiquette book. 87 verses, 170 cartoons as Goops demonstrate virtues of table manners, neatness, courtesy, more. 88pp. 6½ x 9¼. 22233-0 Pa. $1.50

THE BROWNIES, THEIR BOOK, Palmer Cox. Small as mice, cunning as foxes, exuberant, mischievous, Brownies go to zoo, toy shop, seashore, circus, more. 24 verse adventures. 266 illustrations. 144pp. 6⅝ x 9¼. 21265-3 Pa. $1.75

BILLY WHISKERS: THE AUTOBIOGRAPHY OF A GOAT, Frances Trego Montgomery. Escapades of that rambunctious goat. Favorite from turn of the century America. 24 illustrations. 259pp. 22345-0 Pa. $2.75

THE ROCKET BOOK, Peter Newell. Fritz, janitor's kid, sets off rocket in basement of apartment house; an ingenious hole punched through every page traces course of rocket. 22 duotone drawings, verses. 48pp. 6⅞ x 8⅜. 22044-3 Pa. $1.50

PECK'S BAD BOY AND HIS PA, George W. Peck. Complete double-volume of great American childhood classic. Hennery's ingenious pranks against outraged pomposity of pa and the grocery man. 97 illustrations. Introduction by E.F. Bleiler. 347pp. 20497-9 Pa. $2.50

THE TALE OF PETER RABBIT, Beatrix Potter. The inimitable Peter's terrifying adventure in Mr. McGregor's garden, with all 27 wonderful, full-color Potter illustrations. 55pp. 4¼ x 5½. USO 22827-4 Pa. $1.00

THE TALE OF MRS. TIGGY-WINKLE, Beatrix Potter. Your child will love this story about a very special hedgehog and all 27 wonderful, full-color Potter illustrations. 57pp. 4¼ x 5½. USO 20546-0 Pa. $1.00

THE TALE OF BENJAMIN BUNNY, Beatrix Potter. Peter Rabbit's cousin coaxes him back into Mr. McGregor's garden for a whole new set of adventures. A favorite with children. All 27 full-color illustrations. 59pp. 4¼ x 5½. USO 21102-9 Pa. $1.00

THE MERRY ADVENTURES OF ROBIN HOOD, Howard Pyle. Facsimile of original (1883) edition, finest modern version of English outlaw's adventures. 23 illustrations by Pyle. 296pp. 6½ x 9¼. 22043-5 Pa. $2.75

TWO LITTLE SAVAGES, Ernest Thompson Seton. Adventures of two boys who lived as Indians; explaining Indian ways, woodlore, pioneer methods. 293 illustrations. 286pp. 20985-7 Pa. $3.00

CATALOGUE OF DOVER BOOKS

EGYPTIAN MAGIC, E.A. Wallis Budge. Foremost Egyptologist, curator at British Museum, on charms, curses, amulets, doll magic, transformations, control of demons, deific appearances, feats of great magicians. Many texts cited. 19 illustrations. 234pp. USO 22681-6 Pa. $2.50

THE LEYDEN PAPYRUS: AN EGYPTIAN MAGICAL BOOK, edited by F. Ll. Griffith, Herbert Thompson. Egyptian sorcerer's manual contains scores of spells: sex magic of various sorts, occult information, evoking visions, removing evil magic, etc. Transliteration faces translation. 207pp. 22994-7 Pa. $2.50

THE MALLEUS MALEFICARUM OF KRAMER AND SPRENGER, translated, edited by Montague Summers. Full text of most important witchhunter's "Bible," used by both Catholics and Protestants. Theory of witches, manifestations, remedies, etc. Indispensable to serious student. 278pp. 6⅝ x 10. USO 22802-9 Pa. $3.95

LOST CONTINENTS, L. Sprague de Camp. Great science-fiction author, finest, fullest study: Atlantis, Lemuria, Mu, Hyperborea, etc. Lost Tribes, Irish in pre-Columbian America, root races; in history, literature, art, occultism. Necessary to everyone concerned with theme. 17 illustrations. 348pp. 22668-9 Pa. $3.50

THE COMPLETE BOOKS OF CHARLES FORT, Charles Fort. Book of the Damned, Lo!, Wild Talents, New Lands. Greatest compilation of data: celestial appearances, flying saucers, falls of frogs, strange disappearances, inexplicable data not recognized by science. Inexhaustible, painstakingly documented. Do not confuse with modern charlatanry. Introduction by Damon Knight. Total of 1126pp. 23094-5 Clothbd. $15.00

FADS AND FALLACIES IN THE NAME OF SCIENCE, Martin Gardner. Fair, witty appraisal of cranks and quacks of science: Atlantis, Lemuria, flat earth, Velikovsky, orgone energy, Bridey Murphy, medical fads, etc. 373pp. 20394-8 Pa. $3.00

HOAXES, Curtis D. MacDougall. Unbelievably rich account of great hoaxes: Locke's moon hoax, Shakespearean forgeries, Loch Ness monster, Disumbrationist school of art, dozens more; also psychology of hoaxing. 54 illustrations. 338pp. 20465-0 Pa. $3.50

THE GENTLE ART OF MAKING ENEMIES, James A.M. Whistler. Greatest wit of his day deflates Wilde, Ruskin, Swinburne; strikes back at inane critics, exhibitions. Highly readable classic of impressionist revolution by great painter. Introduction by Alfred Werner. 334pp. 21875-9 Pa. $4.00

THE BOOK OF TEA, Kakuzo Okakura. Minor classic of the Orient: entertaining, charming explanation, interpretation of traditional Japanese culture in terms of tea ceremony. Edited by E.F. Bleiler. Total of 94pp. 20070-1 Pa. $1.25

Prices subject to change without notice.
Available at your book dealer or write for free catalogue to Dept. GI, Dover Publications, Inc., 180 Varick St., N.Y., N.Y. 10014. Dover publishes more than 150 books each year on science, elementary and advanced mathematics, biology, music, art, literary history, social sciences and other areas.